Black Men from behind the Veil

Philosophy of Race

Series Editor: George Yancy, Emory University

Editorial Board: Sybol Anderson, Barbara Applebaum, Alison Bailey, Chike Jeffers, Janine Jones, David Kim, Emily S. Lee, Zeus Leonardo, Falguni A. Sheth, Grant Silva

The Philosophy of Race book series publishes interdisciplinary projects that center upon the concept of race, a concept that continues to have very profound contemporary implications. Philosophers and other scholars, more generally, are strongly encouraged to submit book projects that seriously address race and the process of racialization as a deeply embodied, existential, political, social, and historical phenomenon. The series is open to examine monographs, edited collections, and revised dissertations that critically engage the concept of race from multiple perspectives: sociopolitical, feminist, existential, phenomenological, theological, and historical.

Recent Titles in the Series

Black Men from Behind the Veil: Ontological Interrogations, by George Yancy
White Educators Negotiating Complicity: Roadblocks Paved with Good Intentions, by Barbara Applebaum
White Ignorance and Complicit Responsibility: Transforming Collective Harm Beyond the Punishment Paradigm, by Eva Boodman
Iranian Identity, American Experience: Philosophical Reflections on Race, Rights, Capabilities, and Oppression, by Roksana Alavi
The Weight of Whiteness: A Feminist Engagement with Privilege, Race, and Ignorance, by Alison Bailey
The Logic of Racial Practice: Explorations in the Habituation of Racism, edited by Brock Bahler
Hip-Hop as Philosophical Text and Testimony: Can I Get a Witness?, by Lissa Skitolsky
The Blackness of Black: Key Concepts in Critical Discourse, by William David Hart
Self-Definition: A Philosophical Inquiry from the Global South and Global North, by Teodros Kiros
A Phenomenological Hermeneutic of Antiblack Racism in The Autobiography of Malcolm X, by David Polizzi
Buddhism and Whiteness, edited by George Yancy and Emily McRae
Black Christology and the Quest for Authenticity: A Philosophical Appraisal, by John H. McClendon III
For Equals Only: Race, Equality, and the Equal Protection Clause, by Tina Fernandes Botts
Politics and Affect in Black Women's Fiction, by Kathy Glass

Black Men from behind the Veil

Ontological Interrogations

Edited by
George Yancy

LEXINGTON BOOKS
Lanham • Boulder • New York • London

Published by Lexington Books
An imprint of The Rowman & Littlefield Publishing Group, Inc.
4501 Forbes Boulevard, Suite 200, Lanham, Maryland 20706
www.rowman.com

86-90 Paul Street, London EC2A 4NE

Copyright © 2022 by The Rowman & Littlefield Publishing Group, Inc.

All rights reserved. No part of this book may be reproduced in any form or by any electronic or mechanical means, including information storage and retrieval systems, without written permission from the publisher, except by a reviewer who may quote passages in a review.

British Library Cataloguing in Publication Information Available

Library of Congress Cataloging-in-Publication Data

Names: Yancy, George, editor.
Title: Black men from behind the veil : ontological interrogations / George Yancy.
Description: Lanham : Lexington Books, [2021] | Series: Philosophy of race | Includes bibliographical references and index. | Summary: "Black Men from Behind the Veil bears witness to anti-Black male violence and does so from the perspective of Black male scholars who disclose their fears and what it means to suffer as Black men, courageously marking the deep material, institutional, and epistemic structures that amplify that fear and suffering"— Provided by publisher.
Identifiers: LCCN 2021044330 (print) | LCCN 2021044331 (ebook) | ISBN 9781666906479 (cloth) | ISBN 9781666906493 (paper) | ISBN 9781666906486 (ebook)
Subjects: LCSH: African American men—United States—Social conditions—21st century. | Racial profiling in law enforcement—United States. | United States—Race relations. | African Americans—Social conditions—21st century. | Racism—United States.
Classification: LCC E185.86 .B52625 2021 (print) | LCC E185.86 (ebook) | DDC 305.896/073—dc23
LC record available at https://lccn.loc.gov/2021044330
LC ebook record available at https://lccn.loc.gov/2021044331

*This book is dedicated to the memory of
George Floyd and Breonna Taylor*

Contents

Acknowledgments ix

Introduction: Speaking *Behind* and *To* the Veil 1
George Yancy

1 Incarcerating Blackness: My Nephew, His Letter from an Arizona Prison, Our Reflections 11
William David Hart

2 Philosophy as Excited Delirium and the Credibility Deficit of the Black Male 27
Clevis Headley

3 Emmett Till's Body 39
A. Todd Franklin

4 The War on Blackness: Black Men and the State of the Union 49
Arnold L. Farr

5 Blues Sons and Sorrow's Kitchen 59
Houston A. Baker Jr.

6 Disaggregating Death: George Floyd and the Significance of Black Male Mortality in Police Encounters 65
Tommy J. Curry

7 Theory, Epistemic Failure, and the Problem of (Hue)Man Suffering: A Phenomenology of Breathlessness 81
Timothy J. Golden

8	What's Happening Brother? *Josiah Ulysses Young III*	97
9	To be Overdetermined from Without: Negotiating White Supremacy from Corporeal Blackness *Linden F. Lewis*	109
10	Navigating the Aguala: Blackness, Shamans, and Drag Queens *Sterlin Mosley*	119
11	Power, Divorce, and Trauma: Law and Loss *Floyd W. Hayes III*	131
12	Black Subversive Memory and a Black Progressive Leadership as Resources for Black Male Engagement in Prolonged Resistance against White Power Structures *Joseph L. Smith*	149
13	Alternative Hip Hop Masculinity: On Hip Hop Hypermasculinity, Heteronormativity, and Radical Humanism *Reiland Rabaka*	163
14	How Black Lives Matter and Why Revolutionary Philosophy Is Relevant: Philosophical Considerations on Ideological and Political Economic Contradictions *John H. McClendon III*	179
15	The Spectacle Lynching and Modern-Day Crucifixion of George Floyd: When the World Is a Witness to Murder *Aaron X. Smith*	195
16	Blood on the Check *Semassa Boko*	203

Index	213
About the Contributors	221

Acknowledgments

I thank Jana Hodges-Kluck, senior acquisitions editor at Lexington Books (within the areas of philosophy, classics, and linguistics), for her deep commitment to publishing outstanding books and working with authors with such professionalism, patience, and generosity. Jana is a gift to work with. I would also like to thank Sydney Wedbush, assistant acquisitions editor, for her care and logistical excellence in regard to bringing this book to fruition. I especially thank all the contributors who understand the political, personal, and existential importance of this book, those who are courageous in their voices and praxes. This book does not operate within a zero-sum framework. That would entail a failed project, a false start. Rather, we understand the importance of Black pain and suffering even as we acknowledge the shared and yet specific ways that we magnetize bullets and are the targets of racist misandry. I am thankful for our collective effort within this text. I would also like to thank Andrea Warmack who is a formidable Black feminist philosopher who continues to keep me critically engaged. Her presence in the world makes a difference, and her philosophical voice will creatively mess things up. I, for one, can't wait. I would also like to thank my parents for giving birth to me, *not* a criminal, a thug, a rapist, a sub-person. Their hearts, voices, and arms spoke my name and shaped by being in a country (nay, a world) that would rather call me an abject monster, a thing unfit for civil (read: white) society. Because of this, I thank my Black sons for who they are and who they will become. Please know that "the talk," which should now be indelibly fixed into your psyches, was not what I desired. It is what is necessary for you to stay alive, to return home, to live for another day. Never forget these numbers: 9:29. And whatever you do, remember 1619. I love you, but even that love can't stop a bullet, a chokehold, or a knee that refuses to see your humanity, or grant its self-evidence. So, stay alive. That is your counter-weapon; that is your defiance. I especially would like to thank Susan for her love. Our Black sons are bone of her bone, flesh of her flesh. Thanks for literally bearing and giving birth to such beautiful possibilities, because that is what our Black sons are. Also, thanks for your indispensable editorial work to see that this book was ready for publication. That was a challenge. I know that and I appreciate that. I am indebted in more ways than one. Lastly, I would like to thank those deeply committed and brilliant participants in my intense six-week seminar on Whiteness and Phenomenology of Race at Cornell University's School of Criticism and Theory (Summer 2021). I could not have asked for more. Your critical voices will remain with me, and I hope mine with you.

Introduction

Speaking Behind *and* To *the Veil*

George Yancy

I have watched the video of George Floyd's death in its entirety at least once. Perhaps once is too much. Needless to say, it is hard to watch. For me, watching it generates multiple states of being: rage, fury, anger, outrage, frustration, exhaustion, defeat, fear, pessimism, grief, sadness, and deep sorrow and pain. These modes of being are not experienced serially, but simultaneously, more like an immediate influx. All these emotions are grueling to hold in one Black male body. One gets the sense that one doesn't truly have the "dogged strength" and that one will be, sooner or later, torn asunder. Part of what fuels this pain, this sorrow, is that it is ongoing, perhaps without end. Given this, any sense of closure is deferred, postponed. The white State, along with its deputized citizens, is relentless, and skilled at maintaining white social and civic equilibrium, white normativity, and white normalcy. Hence, there will be another unarmed Black body killed later today, tomorrow, the day after tomorrow, the day after tomorrow's tomorrow, etc., etc., etc., etc., etc., etc., etc., etc., etc., etc., etc., etc., etc., etc., etc., etc., etc., etc., etc. The Latin, et cetera, communicates "that which remains." It is the *to-be-killed* Black male body that remains, the prone Black male corpse captured on video that remains, the a priori sense of certainty that there is a line of unnamed Black men who are targeted for death by the State and its functionaries that remains. Unnamed because we come to know their names only *after* their deaths. Then again, is there ever a *before* that is not always already an *after*? As William Hart writes, "Trayvon Martin was dead before his deadly encounter with George Zimmerman. His execution (I use this loaded word intentionally) was a postmortem event; a ratification after the fact of the facts of black male being-in-America."[1] In short, within this tragic situation, there is a species of death *before* physical death. W. E. B. Du Bois, in his deeply probing and heartfelt essay, "Of the Passing of the First-Born," suggests that the death of his firstborn child has escaped the *before* of that species of death behind the veil. He writes of his son's physical death as an escape and as a mode of freedom. Du Bois writes, "Perhaps now he knows the All-love, and needs not to be wise. Sleep, then, child,—sleep till I sleep and waken to a baby voice and the ceaseless patter of little feet—above the Veil."²

Is this what it means for us, Black men and Black boys, "to be" behind the veil, that deep shroud that while not having a univocal meaning keeps us in "our place," a place where the *ontos* of Black male existence is fundamentally unstable? While W. E. B. Du Bois is not hopeless, though he certainly knew what it meant to be unhopeful, one can feel the sheer weight of his pain and suffering (and yet a sense of joy) where he construes death as a site of refuge vis-à-vis the death of his firstborn. Du Bois is not bound by some morbid death wish; rather, he powerfully articulates the pain of being Black behind the veil in a country which was/is predicated upon the ontological diminution of Black people, where to be Black is to be reduced to the status of a "nigger" who has "No Rights a White Man is Bound to Respect."³ He writes, "All that day and all that night there sat an awful gladness in my heart,—nay, blame me not if I see the world thus darkly through the Veil,—and my soul whispers ever to me, saying, 'Not dead, not dead, but escaped; not bond, but free.'"⁴

The Black men within this text stand in the shadow of the affectively haunting and brutally tragic deaths of forty-six-year-old George Floyd (2020), twenty-five-year-old Ahmaud Arbery (2020), thirty-two-year-old Philando Castile (2016), forty-three-year-old Eric Garner (2014), twelve-year-old Tamir Rice (2014), seventeen-year-old Trayvon Martin (2012), twenty-three-year-old Amadou Diallo (1999), fourteen-year-old Emmett Till (1955), fourteen-year-old George Stinney Jr. (1944), twenty-three-year-old Claude Neal (1934), and all of those countless Black embodied persons who were murdered or who were always already about to be murdered because they were deemed ontologically criminal, up to no good, ersatz, subhuman, and ungrievable. As Black men, as Black bodies, we are the un-killed,⁵ which, for me, suggests a mode of existential temporal reprieve, a racially precarious mode of existence that *isn't* simply precarious because *all* human beings are precariously finite by nature. Our finitude is, as it were, accelerated by our being *Black men*, our finitude is sped up because of an epidermal and gendered distorted meaning that has been historically installed, reinforced through an anti-Black male episteme that is predicated upon whiteness, though by no means limited to whiteness. The problem (or *being* a problem) is not because we are "monstrous" and "dangerous" Black men *simpliciter*. Rather, our portrayal as the global "Black monster," the frightening things of nightmares, is because of *relational* epistemic, libidinal, patriarchal, aesthetic, ethical, political, social, theological, and material white hegemonic orders and investments that we didn't create. And yet, we suffer, we bleed, we weep, we mourn, we die, because we have socially inherited the death-dealing weight of the Black male imago vis-à-vis the white imaginary. That inheritance, that indelible mark of "criminality," often feels, though, as if it has weighed our bodies down forever. W. E. B. Du Bois understood the gravitas of an epidermis construed as a misdeed, a crime. He wrote, "I realized that some folks, a few, even several, actually considered my brown skin a misfortune; once or twice I became painfully aware that some human beings even thought it a crime."[6]

The future doesn't look any better, either. So, I am not an optimist. If in fact we are the un-killed (and the fungible), then we also cast a shadow forward, one that covers those Black men, Black boys, Black bodies, that have yet to be born, yet to become the un-killed. Notice how the un-killed captures something that is neither the plenitude of life nor the absolute nullification that is death. The prefix, "un," means not. More specifically, the sense of "not" bespeaks how the Black body waits in line, so to speak, *to be killed*. To be within that "not" is precisely not (quite) to be; one is paradoxically, but always terribly and revoltingly, both dead and alive. The Hamletian disjunction ("to be or not to be") is too unambiguous, there isn't room for a muddied, racially lived logics where, as a Black male, I am the *being of not* and the *not of being*. Hart calls this mode of being-*not*-being, "an in-between thing, a *tertium quid*."[7]

What feels like an inexorable trap does not cut at the joints of reality. In other words, anti-Blackness or racial misandry is not metaphysical; it is not the same as the "basic furniture of the universe," as some scientific realist philosophers like to say. Rather, anti-Blackness or racial misandry is socially constituted, historically constructed, and materially and institutionally maintained; it is a dynamic process of semiotic meaning-making or white nation building. In this way, the "rapacious Black male" is not a (timeless) Platonic form, but a (temporally indexed) phenomenon that is more like an *event*,[8] an event that involves the confluence of white toxic ejecta, white projections of white phantasmal creations, white libidinal forces, white colonial desires, white gratuitous violence, white forms of panoptic surveillance, a racial Manichean divide, ship holds, chains, spatial confinement, inhibited motility, carceral logics, ocean crossings, and the denigration and terrorization of Black bodies, the "creation" of the myth of racialized Black "impurity" vis-à-vis white racialized "purity." I would argue that given the white consumptive logics that sustain anti-Blackness, the Black male body functions like a disposable plastic cup, recyclable and fungible ad infinitum, and yet necessary for sustaining whiteness, which appears to have a voracious and insatiable gut for "ingesting" Black bodies. It is as if we are part of a Fanonian recursive loop where we desire to come into the world lithely, be and move with effortless grace, yet we are stopped—*dead*. We are embedded within a white anti-Black male saturated and structural space within which we have become objects "in the midst of other objects,"[9] where white perception, white epistemology, and white ontology are collapsed, and where the Black male body is constantly inundated by white falsehoods, white myths, white violence. Indeed, we find ourselves interwoven "out of a thousand [white] details, anecdotes, stories."[10]

We are taught to believe that it is through our agency that we are responsible for the psychic, cultural, and historical debris and wreckage which surrounds our lives. On this score, as a problem people, we are said to stand in the way of our own potential emergence within the world. These are but lies, modes of displacement, bad faith, and scapegoating, where white people ritualistically *escape* what it means that their humanity is purchased at the expense of Black bodies, where the psychic architecture of civil society is what it is because some of us (too many to name) are Black. In this way, Black male racial embodiment is instrumentalized for the purpose of white America's sense of itself as "virtuous," "civilized." Frank B. Wilderson writes, "For years I had seen myself as a degraded Human, seen my plight as analogous to the plight of Palestinians, Native Americans, and the working class. Now, I understood that analogy was a ruse. I was the foil of Humanity."[11] He continues, "Humanity looked to me when it was unsure of itself."[12] Our alleged self-generated debris and wreckage can best be stated in terms of someone else's waste or refuse, which accurately signifies a foul-smelling odor of lies upon lies, a history of white shit that white people, through processes of mythopoetic obfuscation, fail or refuse to smell. In this way, whiteness *needs* the Black male body for its own social ontological integrity, coherence, and unity. Toni Morrison is aware of this social ontological dependency and voraciousness that is marked through negation or the *not*. Through the conceptual lens provided here, I would argue in stream with Morrison that it is whiteness whereby

> the American self knows itself as not enslaved, but free; not repulsive, but desirable; not helpless, but licensed and powerful; not history-less, but historical; not damned, but innocent; not a blind accident of evolution, but a progressive fulfillment of destiny.[13]

It is this *not* that resides at the core of whiteness, which forces a deep and important existential question: What is whiteness without that *not*, without anti-Black racism, without the Black man/person functioning, as James Baldwin would say, "in the white man's world as a fixed star"?[14] Perhaps the answer is painfully clear to white people—*nothing!*

It is important to note that when I talk about whiteness, I am not speaking exclusively to those white people who identify with the KKK, the Proud Boys, Neo-Nazism, or the boogaloo movement. I am not speaking exclusively to those white people who, in Washington, DC, stormed the U.S. Capitol on January 6, 2021. Their aim, as we must *never forget*, was to subvert democracy on behalf of a white, neofascist, and dangerous narcissistic would-be strongman. I am not referring singularly to those white supremacists who on August 11 and 12, 2017, came together in Charlottesville, Virginia, to Unite the Right through racist discourse and violence. Whiteness, while inclusive of these groups and events, constitutes a larger and historically dynamic social ontological structural binary. To be white and to fight against white supremacy in its spectacular forms does not entail that one is exhaustively fighting against anti-Blackness. After all, one is still white. One is still within the binary, and it positions one beyond voluntaristic moral efforts to undo the structural insidiousness of whiteness. As white, you probably still think that your moral state is simply dependent upon your moral will.[15] I would argue that you are more like the "benevolent" slave master who feeds me well, provides me with plenty of clothes, who doesn't whip me, who advocates on behalf of the Black Lives Matter movement. Yet, you don't stop to see how my Blackness continues to function as the underside of your everyday (non-spectacularly racist) white modes of being-in-the-world, how your unquestioned humanity is predicated upon my being as Black, as the "wretched," the "sub-person." I hear you. "But I am a *poor* white." "I am white trash." I get it, but that doesn't complicate the binary. The binary remains. You are deemed a failed white person. Note, though, that the conceptualization of a *failed* Black person or *failed* Blackness is not the same as a state of failed whiteness. Indeed, there is no "failed Blackness" as I'm theorizing the white structural binary. To fail would imply that Blackness is somehow situationally inhibited to move forward based upon a real sustainable promise. Yet, there is something that is ontologically at stake here. Blackness and its relationship to failure would amount to more than a missed opportunity, more than having not received an economic promise. Rather, Blackness is always already without genuine ontological (human) grounding. Blackness, ipso facto, is the site of nullification, where one's humanity is not simply suspended, but structurally barred from the human (read: white humanity). Poor whiteness is at least covered by a halo of a promise, a strategic corrective. After all, to be poor and white is still to be white. If one takes away trash, whiteness remains intact. To be poor and Black is still to be Black. Take away poverty, and yet Blackness remains intact, that is, one remains the ontologically ersatz. Indeed, poor whiteness is even a mark of shame.[16] Blackness is not shame as shame implies an anterior mode of dignity. Blackness, read through the lens of an anti-Black structural binary, undercuts dignity and thereby shame.

This conceptual mapping implies the weight of white responsibility. If we as Black men, as Black people, must carry and be haunted by the weight of the Black dead killed by your whiteness, then it is you who must carry the weight of those white killers and be haunted by their actions. When I think about who I am as a Black man, I carry the history of those Black men, those Black bodies, that have been murdered under anti-Black logics. When I think about George Floyd, I carry the memory of his death, the memory of his pain and suffering, the memory of his calling for his mama. If you are white, what memories do you, or should you, carry? What is your relationship to the history of whiteness and its crimes against Black bodies? Baldwin suggests part of the obstacle to answering these questions. He writes that "people who imagine that history flatters them (as it does, indeed, since they wrote it) are impaled on their history like a butterfly on a pin and become incapable of seeing or changing themselves, or the world."[17] I think that Baldwin is correct. So, let me help. Tarry with the indifference (and yet targeted effort) of Derek Chauvin as he killed Floyd. Chauvin is your burden; carry him. I've already got too many postmortem Black men and Black boys to carry. Chauvin is a product of the same whiteness, the same structural binary, that oppresses Black bodies, that took Floyd's life, that has no edges and thereby touches black bodies to the point of a cruel and painful asphyxiation: "I can't breathe!" "I can't breathe!" "I can't breathe!" "I can't breathe!" "I can't breathe!" "I can't breathe!" "I can't breathe!" "I can't breathe!" "I can't breathe!" "I can't breathe!" How does whiteness, *your* whiteness, enable you to breathe? More powerfully and hauntingly: What if your being able to breathe is possible because some of us cannot breathe? If this is true, and I have come to the nontrivial conclusion that it is, then the relationship is one of parasitism; you get to breathe in the capacity of those who are spirit-eaters, as it were. The consumptive, gastronomical implications are intentional. Our spirits (Latin, *spiritus* or breath) are ingested so that you might live. Guilt is a nonstarter; it is too easy. Just breathe. Take in the air. Feel your lungs and your chest expand. The power and violence of whiteness is just that simple; it is that normal; it is that effortless; and it is that close and invisible. That is what whiteness provides—breath, life, "innocence," humanity, bodily expansion into a white America, a white world meant for you. It is a space within which you get to *stand your ground*, and where Black bodies are reduced to lying face down *on the ground*.

The initial aims of *Black Men from Behind the Veil: Ontological Interrogations* were limited compared to what obtained. While each of us writes within the shadow of George Floyd's death, the contributions are varied in their conceptual and narrative fecundity. In this regard, this book proves to be a collective powerful meditation, though not of the Cartesian kind, on various aspects of Black male trauma, identity, performance, and situatedness. The text does not assume an abstract and ahistorical conception of what it means to be Black men. The text takes seriously lived history and how that history is structured by constitutive (not deterministic) material and discursive vectors. Hence, the text moves the reader through the complexities of Black male lived experiences without reducing experiences wedded to neoliberal subjects. The text also reveals forms of grieving that are not shaped by perfunctory modes of self-confession or self-flagellation. The text explores questions of death, pain and sorrow, racial injustice, and loss of family. It critically explores and challenges various forms of credibility deficit/epistemic injustice as they negatively impact Black men, engages meditative reflections on the life and meaning of Emmett Till, and the war on Blackness, the depth of family trauma, and the pain experienced as a Black son struggles, for example, with mental illness and the joy of transformation and transcendence that captures the dynamic movement of a powerful blues motif. The text explores the importance of disaggregating death and how racial misandry has been overlooked and undertheorized. It provides an engaging meditation on epistemic failures that don't generate productive modes of vision that see Black men as they are, but instead theorize Black men as ahistorical essences. The text tarries with the death of Black male friends within social spaces that are inundated with necro-political violence, and yet identifies the importance of a guiding paternal hand. The text also captures what it means to walk a tightrope of being overdetermined as a problem not only in the United States, but throughout the Black Diaspora, and also challenges the "fixity" of Black male identity vis-à-vis a multiplicity of Black male social locations: Black man, bisexual, academic, poet, seeker, and queer who fights to undo and deconstruct larger Western binaries. In stream with this theme, the text explores hop hop culture and its possibilities and limits as we are called to rethink the hegemonic orders of hyper-masculinity and heteronormativity. In this way, as is argued, room is made for a radical humanism that deconstructs sites that place under erasure Black feminist, Black queer, and Black trans modes of hip hop performativity. What is clear is that the text doesn't attempt to understand Black male modes of being-in-the-world from nowhere. There is no such place. The text tarries within the quotidian. Within this context, the text explores the predicament of being a Black father who loves his Black children and finds himself facing a judicial system designed for him to fail; it explores rethinking Black nihilism not as a social pathology intrinsic to Black male identity, but as a configured social reality that is shaped by specific market values and the deracination of robust and viable Black support systems. The text demonstrates the recursive and painful truth regarding the fact of the spurious American social contract that values Black life on the cheap; it explicates the ways in which various dimensions of professional philosophy have failed to philosophically engage the ethical, political, and existential significance of Black lives and have failed to engage the reality that Black lives don't matter under specific racist and capitalist modes of production. With accounts of personal and collective pain and suffering, the text asks us to tarry with Black death, and to comprehend the power and scope of the claim that we, as Black people, all die because of the logics of anti-Blackness.

Black Men from Behind the Veil: Ontological Interrogations consists of Black men who courageously engage the complex social locational cartography within which they have been *thrown*. Each chapter begins with that fundamental assumption. In this way, ideal theory is of no use when what is at stake has to do with our very lives, and the lives of those whom we love. Grounded within the facticity of anti-Black racism, specifically within the context of its implications for Black men, each of us has been painfully impacted by the brutal death of George Floyd. I imagine that some of us carry that pain in ways that manifest itself unannounced. As intimated, though, we collectively understand that Floyd was not the first and he will not be the last Black male killed by the State, and by the larger systemic logics of racial capitalism where the Black body is both abject (etymologically, that which is cast out) and yet usable, exploitable. Each of us has felt the toxic sting of racial misandry. The myths are in the DNA of America's white body politic. Black men are always already rendered "criminal," "hypersexual," "thugs," and "pathologically violent." The knee pressed against Floyd's neck, within the context of anti-Black racism, functions as a synecdoche, an entire anti-Black male system that creates a situation in which we find it hard to breathe or where so many of us cannot breathe at all. This book refuses the violence of anti-Black male anonymity and brings attention to the quotidian ways in which Black men suffer within the encasement of their/our Black skin (I almost wrote, "sin"). It is a crucial and imperative text as older Black men and young Black men in the United States attempt to negotiate their lives within a society that *doesn't* want them to succeed, advance, mature—indeed, that *doesn't* want them to live, *to be*. Then again, on their terms, on their white terms, we are the being of not and the not of being. As argued, this means that the problem facing Black men is not just a social one, but an *ontological* one. We face a situation in which we are told that our lives have never mattered and will never matter. That is what it means, inter alia, to be a Black male who lives behind the veil; and, yet, who speaks (must speak) *to* the veil.

NOTES

1. William David Hart, "Dead Black Man, Just Walking" in *Pursuing Trayvon Martin: Historical Contexts and Contemporary Manifestations of Racial Dynamics*, eds. George Yancy and Janine Jones (Lanham, MD: Lexington Books, 2013), 91.

2. W. E. B. Du Bois, *The Souls of Black Folk* (1903; reprint, New York: New American Library, 1982), 232.

3. This judicial decision, which is considered by many to have been the worst decision declared by the Supreme Court, was made on March 6, 1857, by Chief

Justice Roger Taney in the case of *Dred Scott v. John Sanford*. Taney argued that Black people were mere articles of merchandise, inferior, and were not fit to associate with white people as equals.

4. Du Bois, *The Souls of Black Folk*, 231.

5. I thank literary scholar and intellectual Micaiah Johnson for this term. Micaiah used this term in a seminar that I taught at Cornell University's School of Criticism and Theory in the summer of 2021.

6. W. E. B. Du Bois, *Darkwater: The Givens Collection* (New York: Washington Square Press, 2004), 7.

7. William David Hart, "Dead Black Man, Just Walking" in *Pursuing Trayvon Martin: Historical Contexts and Contemporary Manifestations of Racial Dynamics*, eds. George Yancy and Janine Jones (Lanham, MD: Lexington Books, 2013), 92.

8. I thank the philosopher R. A. Judy for the suggestive implications of the term "event" within this context.

9. Frantz Fanon, *Black Skin, White Masks*, trans. Charles Lam Markmann (New York: Grove Press, Inc., 1967), 109.

10. Fanon, *Black Skin*, 111.

11. Frank B. Wilderson III, "Afropessimism and the Ruse of Analogy: Violence, Freedom, Struggles, and the Death of Black Desire" in *Antiblackness*, eds. Moon-Kie Jung and João H. Costa Vargas (Durham: Duke University Press, 2021), 56.

12. Wilderson lll, "Afropessimism and the Ruse of Analogy: Violence, Freedom, Struggles, and the Death of Black Desire", 56.

13. Toni Morrison, *Playing in the Dark: Whiteness and the Literary Imagination* (New York: Vintage, 1990), 52.

14. James Baldwin, *The Fire Next Time* (New York: The Modern Library, 1995), 8.

15. Peggy McIntosh, "White Privilege and Male Privilege: A Personal Account of Coming to See Correspondences through Work in Woman's Studies" in *Critical Whiteness Studies: Looking behind the Mirror*, eds. Richard Delgardo and Jean Stefancic (Philadelphia: Temple University Press, 1997), 292.

16. Thinking about shame in this way was made explicit within the context of a seminar that I taught at Cornell University's School of Criticism and Theory in the summer of 2021. I thank the participants and especially Micaiah Johnson. Our objective was not to deny the reality of poor white people, but to avoid the error of conflation vis-à-vis anti-Black racism. To solve the problem of white poverty does not guarantee the end of an anti-Black world. It seems reasonable to me, though, that the end of an anti-Black world would necessarily trouble the continuation of the misery and pain of poverty experienced by poor white people.

17. James Baldwin, *Baldwin—Collected Essays / Notes of A Native Son / Nobody Knows My Name / The Fire Next Time / No Name in the Street / The Devil Finds Work* (New York: The Library of America, 1998), 723.

BIBLIOGRAPHY

Baldwin, James. *The Fire Next Time* (New York: The Modern Library, 1995).

Baldwin, James. *Baldwin—Collected Essays / Notes of A Native Son / Nobody Knows My Name / The Fire Next Time / No Name in the Street / The Devil Finds Work* (New York: The Library of America, 1998).

Du Bois, W. E. B. *The Souls of Black Folk* (1903; reprint, New York: New American Library, 1982).

Du Bois, W. E. B. *Darkwater: The Givens Collection* (New York: Washington Square Press, 2004).

Fanon, Frantz. *Black Skin, White Masks*, trans. Charles Lam Markmann (New York: Grove Press, Inc., 1967).

Hart, William David. "Dead Black Man, Just Walking" in *Pursuing Trayvon Martin: Historical Contexts and Contemporary Manifestations of Racial Dynamics*, eds. George Yancy and Janine Jones (Lanham, MD: Lexington Books, 2013).

McIntosh, Peggy. "White Privilege and Male Privilege: A Personal Account of Coming to See Correspondences through Work in Woman's Studies," in *Critical Whiteness Studies: Looking behind the Mirror*, ed. Richard Delgardo and Jean Stefancic (Philadelphia: Temple University Press, 1997).

Morrison, Toni. *Playing in the Dark: Whiteness and the Literary Imagination* (New York: Vintage, 1990).

Wilderson, Frank B., III. "Afropessimism and the Ruse of Analogy: Violence, Freedom, Struggles, and the Death of Black Desire" in *Antiblackness*, eds. Moon-Kie Jung and João H. Costa Vargas (Durham: Duke University Press, 2021).

Chapter 1

Incarcerating Blackness

My Nephew, His Letter from an Arizona Prison, Our Reflections

William David Hart

When Officer Derek Chauvin of the Minneapolis police department pressed his knee against George Floyd's neck, he murdered a man with a life, family, and history. Floyd is a man not a metaphor. Nevertheless, the knee on Floyd's neck instantiates the deadly weight on the collective neck of Black people in the United States and around the world. Police are the most conspicuous organ of antiblackness and the carceral state, and policing blackness is its basic work. Whether through police, prison, jail, parole, probation, electronic monitoring, or the racists algorithms of surveillance technologies, Black people are subject to a carceral logic, gaze, and apparatus. The criminogenic gaze of antiblackness followed Ahmaud Arbery as he jogged through a Georgia neighborhood where the subjects of that antiblack way of seeing, three white men, one a retired police officer, murdered him. As he jogged, Arbery did not realize that he was on the run from modern-day slave patrollers, the police and their White citizen deputies. Black people have no sanctuary, no sanctum, no inviolable sacred space. Even home becomes a prison, a death chamber where Blacks are violated with impunity, as was Breonna Taylor who was murdered by the Louisville police as they "served" an early morning no-knock warrant. Where blackness is constructed as dangerous and criminal, and where black people have no rights that an antiblack carceral state is bound to respect, "mistakes will be made." These mistakes that extinguish Black life are indistinguishable from intention under the purview of the criminology industry that reduces Black life to a math problem.

> We have seen that, in penal justice, the prison transformed the punitive procedure into a penitentiary technique; the carceral archipelago transported this technique from the penal institution to the entire social body.[1]

> Throughout the criminal justice system, as well as in our schools and public spaces, young + black + male is equated with reasonable suspicion, justifying the arrest, interrogation, search, and detention of thousands of African Americans every year, as well as their exclusion from employment and housing and the denial of educational opportunity. Because black youth are viewed as criminals, they face severe employment discrimination and are "pushed out" of schools through racially biased school discipline policies.[2]

> Dear Uncle Bill,
> Before I commence let me extend my apologies to you for asking you for money. . . . But the help I am going to ask you for will have a long-term effect on my remaining life. Before I make my request, I want to give you an idea of where I am mentally and spiritually so you can decide if I am worth your "sponsorship" or not.[3]

The news that my nephew had been shot and killed left me shocked and sad, but not surprised. It is possible to be both: shocked but not surprised. I knew that the kind of life he had led might end the way it did. Still, learning that he had died so violently and senselessly was shocking; not, to repeat, because I was unaware of the possibility, even the probability; rather, it was the actuality and finality of his death that struck me as novel. It was a new event in my experience. While striving not to violate my obligations of kinship piety to my deceased nephew, I wish to reflect on some of what it means to be a Black male in America. I pursue this inquiry by triangulating personal reflections with Michel Foucault's prescient analysis of the "carceral society," that is, prison-inspired techniques of social control (discipline) that colonize institutions writ large, forming an archipelago that creates the modern self, and Michelle Alexander's account of the Jim Crow-like[4] effects of mass incarceration.

While this chapter is about a systematic form of injustice, I do not deny the culpability of individual actors. On the contrary, it is the relationship between structure and agent—systemic habits, incentives, and constraints, on the one side and individual, circumstantial agency, on the other—that interests me. This chapter is not an argument about the actual innocence of my nephew. On the contrary, I hope to show that actual, individual guilt and systematic, racial injustice are compatible, and even integrally related. Everyone makes choices under circumstances they do not choose.[5] The institutional, structural, and systematic conditions (both enabling and disabling) that govern our choices are the unavoidable consequences of social life. However, everyone is not equally conditioned. The carceral society and its dominant expression in the regime of mass incarceration capture this structure/agent relationship—anonymous social structures, intersubjective habits, and individual agency—in the lives of Black people. But the focus of this chapter is the Black Male. Finally, a cautionary note directed as much to myself as to the reader: I will not act and hope not to be used as a weapon against my nephew; here I refer to the comparative trope of the so-called good Black versus the bad nigger that obscures the complexities and ambiguities of my life and his. This is a reminder of seductive tropes and story lines regarding Black males, crime, and punishment that must be resisted. I know that a host of contingencies, and not my preternaturally superior character, wisdom, or judgment, landed me in college and my nephew in prison. A religious person might call it "grace," a gambler, "luck." Through serendipity, I received the grace of being lucky, my nephew did not.

In some kinship systems, uncles have special duties toward their sister's children. They are part of the child's descent group in a way that the biological father is not. Uncles are the spiritual fathers, so to speak, of their sister's children. One finds this notion among the Akan people of West Africa, whose culture influenced African Americans in various ways. I have always experienced my role as an uncle in this manner, felt the obligation to care and guide. My job was to set an example, to mentor. So I was keen on helping my nephew, Corey D. Hunter, then twenty-nine years old and serving time for a felony robbery conviction in the Arizona State Prison. I had rebuffed an earlier request for money after judging his purposes to be trivial and self-indulgent. He seemed to be bullshitting, behavior I had seen before, and I did not wish to be played. Postmarked July 10, 2000, this letter,[6] which I present in serial form, was a follow-up request:

> When you last saw me I was in very bad shape, and I am sure when you first heard from me, the image of that "parasitic vagabond" flashed across your mental screen. Well that person no longer exists. Above, I said "when you last saw me," because I vaguely recall seeing you. One thing that I do recall with clarity is when you said to me, "I saw your daughter and she is beautiful." The lack of concern that I conveyed on that day, sticks in my heart and soul like a dagger. She is and always has been the axle to my earth, but you would not have known that by my response on that day.
>
> The reason I recall that moment is so that I could give you an idea of how far gone I was, and to also set a premise to show how far I have come. It was not incarceration, so much, that began my reconstruction, because I was at a point where I felt incarceration or death did not affect me or anyone else. That is how far removed, emotionally, I was. The thing or person that was the catalyst in

my reconstruction was the love and responsibility I felt toward my daughter (De'Antrea). After the smoke in my head cleared and my common sense was able to find solid ground, I begin to realize that although prison or death didn't seem to affect me, it did affect De'Antrea, and that in turn affected me in a profound way.

I met my niece, De'Antrea, in the late 1990s when she was about five. Her mother and Corey never married, and their relationship did not survive his imprisonment. I lost contact when her mother moved the family to Texas. Fortunately, my sister did not lose contact with her granddaughter; De'Antrea is a thriving, well-adjusted adult despite her father's incarceration and death. As is true of many who experience imprisonment, Corey's confinement, perhaps its penitential qualities, as generations of prison theorists and reformers hoped, goaded him toward self-reflection and reform.

> I don't think I can tell you of the particular system I used to set myself straight since the prison I am in does not offer a real program to help a person make an honest change. I can only attribute my change to the exhaustion I felt, of being a failure. That, along with the innocent soul I left out there, who didn't ask to be born, and definitely didn't ask to be born to an irresponsible loser for a father. All these things were my reasons or driving force for reconstructing my thoughts and conduct. Higher education has become an important aspect of all of this because when a person has lifted his pride and self-worth, education becomes a must if he/she plans to go higher and remain prideful and self-worthy. This is my personal philosophy, but I do believe it can and should be applied universally. The way it applies to me is that I've become a person who thinks better of himself and one who sees himself being an example setter for others who might travel the same destructive path as I did. Except, I do not want just to be a person who gets out and abstains from criminal activity. I want to be a person who can overcome great odds and I think the way to do that is by expanding my education.

Corey was always intelligent. But school was less attractive than the tough and rowdy company he kept. That company's codes of honor and manliness, cultivated far too often in fatherless homes, spoke to him in ways that the structure and decorum of the classroom did not. The classroom could not contain his rambunctious energy and did not provide avenues for his risk-taking sense of adventure. The street spoke his name. Early on he got caught up with the wrong crowd, became the wrong crowd, and found himself flowing through the school-to-prison pipeline before the term was even coined. (I should note that the pressure within that pipeline is more intense now than then; thus students are incarcerated for offenses as trivial as using profane language or texting in class. Criminalizing behaviors such as these, bypassing the principal and issuing police citations for normal if disrespectful adolescent behavior, and directing these punitive measures disproportionately toward Black children, creates a vicious cycle that makes future incarceration more likely.) In his request for financial assistance, my nephew appealed to our common humanity, which means among other things, our propensity to miss the mark.

> Do you remember your accident after your fire fighter's academy graduation? That could have been the death of you, and you would not have had the chance to be as great a man as you are now. No doubt you were a great man then, but your level of elevation now would not be possible. You may not know this but me and Theodore[7] thought you were some type of superman or something. To be able to kick out the windows and swim in fast moving waters to safety—Man! We were like, "I knew he was big and strong but I didn't know he was superman."

I had recently completed training at the Phoenix Firefighter's Academy and was now a probationary firefighter and emergency medical technician. After leaving a party for academy graduates extremely drunk, I nearly killed myself when I fell asleep and drove my car into a river. After escaping the car, swimming to shore, and enduring a fitful night, I retrieved my firefighting gear from the truck of my partially submerged car, the following morning. My younger brothers helped me. Construction workers in the area saw three young black men prying open the car truck, assumed that we were burglars, and called the police. Only my status as a firefighter and dumb luck (one of the officers and I had attended the same elementary school where we served together in student government) prevented my arrest and, since I was a probationary firefighter, the probable loss of my job. As my nephew reminded me, none of us live perfect lives. His youthful exaggerations of my talents notwithstanding, a different set of contingencies might have landed me in the clutches of a mass incarcerating society. Corey adds:

> The reason I brought this up was so I could sort of draw a parallel between that almost fatal incident and my nearly destructive life. Not to say that we are similar in anyway, because I could never be who you are. But I would like to overcome my situation with the capability to be all that I can. *For certain I do not want to come back here.* (Emphasis added)

Corey is sure that he does not want to return to the Arizona State Prison. Any romantic notions of prison that he may have had are gone. He knows that prison is no frolic in the park. For thousands of African American boys and men and increasingly for Black women and girls, prison is a cruel joke. Mass incarceration is the punitive activity of a society that has always criminalized blackness and punished Black people. Since Black people are presumptively guilty, whether subjects of the criminal justice system or not, only the system can properly establish innocence. Actual innocence derives from presumptive guilt. Always on trial, Black people are guilty until proven innocent. *There is no presumption of innocence.* This kind of thinking lies behind the regime of stop and frisk. This is why the lives of Black people, especially Black males, are precarious; it is why, hoping against hope, many regard education as a reliable way out.

> The bottom line to all this is I do not want to get out without a higher level of education. I would love to exit with at least an associate's degree in business. Since this goal of mine can only be accomplished through outside assistance, I was hoping that a person such as you, who can appreciate a second chance, can be helpful to an ambitious nephew. What I am getting at Uncle Bill is, if it is possible, I would like for you to sponsor me in this educational endeavor. Tell the family I said hello and to take care.
>
> P.S. Sorry for such a long letter
Your striving nephew
Corey D. Hunter
7/8/00

I helped my nephew. A few years later he was released from prison and began the difficult task as an ex-convict, especially as a young Black man, of building a new life. For a time he seemed to be successful. I was very proud of him. But on April 30, 2008, he was shot and killed. His inability to leave behind a grudge cultivated in prison against another former inmate led to a deadly altercation. Caught up in distorted notions of manhood and honor that only metastasized in prison, he was both a victim and a perpetrator in his own death. Though I shall argue that the script was already written, the suspicious regard preordained and, therefore, that the "deck was stacked," my nephew behaved in ways that properly brought him to the attention of the criminal justice system. But the carceral realities that condition the lives of Black men in America are remarkably indifferent to actual innocence. They operate independently of the actual behavior of Black boys and men. These carceral realities manifest as an all-pervasive visibility and surveillance. Black people are made visible, their presence conspicuous. Even a cursory exploration of American history reveals this panoptic whiteness at work, controlling the free movement of Black people in social space. The presence of masterless, nonservile, and nondocile Black bodies—male, female, or transgender—triggers a suspicious and punitive response: keep the nigger down. Rooted in a deeply ingrained mental habit, this response signifies that something in the social order is awry—danger lurks. The default response is to call the slave catcher or the police. By the Civil War, Black bodies were an immensely valuable commodity in the form of free labor, cheap labor, and enhanced social status. Second only to the dollar value of the land, of which the Native Peoples were brutally dispossessed, Black bodies circulated in the slave economy and the neo-slave economy that followed as both a commodity and a living form of capital that required discipline and control. From the very beginning, panoptic whiteness—surveilling Black bodies with the aim of making them docile and useful—married the profit motif of the new world planter capitalist class and various profiteers in the Atlantic world who were complicit with them. So the surveillance of Black bodies, especially males, is to reiterate a deeply ingrained American habit. It constitutes the American habitus, America's common sense.

To characterize matters this way might seem overly pessimistic and suggests that American society strongly resists perceptions of Black bodies that are not coded as dangerous when unchained. But this is precisely what an unblinkered assessment shows. My nephew may in fact have been dangerous. But he was perceived as dangerous before the fact of his actual criminality and would have been so perceived even if he had led an exemplary life. The whole point of panoptic whiteness lies in its *counter-empirical* phenomenology.[8] It constructs Black males as dangerous in opposition to the facts.[9] It prefigures Black boys and men as criminals; through biased perception and targeted surveillance, it creates the conditions of a self-fulfilling prophecy—the mass incarceration of Black people. Complete with animosity, guilt, and denial, this construction of Black people is an American habit.

New York City police officers sweep through Black neighborhoods, and especially through the "contact zones" where such neighborhoods are white-defined social spaces, stopping, questioning, frisking, and humiliating Black men at an exceptionally high rate. On this antiblack view, the dragnet approach to policing is especially apropos since the agency of a single Black person is isomorphic with the group: to know how one behaves is to know the group; indeed, because one *knows* the group, individuals do not matter. Thus antiblackness stigmatizes the group and renders the individual indistinct and imperceptible as an individual. In the vernacular of some urban police departments, the Black individual is just one more "Yo." In these encounters, police attempt to impose Jim Crow etiquette by demanding an ostentatious performance of Black docility. Failure to perform may lead to insult, humiliation, and deadly violence. Blacks are routinely treated the way Dylan Roof, the neo-Confederate white supremacists would have been treated if he were black, that is, like the mass murderer he was. In contrast to the typical Black person's experience, he was treated with dignity and respect. Roof may have been a white terroristic murderous danger to Blacks several of whom he had just killed, but the police officers who arrested him did not regard him archetypically as a threat to them. As police sweep the streets, school officials sweep through classrooms and hallways criminalizing adolescence. The surveillance of Black adolescents *of all genders*, boys in particular, is especially intense. As everyone *knows*, Black people, adult and child, are disposed to criminality. So school officials find what they are looking for, behavior that "merits" zero tolerance, suspension, expulsion, and arrest.

Within a racially driven carceral society, Black people are judged abnormal, aggressive, surly, and insubordinate. Black boys and men are judged to be especially dangerous and violent (and so are Black girls, given video evidence of the manhandling violence toward them of school resource officers). *They are caught in a carceral pincher movement of stop and frisk and the school to prison pipeline.* This pipeline, through which the prison industrial complex acquires ever younger targeted victims, is the latest and, perhaps, the most pernicious example of the carceral society at work. In an institutional space, second only to home, where Black boys ought to receive care and encouragement, they are vulnerable to punitive practices that place them in the hands of the juvenile and adult "justice" system. Adolescents can test the patience and composure of the most even-tempered adult. And of course, there are extreme behaviors that genuinely merit suspension, expulsion, or arrest. What ought to be exceptional measures have become all to routine, especially for Black adolescents *of all genders*—even for Black preadolescents. Once approached developmentally, the effervescence and boisterousness of boyhood are now treated punitively. And some boys are not recognized as boys at all. According to a recent study, White middle-class males "are not held fully responsible for their actions" until their late twenties, long past the traditional age of college graduation, before which, of course, *White boys* will be boys, are allowed to be boys. In contrast, Black children may be perceived as adults as early as thirteen. On average, in some cases, observers overestimate the age of Black children by more than four and a half years. Unlike most children, perceived as "innocent until adulthood"—this includes eighteen- to twenty-two-year-old *White kids* in colleges and universities whose lives should not be ruined by youthful indiscretions—Black children may be deemed suspicious and judged worthy of a punitive response while still in elementary school.[10] This frightening picture underscores the harsh reality of the school-to-prison pipeline. Through zero tolerance policies and the inappropriate and excessive use of suspension, expulsion, and arrest, the disciplines and penalties of the prison invade and reorganize the environment of the schoolhouse. These prison protocols pipeline students into the "justice system." Black boys are disproportionately subjected to this fate.

In the late nineteenth and early twentieth centuries, America's Jim Crow justice system routinely and systematically arrested Black people, marginalized by the Jim Crow economy, for the crime of vagrancy. These manufactured criminals, created by and for the Jim Crow political economy, were then leased to mines and other commercial corporations. This "slavery by another name,"[11] as it is aptly called, was the cruel fate of many Black people after the end of Reconstruction and the "redemption" of the south. Along with peonage, Jim Crow vagrancy laws and the Jim Crow convict lease system became dominant techniques for disciplining "free" Black labor. This was a "job market exclusion to prison pipeline." In the late twentieth and early twenty-first centuries, the school age descendants of these African Americans, enslaved post-emancipation, are caught in a new prison pipeline. Incarcerated Black children are the new vagrants, this time in the form of superfluous labor, of the twenty-first century.

In *Burning Down the House: The End of Juvenile Prison*, investigative journalist Nell Bernstein counts the costs.

> Fully 80 to 90 percent of American teenagers have committed an illegal act that could qualify them for time behind bars, and one third of all teens have committed a serious crime. Most, however, never see the inside of a jail, or even a police car.
> . . . .
> Black and brown youth, especially those from impoverished communities, face far different prospects than their white counterparts on this front. Those who live in poor neighborhoods are subject to what sociologist Victor Rios calls a "culture of control"—treated with suspicion and harsh discipline at school, on the street, and even in the community.
> . . . .
> Disproportionately black and brown, they are more likely to have been victims of violence than they are to have perpetrated it. Incarceration not only exacerbates the vulnerabilities with which they arrive but exposes them to all manner of new challenges: post-traumatic stress syndrome, curtailed education; gang affiliation and a warrior mentality enforced by prison culture; the unraveling effects of social isolation and a lifetime of stigma and further isolation.[12]

Incarceration shadows the Black male coming of age genre and other narratives that explore the Black male experience in America: from Richard Wright's *Black Boy* (1945) to Claude Brown's *Manchild in the Promised Land* (1965), Brent Staples's *Parallel Time: Growing Up in Black and White* (1993), Nathan McCall's *Makes Me Wanna Holler: A Young Black Man in*

America (1995), Ellis Cose's *The Envy of the World: On Being a Black Man in America* (2002), to Wes Moore's *The Other Wes Moore: One Name, Two Fates* (2010). After a youthful encounter with reform school, the pivotal event in Brown's life was his resolution not to go to jail or kill anyone.[13] I wonder about the contingencies that enabled his resolution and can't help but think of my nephew. After his arrest for armed robbery, McCall's holding cell, full of black faces, reminded him of the "Motherland."[14] Without denying that Black men are targeted by the criminal justice system in a racially discriminatory way, Cose fears that contemporary Black men, unlike their predecessors, are coconspirators in their own subjugation.[15] Staples contemplates the absurdities of parallel time: his pursuit of a PhD and entry into a world of status and achievement and his brother's death from a drug deal gone awry. Despite differences, these texts show the extent to which the Black male experience is a history of carceral surveillance, discipline, and mass incarceration. They exhibit what the historian Khalil Muhammad calls the "condemnation of blackness," how constructing Black people as dangerous criminals affected urbanization.[16] These books are at their best when the authors refuse to embrace a heroic narrative, when they avoid exceptionalist, Horatio Alger, up by your boot straps accounts. In this regard, none of these authors is more effective than Moore who compares his fate as a Rhodes Scholar with another Wes Moore, who grew up on the same Baltimore streets and is now serving a sentence of life in prison for murder: "The chilling truth is that Wes's story could have been mine; the tragedy is that mine could have been his."[17]

If I am pessimistic, to take up this issue again, then it reflects my realism. The numbers do not lie. One—the United States incarcerates more people than any country in the world.[18] Two—black people are disproportionately incarcerated: 13 percent of the population, roughly 39 percent of those incarcerated. Three—by the 1990s, the emergent era of colorblindness, Black men were incarcerated at seven times the rate of White men; more than twice as high as the comparative rates of the 1930s during the official era of Jim Crow.[19] Though imprisonment is overwhelmingly a male phenomenon, rates of Black female incarceration are also disproportionate: one in every eighteen Black women versus one in every 111 White women.[20] Four—though the rate of drug offenses among Blacks is both proportionate to their percentage of the population (13%) and lower than the rate among Whites, Blacks are arrested (38%) and convicted (59%) at much higher rates.[21] Five—*the numbers do lie* insofar as data on black social progress routinely excludes the prison and jail population and thus, in the age of Obama, creates the illusion that African Americans are doing better than they are.[22] At every stage of the criminal justice system—from assumptions about who commits crime to police surveillance, incarceration, and parole—black people are treated in a racially disparate manner.[23] Yes, there are icons of Black achievement in virtually every sector of American life. Counterstereotypical black achievers—what we once called "black firsts," the first this or that—have become routine. A Black man has served as president of the United States, an occurrence that many thought impossible in their lifetimes, though they no doubt overestimated its significance.[24] Such Black achievement notwithstanding, an extraordinary wealth disparity between Black and White persists. Even when adjusted for income and educational attainment, the wealth disparity persists, a legacy of slavery, Jim Crow economics and banking practices, government social policies such as the New Deal, the Federal Housing Administration, and the destruction of Black communities and wealth through Negro removal, also known as urban renewal.[25] These practices created a large thriving White middle class and impoverished Black ghettos.[26] Created by slavery, Jim Crow, and government, this wealth disparity is "the changing same" beneath important but superficial changes in law, educational attainment, and reductions in income inequality.

These are the realities into which the contingencies of history threw my nephew. He came of age in the late 1970s and 1980s during the birth of mass incarceration, what Michelle Alexander calls the New Jim Crow. Like "the other Wes Moore," the choices that Corey made (under circumstances he did not choose) exacerbated the negative contingencies in his environment. Of course, everyone's choices are constrained. This is our common existential condition. However, in a society governed by the carceral gaze of panoptic whiteness, the choices of black people are differentially and invidiously constrained. To use Nell Bernstein's phrase, Corey died in large part because of "a warrior mentality enforced by prison culture."[27] Warriors fight, kill, rape, and pillage. *One finds this warrior ethos within various cultures of hypermasculinity: military, prisons, gangs, sports, and fraternities among others.* For this reason, we are under ethical obligation to reduce the occasions for war: actual warfare conducted by militants and its iconic and metastatic effects within hypermasculine cultures and across the social body.[28] I ache thinking about what might have been, the life my nephew might have lived, and the person he might have become. Corey was more than an ex-convict. He had a way about him, a captivating smile, a twinkle in his eye.

Antiblackness renders Black people hypervisible while concealing the process of race-making. This act of concealing is so effective that many intelligent White people convinced themselves that racism only exists in isolated and vestigial forms or in the fervid and disordered imaginations of Black people.[29] They view racism, primarily if not exclusively, as a matter of individual subjectivity, bad intentions, and ostentatious signs such as the use of the word nigger. They deny the reality of racism as a material, structural, and systematic phenomenon when they say things such as "I do not hate Black people" or "I have Black friends and family members." These claims are logically identical to the claims often made by men that they are not sexist because they love women. Loving, marrying, and sharing all manner of intimacy with women does not mitigate habits, institutions, and disciplines that systematically advantage men and disadvantage women. Love abides with catastrophic levels of domestic, sexual, and psychic violence against women, and with blaming them for their victimization and for our violence. Even if, individually, we are not misogynists and do not victimize women, we are advantaged by the systematic effects of male dominance. Men may not be guilty but they are responsible. Male advantage and female disadvantage play within the complexities of intersectionality. To illustrate this point consider this analogy. Though individual white people may not behave in an antiblack manner, they are advantaged by the systematic effects of racism and have an obligation to work collectively to change that social reality. In the same way that advantaged men of all races bear more responsibility for confronting misogyny than disadvantaged men, White elites bear more responsibility than do disadvantaged White people for confronting antiblackness. Intersectional differences among White people are relevant to attributions of responsibility.

Liberation from the carceral gaze of colorblind white supremacy is inseparable from the destruction of distorted notions of manhood: masculinity as an invidious relation to femininity, the subjection and diminution of women, womanliness, transgender persons, and intersexed bodies. Those who deny the reality of racism structured by white supremacy, that is, antiblackness or who relegate it to the subjectivity of isolated individuals, ignore habits, institutional arrangements, and disciplines that systematically advantage White people and disadvantage Black people. Captive to a kind of *racial dyslexia*, they cannot read what is in plain view, ubiquitous signs of white supremacy. They refuse to connect the data points, indices found virtually everywhere, that reveal, *in the absence of conscious intent*, the systematic effects of racist habits, institutions, and disciplines. Absent individual intent, they see such indices as indicating nothing—except, perhaps, an unfortunate coincidence or the pathology of Black people. They deny the implicit dimensions of human motivation. The ignorant and the knowledgeable alike skate along the surface of explicit motivations: the former because they do not know what lies beneath; the latter because they do know but do not wish to acknowledge what they know.[30] They reduce racism to hate. But antiblackness is more complicated, protean, cunning, and powerful than hate. Though important, animus is only one disposition among many that an antiblack racist can have. When some White supremacists say that they do not hate Black people or that some of their friends or family members are black, they speak the truth. White supremacy cannot be reduced to hate. It is a more complicated phenomenon than that. White supremacy is compatible with kinship, love, and friendship, however degraded. As I remarked elsewhere, I have no doubt that the arch white supremacist Strom Thurmond loved the daughter that he fathered with his family's Black maid. Though he concealed paternity, Thurmond provided for his daughter, Essie Mae Washington-Williams (1925–2013), throughout his life. We might not like it but there it is.

NOTES

1. Michel Foucault, *Discipline and Punish: The Birth of the Prison* (New York: Vintage Books, 1979), 298.
2. Michelle Alexander, *The New Jim Crow: Mass Incarceration in the Age of Colorblindness* (New York: The New Press, 2012), 199.
3. Corey D. Hunter, "Letter to Uncle Bill," personal communication, July 8, 2000. Printed with permission.
4. I say "Jim Crow-like" to signal a slight disagreement with Alexander.
5. Philosophers debate the nature of choosing and whether constrained choices are choices. I subscribe to the view that all choices are constrained.
6. With the exception of minor editing, this letter is a verbatim transcript of my nephew's letter. One use of "yourself" was changed to "you." I removed some comma splicing and altered one sentence fragment. In the sixth paragraph, two uses of "a" were changed to "an." In the last paragraph, I changed the beginning of the first sentence from "As I digress" to "In conclusion." I capitalized "Uncle" before "Bill." In addition, I made minor corrections of grammar, syntax, and word choice. To retain my nephew's authentic voice, I choose not to clean up everything.
7. Corey's younger brother.
8. Nell Bernstein remarks that "race and class, more than anything else, *including* behavior, determine who gets locked up in this country." See *Burning Down the House: The End of Juvenile Prison* (New York: The New Press, 2014), 99.
9. This perception of criminal danger distorts the real, historically based danger to white supremacy: the prospect of the slave escaping and, under the worse scenario, incarnating the vengeance of Nat Turner or, in the deep background, the revolutionary insurrection of the Haitian people.
10. Phillip Atiba Goff, Matthew Christian Jackson, Brooke Allison Lewis Di Leone, Carmen Marie Culotta, Natalie Ann DiTomasso, "The Essence of Innocence: Consequences of Dehumanizing Black Children," *Journal of Personality and Social Psychology*, Vol. 106, No. 4 (2014): 526–545; DOI: 10.1037/a0035663, 541.
11. See Douglas A. Blackmon, *Slavery by Another Name: The Re-Enslavement of Black Americans from the Civil War to World War II* (New York: Doubleday, 2008).
12. Bernstein, 8–9.
13. Claude Brown, *Manchild in the Promised Land* (New York: Touchstone, 1965), 183.
14. Nathan McCall, *Makes Me Wanna Holler: A Young Black Man in America* (New York: Vintage Books, 1995), 149.
15. Ellis Cose, *The Envy of the World: On Being a Black Man in America* (New York: Washington Square Press, 2002), 99.

16. See Khalil Muhammad, *The Condemnation of Blackness: Race, and Crime and the Making of Modern Urban America* (Cambridge; Harvard University Press, 2011).

17. Wes Moore, *The Other Wes Moore: One Name, Two Fates* (New York: Spiegel and Grau, 2002), 180.

18. http://www.apcca.org/uploads/10th_Edition_2013.pdf; Roy Walmsley, "World Prison Population List" (Tenth Edition), *International Centre for Prison Studies*, 1 (Victoria Charity Centre and University of Essex: London, UK, 2013).

19. Becky Pettit, *Invisible Men: Mass Incarceration and the Myth of Black Progress* (New York: Russell Sage Foundation, 2012), 15

20. http://www.sentencingproject.org/template/page.cfm?id=122 (last accessed June 14, 2014).

21. http://www.civilrights.org/publications/justice-on-trial/; Justice on Trial: Racial Disparities in the American Justice System, 8.

22. Pettit, 33, 46, 50, 52, 79–80.

23. http://www.civilrights.org/publications/justice-on-trial/ (Executive Summary).

24. Clayton R. Critcher and Jane L. Risen, "If He Can Do It, So Can They: Exposure to Counterstereotypically Successful Exemplars Prompts Automatic Inferences," *Journal of Personality and Social Psychology*, Vol. 106, No. 3 (2014): 359.

25. Rebecca Tippett, Avis Jones-DeWeever, Maya Rockeymoore, Darrick Hamilton, William Darity, Jr., "Beyond Broke: Why Closing the Racial Wealth Gap is a Priority for National Economic Security," Center for Global Policy Solutions (May 2014): 1. Accessed on June 28, 2014 at http://globalpolicysolutions.org/wp-content/uploads/2014/04/Beyond_Broke_FINAL.pdf.

26. See Ira Katznelson, *When Affirmative Action Was White: An Untold History of Racial Inequality in Twentieth-Century America* (New York: W.W. Norton and Company, 2005).

27. As Bernstein remarks in the passage I quoted earlier, the first exposure to this culture is often the consequence of school-to-prison pipeline.

28. See General Morrison's blistering comments on a culture of rape and humiliation with the Australian army: https://www.youtube.com/watch?v=QaqpoeVgr8U.

29. Critcher and Risen, 360.

30. See Critcher and Risen's analysis of the relationship between explicit and implicit beliefs, 373.

BIBLIOGRAPHY

Alexander, Michelle. *The New Jim Crow: Mass Incarceration in the Age of Colorblindness* (New York: The New Press, 2012).

Bernstein, Nell. *Burning Down the House: The End of Juvenile Prison* (New York: The New Press, 2014).

Blackmon, Douglas A. *Slavery by Another Name: The Re-Enslavement of Black Americans from the Civil War to World War II* (New York: Doubleday, 2008).

Brown, Claude. *Manchild in the Promised Land* (New York: Touchstone, 1965).

Cose, Ellis. *The Envy of the World: On Being a Black Man in America* (New York: Washington Square Press, 2002).
Critcher, Clayton R. and Jane L. Risen, "If He Can Do It, So Can They: Exposure to Counterstereotypically Successful Exemplars Prompts Automatic Inferences," *Journal of Personality and Social Psychology, 106*(3), (2014): 359.
Foucault, Michel. *Discipline and Punish: The Birth of the Prison* (New York: Vintage Books, 1979).
Goff, Phillip Atiba, Matthew Christian Jackson, Brooke Allison Lewis Di Leone, Carmen Marie Culotta, and Natalie Ann DiTomasso, "The Essence of Innocence: Consequences of Dehumanizing Black Children," *Journal of Personality and Social Psychology, 106*(4), (2014): 526–545; DOI: 10.1037/a0035663, 541.
Hunter, Corey D. "Letter to Uncle Bill," personal communication (2000).
Katznelson, Ira. *When Affirmative Action Was White: An Untold History of Racial Inequality in Twentieth-Century America* (New York: W.W. Norton and Company, 2005).
McCall, Nathan. *Makes Me Wanna Holler: A Young Black Man in America* (New York: Vintage Books, 1995).
Moore, Wes. *The Other Wes Moore: One Name, Two Fates* (New York: Spiegel and Grau, 2002).
Muhammad, Khalil. *The Condemnation of Blackness: Race, and Crime and the Making of Modern Urban America* (Cambridge: Harvard University Press, 2011).
Pettit, Becky. *Invisible Men: Mass Incarceration and the Myth of Black Progress* (New York: Russell Sage Foundation, 2012).
Rovner, Josh, et al. "Racial Justice." *The Sentencing Project*, July 15, 2021, www.sentencingproject.org/issues/racial-disparity/.
Tippett, Rebecca, Avis Jones-DeWeever, Maya Rockeymoore, Darrick Hamilton, William Darity, Jr., "Beyond Broke: Why Closing the Racial Wealth Gap is a Priority for National Economic Security," Center for Global Policy Solutions (May 2014): 1. Accessed on June 28, 2014.
Walmsley, Roy. "World Prison Population List" (Tenth Edition), *International Centre for Prison Studies*, 1 (Victoria Charity Centre and University of Essex: London, UK, 2013).

Chapter 2

Philosophy as Excited Delirium and the Credibility Deficit of the Black Male

Clevis Headley

Writing is a risky and potentially treacherous undertaking. Hence, I want to quickly register a few qualifications. First, my goal is not to engage in the suspect activity of quantitatively measuring levels of oppression and domination in order to identify their victims. Second, I do not use the term "Black male" to privilege a hegemonic Black male subject or to center one specific Black male subjectivity as representative of all Black males. Notwithstanding these qualifications, however, one can identify certain themes that are implicit to the Black male lived experience in spite of its diversity.

I will pursue three goals in this chapter.[1] The first goal is to provide a theoretical framing for philosophizing about Black male existence. The second goal is to utilize Tommy Curry's critical engagement with the disciplinary regimes complicit in the representational assassination of Black male existence. Third, and finally, I will employ Miranda Fricker's notion of credibility injustice, among other notions, to introduce other forms of credibility injustice that afflict Black males.

PHILOSOPHIZING WHILE BLACK

The savage murder of George Floyd at the hands of Derek Chauvin and his complicit and morally impaired cohorts is pregnant with a disturbing superfluity of significance. Indeed, the interpretative challenge of understanding the circumstances of Floyd's tragic death escapes all efforts to limit it to an unimaginative and facile reading of Chauvin's despicable and dreadful behavior. For, in retrospect, George Floyd's murder was not just another causal incident of police brutality; rather, seemingly haunted by a dramatic and paradoxical moment of transcendence, the intrusion of a sneaky epiphany, Floyd's murder came to signal or symbolize a movement beyond mundane existence. Despite the haunting ineffability of the event—a meaning that defies the formal limits of representation—Floyd's murder also registers the strange experience or, rather, the peculiar experience of the being-in-the-world of the Black male.

Linguistic alienation and well as cognitive alienation, which doubly constitute an aggravating and enhanced sense of being exiled from the ordinary order of things, are intimate and relentless companions of the Black male. In another sense, there is also the apparently axiomatic assumption that Black males are perverse agents of trauma; they inflict trauma upon others and unmake their world by rendering it meaningless. However, Black males themselves are seldom, if ever, regarded as the victims of trauma and/or the deserving targets of sympathy; they are seen as the perpetrators of trauma but never as its hallowed victims; they do not and cannot claim any direct experiential awareness of what it means to be a body suffering the convulsions of agonizing pain.

Despite the uncanniness of Being that is characteristic of human existence, that is, the sense of thrownness or of abandonment in the world, the absurdity attendant to the unbearable heaviness of being a Black male, who is already by default an objective enemy of the American State, is inexplicably an apparition of thought and being. We are all already exhausted by the conventional narratives of Black male pathology and dysfunctionality. Although multiple thinkers have rightfully denounced the depraved American social science tradition of imprisoning the Black male in an infinite web of pathologies, there is still something to be gained from metaphorically invoking the notion of the bell curve to fashion an interpretive framing of depictions of Black males. My point here is that, while other groups of human beings conform to the common bell curve distribution to the extent that most of them are characterized as average or normal, Black males are subjected to two extreme characterizations on the curve, both of which are defective. The first, which characterizes the Black male as a "freak of nature," is just as precarious as the second, which characterizes the Black male as "exceptional."

There is, then, no stable pattern indicative of Black male normality. The existence of Black men admits to no norm. There is no credible ontological center, and any appearance of a center is hollow precisely because, again, there is no middle range or virtuous mean. There are only extremes of deviance. Even a Black man located on the extreme side of exceptionality is considered a magical kind of being—a being outside the human norm. However, in spite of being seen as defective in not admitting to a norm, Black men are still subjected to the imperatives of fungibility. If all Black males are defective, they are interchangeable in that one Black male can replace or substitute for the other. Yet, although one Black male can take the place of the other, no Black male can replace or substitute the average human being. Black males remain caricatures imprisoned in a "circus of stereotypes." What I propose to do in this brief chapter is to weave an intertextual narrative of what it means to be a Black male at this moment in time, by blending implicit lived experience with textual accounts. At the same time, I will also endeavor to accomplish what mainstream society considers impossible. For how can a Black male at this historical moment seriously believe that, through writing, he will "find determinacy and meaning where previously there was none"?[2] Is the idea, true for other human beings, that "writing is pivotal to how human beings reorient themselves after they have lost their footing in the world"[3] also true for Black males? Is it the case that the world, by its very nature, is anti-Black male? Is the world structured and does it operate in ways that render the Black male its objective enemy?

Even as I commit to writing the present chapter, it is crucial to establish that I will not employ the documentary style of writing that descriptively names objects of the world. Similarly, I will not render transparent any fully, self-contained subject. My task here is not to make transparent an opaque Black male subject whose particularity must, in turn, assume the burden of suspending its own singularity in order to render possible a universal Black male subjectivity. Contrary to the canonical expectations, the deviant hope is that

> [i]n putting itself to the task of writing, [a Black male] consciousness replaces its former object (the "I" and its immediate experiences) with something new. With this development comes not just a new object for, but also a new *mode* of [Black male] consciousness.[4]

To wrestle with the idea of existing as a Black male, particularly in the aftermath of the death of George Floyd, means to reject the empty rhetoric of liberalism. The very notion of being an "abstract individual" that is purged of contingencies means surrendering one's facticity for the sake of an infinite liberal freedom. This is an offensive imperative. However, resisting the bad faith renunciation of Black male facticity does not entail reduction to a pathetic/pathological/immoral personality that imprisons the Black male in a myopic racial/gender identity. The choice to affirm Black male positionality is a strategic use of one's own subjective position to radically affirm and celebrate the plurality of other positionalities in their enchanting singularity. As James Baldwin once urged, one must have the courage to love not as an abstract individual but, rather, as another vulnerable human being, struggling to navigate the uncertainties and disappointments of a fragile and precarious existence. Perhaps, Black male suffering can have redemptive value, if it awakens society to alternative ways of viewing the world that are not clothed in the rhetoric of a whitewashed liberalism and are not mutated versions of white, heterosexual maleness. If Black males must die, they should choose to die to make a different world possible, rather than to die like white men and for the sake of preserving whiteness.[5]

ACADEMIC POLICING AND THE BLACK MALE

I find it imperative to weave Tommy Curry's *The Man-Not: Race, Class, Genre, and the Dilemmas of Black Manhood* into this work. Curry follows other thinkers who, among other things, seek to center Black male experience within the discipline of philosophy. One such notable thinker is George Yancy who, in his *Black Bodies, White Gazes: The Continuing Significance of Race*, critically, but not exclusively, works through the existential implications of the fact that "Black males still socially embody a lethal and threatening presence in the white imaginary."[6] Yancy also underscores the extent to which hypervisibility does not afford Black males any semblance of ontological rigidity—it only affords ontological vulnerability. He claims that "in the case of hypervisibility, the Black body becomes excessive. Within this racially saturated field of hypervisibility, the Black body still functions as the unseen as it does in the case of its invisibility."[7] Furthermore, the Black male, in this context, becomes ghost like—a seen absence. Yancy writes about being a "seen absence." He also states, "I am visible in my invisibility."[8] And David Marriott, in his *On Black Men*, writes:

> Representations [of Black males in European and American culture] invite us to imagine an imitative perversion of human kind, a being incapable of inhibition, morals or ideas; a being whose supernatural indulgence of pleasure and continued satisfaction cannot deal with the contrary of denial or pain; a being whose violent, sexual criminality is incapable of any lasting, or real relationships, only counterfeit, or trickery; a being who remains a perpetual child, rather than a father. The black man is, in other words, everything that the wishful-shameful fantasies of culture want him to be, an enigma of inversion and of hate—and this is our existence as men, as black men.[9]

Despite sharing much in common with Yancy and Marriott, what is particularly distinctive about Curry's project is his demand for a unique discursive place for Black males—a Black Male Studies disciplinary infrastructure is required in order to combat the intellectual equivalent of physical castration and/or theoretical lynching. Curry denounces the various strategies of containment that deny Black males fundamental characteristics enjoyed by other males. Addressing the desire to strip away the manhood of Black males in academic discourses, Curry writes:

> This paradigm is far too prevalent to not warrant remark. Racist accounts of Black males depict them as lesser males who are lazy, unintelligent, aggressive, and violent toward women and children and who abandon their families physically and cannot provide for them economically, while nonetheless requiring coercive legal and extralegal sanctions to control their hyper-masculinity and predatory inclinations.[10]

One of the peculiar things is not that there are many different forms of scholarly discourses about Black males but the extent to which these paradigms of writing converge upon an ontological disappearance/erasure of the Black male; for even hypervisibility facilitates the perception of the Black male as an object to be feared, a presence to be avoided at all cost. And, in accordance with this way of thinking, the Black male must be feared precisely because he is a monstrous ontological presence, a thing from outside this world. Curry creatively invokes the idea of the Black male as a *Man-Not*. The Black male occupies a zone outside the categories of class, race, and gender. Curry writes:

> The Black man, deprived not only of an identity but also a history and existence that differs from his brute negation, experiences the world as a *Man-Not*.
> *Man-Not(ness)* is a term used to express the specific genre category of the Black male.... The Black male is negated not from an origin of (human) being, but from nihility.... Nonbeing expresses the condition of Black male being—the nihility from which it is birthed.[11]

Whereas the category of maleness, at least in certain circles, represents the human norm and, by default, elevates males to a higher status of being, Curry argues this status is not conferred upon Black males. Through a certain ontological deformation or degeneration, maleness is not a category that extends any meaningful benefits or protection to Black males. Maleness, Curry maintains, has been variously defined. However, efforts to apply "maleness" to Black males result in catastrophic ontological deformations because, in them, maleness is mutated. He states that "instead of being protected by patriarchy, Black men and boys are revealed to be its ... victims under closer examination."[12] The loss of his maleness reveals the extent to which the Black male persistently survives as the paradigmatic enemy of all humanity. In short, the Black male is an unabashed ontological predator—a certain lifeform genetically hardwired to prey upon the innocence of all human forms of life.

Because of his structural and existential commitment to rapacious forms of behavior, the Black male is unworthy of ever being considered a victim. Like maleness, the category of the victim does not legitimately apply to the Black male. Curry dedicates his research project to exploring "how the myth of the super-predator is codified within the disciplinary proliferation of theories about Black masculinity and makes it seemingly impossible to conceptualize the Black male as a victim and disadvantaged when compared with other groups."[13]

Even when Black males seek to express their subjectivity, to escape the zone of nonbeing and to claim an identity, they are still denounced as counterfeit humans. Apparently, their natures are so impaired that, even if they attempt to occupy the role of normal subjectivity, they cannot resist the temptation to engage in unethical behavior. They imitate others and assume identities that do not rightfully belong to them. In this context, Curry focuses on the tendency to frame the Black male as being infected with the jealous desire to embody white patriarchy. Black men, in other words, want what white males have: hyper patriarchy. Curry explains this bizarre yearning in the heart of Black males as follows: "The mimetic thesis, or the idea that Black males seek to emulate and ultimately realize themselves as patriarchs next to white men."[14] As Curry contextualizes this rather bizarre thesis, he explains the torture that Black men endure in attempting to frame their own understanding of maleness from their own distinctive mode of being-in-the-world. Curry writes:

> Academic theory has a passion for Black male mimeticism—so much so that it is analytic, a property of Black maleness itself. This position is little more than a myth disproved by attitudinal studies on Black men since that middle 1980s. In reality, . . . Black males simply do not share the same definitions or hold the same cultural expectations as white men in America.[15]

As opposed to the vulgarity of degrading the Black male's existence to a cheap mimicking of the norm, thus treating Black males as mere existential simians invested in servile imitation, Curry underscores the anguish and vulnerability of Black males. He explains as follows:

> *Black male vulnerability* is the term I use to capture the disadvantages that Black males endure compared with other groups; the erasure of Black males' actual lived experience from theory; and the violence and death Black males suffer in society. . . . The term is also meant to express the vulnerable condition—the sheer fungibility—of the Black male as a living terror able to be killed, raped, or dehumanized at any moment, given the disposition of those who encounter him.[16]

The question emerges: Where precisely do these considerations leave us? Why critically engage with the various ways in which society and the academy construct the Black male as a sinister presence in the world? To be more specific, how do these insights relate to the death of George Floyd? The logic is inescapable: Black males are existential threats to the material and symbolic order of mainstream society. They are threats that inhabit the environment of an organism and so must be eliminated. This entails that Black males, since they are perceived as threats, should similarly be eliminated. They become the walking dead among us. In the eyes of the law and the State, this is one reason why George Floyd necessarily had to die. Curry concludes:

> While an analysis of the super-predator, domestic and sexual violence, and the presumption of Black males as only perpetrators, and not victims, of violence may expose the limitations of academic scholarship, the consequence of such an examination may entail confronting the reality that Black maleness is cemented semiotically, and thereby ontologically, as a category of death and disregarded within the symbolic order of America.[17]

BLACK MALE EXISTENCE, VARIETIES OF CREDIBILITY DEFICITS, AND STRUCTURES OF INJUSTICE

At this point, I also wish to build upon Miranda Fricker's deployment of the trope of credibility to codify unique forms of injustice. In this context, my goal is to stretch the notion of credibility, in order to expand its metaphorical reach and then use it to facilitate a framing of Black male existence. Following Fricker, we must begin with an observation about social power, which is merely the capacity an individual has as a social agent to affect the way things go in the social world.[18] But social power is not generic. There are different types of social power, one of which is "identity social power." Identity social power designates those operations or sites of power that are

> dependent upon agents having shared conceptions of social identity—conceptions alive in the collective social imagination that govern . . . what it means to be [a particular social subject]. Whenever there is an operation of power that depends in some significant degree upon such shared imaginative conceptions of social identity, the *identity power* is at work.[19]

Fricker connects identity power to the phenomenon of testimonial injustice. This relation is obvious precisely because identity power is a critical component of the ritual of testimonial exchange. In a testimonial exchange, a hearer depends, though not exclusively, upon social stereotypes to critically scrutinize the credibility of an interlocutor. Stereotypes, since they are not innocent, are especially harmful when grounded in prejudice. As a result, a speaker can suffer two different types of harm: First, there can be an epistemic dysfunction when the hearer discredits the speaker's credibility and, second, the speaker is discredited in his/her capacity as a knower. When a speaker is the victim of testimonial injustice, degraded in his/her capacity as a knower, the individual suffers a credibility deficit. According to Fricker, "testimonial injustice [is] a distinctively epistemic injustice, . . . a kind of injustice in which someone is *wronged specifically in her capacity as a knower*."[20] Once again, the decisive factor fueling the epistemic injustice, according to Fricker, is prejudice. Consequently, prejudice against another, which is an expression of social identity power, can exclude one from epistemic trust solely because of one's social identity. For example, this phenomenon occurs when a Black male suffers harm in his capacity as a bona fide knower merely because he is Black male. Since, in a racist society, Black males are not seen as credible knowers, they consequentially suffer due to a prejudicial credibility deficit. What is not only epistemically unjust, but also unethical, about testimonial injustice is that it is systematic, rather than accidental. Testimonial injustice degrades an individual's entire life, operating as a stranglehold from which there is no escape; it is an existence in which there is no breathing room. Fricker states:

> Systematic testimonial injustices, then are produced not by prejudice *simpliciter*, but specifically by those prejudices that "track" the subject through different dimensions of social activity—economic, educational, professional, sexual, legal, political, religious, and so on. Being subject to a tracker prejudice renders one susceptible not only to testimonial injustice but to a gamut of different injustices, and so when such a prejudice generates a testimonial injustice, that injustice is systematically connected with other kinds of actual or potential injustice.[21]

Again, Fricker underscores that the most severe kind of prejudice inflicting systematic disadvantage upon an individual is identity prejudice, that is, being harmed as a consequence of one's social identity. She ultimately concludes that "a speaker sustains such testimonial injustice if and only if she receives a credibility deficit owning to identity prejudice in the hearer; so the central case of testimonial injustice is identity-prejudicial credibility deficit."[22]

Building upon Fricker's account of testimonial injustice, I want to extend the notion of credibility deficit to other kinds of harms that are based upon identity prejudice and that specifically target Black males due to their social identity. This involves a discussion of the debilitating kinds of credibility deficit that harm Black males, solely upon the basis of their identity as Black males. In addition to suffering testimonial injustice, which is epistemic in nature, Black males also suffer from an ethical injustice that harms them due to an ethical credibility deficit. To the extent that they are viewed as "naturally born criminals" and "super-predators," Black males suffer an ethical credibility deficit by being considered incapable of engaging in ethical behavior. Thus, Black males emerge as the paradigmatic perpetrators of criminal behavior, precisely because they are perceived as incapable of assuming responsibility for the other or of acting in accordance with basic moral intuitions and norms. Thus, the category of an ethical Black male becomes oxymoronic, a contradiction in terms, because the dictates of morality do not and cannot claim the fidelity of Black males. The contradiction involved in fusing the categories "ethical" and "Black male" explains why Black males are considered as warranting incessant policing. Thus, one primary responsibility of the State is to control Black males by any means necessary.

Another form of ethical credibility deficit attached to Black males is the belief that, since they are naturally unethical, Black males are also incapable of love. Those who are naturally predisposed to harming others are incapable of love, because they lack the emotional capacity to empathize with others. So, for example, we may recall the insistent association of Black males with a hypersexuality savagely expressed in sexual violation and exploitation. To the extent that Black males are so consistently reduced to their sexual organs, they are represented as sexual monsters in a society in which others have rationally mediated their sexual desires through the appropriate categories of civil society. Once again, Black males emerge as beings that are incapable of mustering any healthy expression of human warmth and compassion.

A final category of injustice associated with the credibility deficit that afflicts Black males is their lack of existential credibility. Appreciably, similar to the phenomenon of testimonial injustice, this phenomenon constitutes Black males as persons whose existence is not credible and is, thus, objectively unjustifiable. If it is possible to make a case for the existence of other social groups, Black males belong to a group whose existence is unjustifiable because its members are rapacious perpetrators of death. Hence, in an ironical twist of fate, it is their existence that is rendered not credible. The existential credibility deficit of Black males is also manifested in the spectacle of Black death, in which the display of dead Black bodies signals the fact that the value of Black existence is determined by non-Blacks. Non-Blacks have the power to decide the status or worth of Black male existence. Black males must endure not only the symbolic death of incarceration but also physical death. As was shockingly witnessed in the fateful death of George Floyd—Chauvin's expression of confidence as he mercilessly pressed his knees on Floyd's neck betrays his conviction that Floyd's existence lacks credibility.

In this brief chapter, I have woven an intertextual narrative to situate, partially, the unfortunate circumstances of George Floyd's death, although I have not completely exhausted the possible interpretations of its meaning. I have accomplished this by utilizing Curry's rejection of the academic imprisonment of Black males in the discursive spaces and theoretical caricatures of the social sciences. Additionally, I have metaphorically employed Fricker's notion of injustice as a credibility deficit to temporarily stabilize the extent to which existence as Black male is a daily exercise in existential terror: The terror of knowing that one may leave home and that, even if one does not become the victim of a deadly encounter with the police, one will not be spared the various forms of credibility deficit that police the lives of Black males.

NOTES

1. I use the phrase "excited delirium" in the title of this chapter, because this phrase is often listed as the cause or contributing cause of death of Black males in fatal encounters with police officers.
2. Carolyn Culbertson, *Words Underway: Continental Philosophy of Language* (New York: Rowman & Littlefield International, Ltd, 2019), 50.
3. Culbertson, *Words Underway*, 50.
4. Culbertson, *Words Underway*, 48.
5. See Jonathan Metzl, *Dying of Whiteness: How the Politics of Racial Resentment Is Killing America's Heartland* (New York: Basic Books, 2020).
6. George Yancy, *Black Bodies, White Gazes; The Continuing Significance of Race* (New York: Rowman & Littlefield Publishers, Inc., 2008), 12.
7. Yancy, *Black Bodies, White Gazes*, 75–76.
8. Yancy, *Black Bodies, White Gazes*, 25.
9. David Marriott, *On Black Men* (New York: Columbia University Press, 2000), x.
10. Tommy Curry, *The Man-Not: Race, Class, Genre, and the Dilemmas of Black Manhood* (Temple University Press, 2017), 3–4.
11. Curry, *The Man-Not*, 6–7.
12. Curry, *The Man-Not*, 8.
13. Curry, *The Man-Not*, 9.
14. Curry, *The Man-Not*, 10.
15. Curry, *The Man-Not*, 21.
16. Curry, *The Man-Not*, 29.
17. Curry, *The Man-Not*, 34.
18. Miranda Fricker, *Epistemic Injustice: Power & the Ethics of Knowing* (Oxford: Oxford University Press, 2009), 9.
19. Fricker, *Epistemic Injustice*, 14.
20. Fricker, *Epistemic Injustice*, 20.

21. Fricker, *Epistemic Injustice*, 27.
22. Fricker, *Epistemic Injustice*, 28.

BIBLIOGRAPHY

Culbertson, Carolyn. *Words Underway: Continental Philosophy of Language* (New York: Rowman & Littlefield International, Ltd, 2019).
Curry, Tommy J. *The Man-Not: Race, Class, Genre, and the Dilemmas of Black Manhood* (Temple University Press, 2017).
Fricker, Miranda. *Epistemic Injustice: Power & the Ethics of Knowing* (Oxford: Oxford University Press, 2009).
Marriott, David. *On Black Men* (New York: Columbia University Press, 2000).
Metzl, Jonathan. *Dying of Whiteness: How the Politics of Racial Resentment Is Killing America's Heartland* (New York: Basic Books, 2020).
Yancy, George. *Black Bodies, White Gazes; The Continuing Significance of Race* (New York: Rowman & Littlefield Publishers, Inc., 2008).

Chapter 3

Emmett Till's Body

A. Todd Franklin

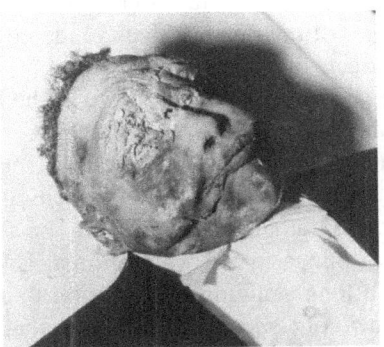

Figure 3.1 Emmett Till's Body. *Jet,* September 22, 1955, Volume VIII Number 20.
Source: Reprinted with the permission of the Johnson Publishing Company, LLC.

Have you ever seen this image? If so, do you remember when you first encountered it? I do. Growing up in the 1970s, I was probably about twenty years removed from the tragedy that gave rise to it. However, despite this historical distance, no image before or since has had such a powerful impact on how I see and understand the dangers and challenges of being a young Black man within a society where anti-Black racism still proves all too prevalent.

Looking back, I'd describe my childhood as rather sheltered. Although the specter of racism loomed large, the patriarchs and matriarchs of my family always did their best to watch over me and prevent me from being in situations that would expose me or render me vulnerable to racism. One of their ways of doing so was by having me spend most of my childhood days nestled among Black folks in and around our family-owned auto body shop.

Principals, politicians, preachers, and all of the other prominent Black people in town would at one time or another bring their cars in to be fixed; and when they did, they always treated my father and uncle with the utmost respect. One of our most memorable customers was Muhammad Ali. Accompanying my father to deliver Ali's freshly painted Cadillac was a real treat; for not only did I get to meet the Champ and hear him playfully spout off a few lines about how he was the greatest, but I also got to listen to him tell everyone that when it came to painting cars, my father was the greatest! Seeing my father and my uncle interact with so many different members of the Black community, and seeing how well treated and well regarded they were, filled me with a sense of pride and left me blissfully ignorant of the dangers associated with being Black. My bliss, however, proved short-lived. Soon after meeting the Champ and marveling at how lucky I was to come face to face with one of the most awe-inspiring exemplars of Black manhood, I sadly happened by chance to come face to face with one of the most heinous and horrifying examples of how being Black rendered a boy like me vulnerable to blatantly racist acts of violence.

Hanging out at the body shop on Saturdays was the highlight of my week. Usually, I'd spend most of my time there fetching tools, sanding fenders, and snickering in the background as the colorful cast of characters who worked there played the dozens and took turns telling Richard Pryor jokes. Sometimes, however, my father would send me up front to the office and have me straighten up things in the waiting area. Like most Black-owned businesses, ours had a long-standing subscription to *Jet* magazine, and we always had an assortment of issues on hand. Given that a new issue came out every week, the magazines always piled up fast. One day, while I was moving a stack of them to a big box where we saved all the old issues, I started to pull out a few at random and flip through them. As it turned out, one of the issues I happened to grab was the one dated September 22, 1955.

Many years have passed since my youth and many of my memories of those days have become fuzzy and faded, but one of the things that I will never forget is flipping through that magazine and seeing that gruesome and grotesque image of Emmett Till's face. Seeing that image scared the hell out of me. Who could do such a thing to a fourteen-year-old boy? What in the world could he have done to deserve something like this? As I turned to the article in search of answers nothing about the case seemed to register. The more I read and the more I looked at the photos, the more I couldn't help thinking about how similar he was to me. Emmett was just a young boy, he was Black, and he was his mother's only child. I was just a young boy, I was Black, and I was my mother's only child. Looking at Emmett was like looking at myself—and seeing what happened to him gave rise to the terrible and terrifying thought that something like that could just as well happen to me.

The sight of Emmett's bloated, bludgeoned, and bullet-torn face frightened me so much that I never spoke of it to my parents or anyone else. Instead, I simply tried to forget about it and put it out of my mind. Ironically, now that I've become a professor with a tragic sense of the social significance of young Emmett's demise, I often use his story and the images associated with it to trouble the minds of my students in the hope that doing so will stir them to combat the anti-Black racism that so violently took his life and so viciously continues to threaten and take the lives of others like him. Although there are a number of ways in which I could introduce the horror of what happened to Emmett, nothing brings it to life more powerfully, more personally, and more poignantly than Stanley Nelson's documentary featuring the boy's mother, Mrs. Mamie Till.

For many, watching this documentary ends up being one of the most disturbing experiences they've ever had in a classroom. In it, Emmett's cousins and classmates describe him as a playful young fellow who had just turned fourteen shortly before taking a train from Chicago to Mississippi in order to spend part of his summer vacation visiting with relatives. Prior to his departure, his mother tried her best to make him understand that the rules for Black boys in the South were vastly different than they were in the North. Furthermore, she did everything she could to let him know that violent racism was real and that, "You have to be very careful." Unfortunately, Emmett wasn't careful enough; for one afternoon, he was accused of breaking the rules of southern social convention by carelessly whistling at a white woman. Outraged by Emmett's alleged action, the woman's husband and his brother later snatched him away from his grandfather's home in the middle of night, drove him to a barn back in town and took turns savagely beating him before eventually driving him to the banks of the Tallahatchie river, shooting him through the head, and tossing his body into the water with an iron gin mill fan tied around his neck.

Needless to say, Mamie Till was heartbroken when she heard the news of what had happened to her son. Despite hearing about how he was found and the horrible condition of his body, nothing was going to stop her from seeing her only son and seeing what they did to him for herself. Sharing her painful recollection of standing there as the sealed casket containing his body was pried open, she describes how she confronted the situation as follows:

> I decided then that I would start at his feet and work my way up, maybe gathering strength as I went. I paused at his midsection, because I knew he would not want me looking at him. But I saw enough that I knew he was intact. I kept on up until I got to his chin and then I—I was forced to deal with his face. I saw that his tongue was choked out. I noticed that the right eye was lying on midway his cheek, I noticed that his nose had been broken like somebody took a meat

chopper and chopped his nose in several places. As I kept looking, I saw a hole, which I presumed, was a bullet hole and I could look through that hole and see daylight on the other side. And I wondered was it necessary to shoot him? Mr. Rayner asked me, he said "Do you want me to touch the body up?" I said, "No, Mr. Rayner, let the people see what I've seen." I was just willing to bear it all. I think everybody needed to know what had happened to Emmett Till.[1]

It is at this point in the documentary that you first see the gruesome images of Emmett Till's body. And it is at this point that his mother gives emphatic voice to the importance of letting the people see what she was so tragically forced to see.

Hearing his story and seeing his body, those unfamiliar with it all watch the rest of the documentary intently in hopes of seeing the heartless racists responsible for it brought to justice. By the end, however, they are left shocked and dumbfounded as they learn that although the two brothers, Roy Bryant and J. W. Milam, were swiftly tried for Emmett's murder, the Anglo-Saxon community of Mississippi closed ranks and acquitted them of the charge.

In contrast, those familiar with the heinous murder and the legal mockery that followed react rather differently. Rarely if ever do I come across a white student familiar with the story of Emmett Till. All too often, the only ones who have some sense of who he was and what transpired are the ones who are Black. For these students, the horror of seeing Emmett's face never fades, but the sense of shock that others feel is nonexistent. Moreover, for those who are Black and already well versed in the vicious history of American racism, sentiments of shock and amazement have long since given way to somber disillusionment.

Highlighting this contrast, a promising young Black brother named Branden Miles writes as follows:

After watching the Emmett Till documentary in class on Tuesday, I really didn't have anything to say. First, it wasn't my first time seeing the documentary, second, it is something that still happens today, and finally, the overarching negative perception of young Black men in America is still something I have to face on a daily basis.[2]

As Branden rightly points out, what happened to Emmett tragically still happens today. Sadly, two examples at the time were the murders of Trayvon Martin and Jordan Davis. Both of these boys were Black and both of their murderers perniciously perceived them as imminent dangers that warranted the deployment of deadly force. Thus, for Branden and other young Black males like him, the imminent danger associated with being perceived as an imminent danger is a danger with which they are all too familiar.

For Branden, his position behind the veil of anti-Black racism gives rise to a perspective on the events depicted that differs radically from the perspective of those positioned beyond it. Subsequently, the only thing that Branden does find shocking as he watches the documentary is the reaction of his white classmates. Sharing this experience, he writes,

> In class, I was shocked at the amount of surprise people had in reaction to the film because it is something I or most any other Black male on campus could have described to them in one way or another. What makes Emmett's story so terrible to me is not the fact that he was killed but the way in which these men mutilated his body. Every time I see his face, it sends a shock down my body because I know that's something my ancestors faced and something I still have to face today.

Here again, Branden stresses the fact that what those beyond the racist veil find shocking, those behind it find commonplace. However, summarizing what he sees as the grim significance that stories like Emmett's hold for him and other young men of his hue, Branden stoically states that when he sees "what happened to Emmett Till or what has happened to Trayvon Martin and Jordan Davis," it serves as a visceral reminder of what he refers to as "the silent daily battle" that preoccupies his life and the lives of those like him.

Silence, however, is no solution. For far too long, far too many have silently sheltered in place and suffered the slights and indignations of racism for fear of suffering far worse. Indeed, the battle that young Black men face is daily, but if this battle is to be won—that is to say, if the socially progressive sentiments of respect and fellow feeling are to someday take pride of place over the racist and regressive dispositions of disdain and indifference—then it cannot be a battle waged in silence. On the contrary, the only way to win this battle is to break the silence by exposing the indignities, inequities, and inconceivable cruelties suffered by those behind the veil in ways that effectively enlighten and transform the racial consciousness of those who live beyond it.

One of the ways I try to do this is by using the Emmett Till documentary to encourage those who are racially privileged to conceptually and emotionally grapple with both the lived experiences of Black folks and the privileged relation in which they stand to the anti-Black racism that frames those experiences. For many, these encounters prove deeply meaningful and moving. One case in point is that of a young white woman named Morgan Markman. Shortly after seeing and discussing the documentary, Morgan writes:

> When Professor Franklin asked the class, "who's heard of the Emmett Till murder?" I shook my head no and tried to think back to the history lessons I had in high school. I thought to myself, "did that name ever pop up in AP American history class?" However, after watching the Emmett Till documentary, I became angry with myself for not knowing this important piece of history. My question is, "why did I not have a single clue to who Emmett Till was?"

Interestingly enough, Morgan found her cluelessness so troubling that she decided to check with a few of her friends to see if they were clueless too:

> "Why do I have a vivid memory of Rosa Parks but not Emmett Till?" I asked five of my white friends if they had ever heard of Rosa Parks and they all said yes. However, when I asked them if they knew who Emmett Till was—they all said no. It saddens me that my white friends and I do not know this important piece of history.

In the end, Morgan's discovery of her own ignorance and that of her white friends did more than sadden her. Happily, it also inspired her to "inform them about Emmett Till's story" in order to help give the horrific nature of racism the attention it deserves.

For Mercy Corredor, another student in the course, what proves troubling is not her ignorance of the horrific nature of racism, but rather her failure to face up to it. Although keenly aware of "the many injustices, the racist aggressions, [and] the gruesome murders that occur every single day," her daily life is so far removed from it all that she only thinks of such matters in terms of empirical studies and conceptual analyses. However, moved by the way the very visceral encounter with Emmett's story "forced [her] to view him as human," Mercy shamefully realizes the inauthenticity of her attempt to take emotional refuge in "a world radically distant from Emmett's" by casting and taking up racism solely as "a concept, or an idea, or a set of statistics." Moreover, viewing the documentary moved Mercy to realize that although she had "done plenty of theorizing *about*" racism, she hadn't done nearly "enough listening to and learning *from* others and their experience" to fulfill what she herself laudably describes as her "responsibility" to truly fathom it "for what it is."

While many of the students who live beyond the veil view the documentary of Emmett Till as a lens through which they can glimpse and then grapple with the horrors of American racism, for some it can also serve as a mirror that helps them glimpse and begin to grapple with the racist enemy that lies within. One student for whom the film served as such is a promising young ally named Robbie Fagan. As Robbie writes:

> The Emmett Till documentary struck me, but I think I responded to the story of Emmett Till in an atypical way because I was not directly struck by the death or pictures of Emmett Till. For example, the first time I saw Emmett Till's mutilated face I had no reaction. The boy's face was simply there, just like any other image of a mutilated body. I felt nothing, which seemed peculiar to me.

Rightly pointing out the peculiar nature of such a cold response, Robbie goes on to describe how what really struck him was the way he identified with the murderers:

> Their faces are still emblazoned in my mind. These monsters! My monsters. I felt connected to these men through their whiteness, their privilege, and their racism. I saw these men as more of my own than the outraged Black community or Emmett Till's grieving mother. I saw these monsters as more of my own than [those who were] compassionate [and] loving humans. I saw my own monsters. My racism, my whiteness, my privilege.

For Robbie, seeing himself as he saw the monsters who murdered Emmett proves so devastating that he writes:

> I am scared of what I can do and who I am disgusts me. Now the question seems to be: how do I live with myself?
> I cried at the prospect that I am going to have to live with hate in my heart, a disregard for others, ignorance, selfishness, fear, and desire. I cried at the fact that I did not feel for Emmett. I cried because I sympathize with monsters. I cried.

Reading Robbie's words, I cried as well. In reading them, I discovered a young man desperate to disavow a racism that he rightly recognized as deeply rooted in his very being. Fortunately, however, Robbie chose not to resign himself to this racism. Indeed, as he then goes on to say:

> I know there is hope. Emmett Till's death generated a great and important response for American society. But, right now, that is not enough for me. I am greedy. I do not want to have to live with my racism, my whiteness, my privilege. I can fight white supremacy [and] even hope to change myself.

For me, the most hopeful thing about Robbie's newfound hope is its honesty. Robbie doesn't fool himself into believing that he will ever be able to completely rid himself of his racism, his whiteness, or his privilege. On the contrary, despite his best efforts to do so, he knows full well that he will often fail and fall short:

> Maybe I can lessen the pain I feel when I face my monstrous self. . . . But how can I fight when I know that I will fail, because I will fail. I am surrounded by white supremacy and I am still, in part, a white supremacist. Whether I know it or not, I will once again view Black persons as less than human. I feel blue. I ask myself: is it worth it?

Thankfully, Robbie finds that despite the difficulty of doing so, facing and fighting the dispositions of white supremacy so deeply rooted in American society, and so deeply rooted in his soul, is a task well worth the effort. Moreover, as he himself concludes:

> Of course it is. Because each time I struggle and I fail, I fail harder. Each time I fight, I push back the enclosing circle of racist thought and privilege that threatens to choke out my humanity [just] a little farther. At least I can loosen the bonds of necessity and create a space for my future. Maybe I will never be free but at least I might someday take a labored breath.

In the end, the freedom that Robbie seeks as he struggles against his racism is similar to the freedom that we who are dark seek as we struggle against it as well; for like Robbie, we too find ourselves gasping for breath as we battle against the vicious and violent racism that constantly threatens to choke out our humanity.

Tragically, one of the most memorable casualties of this racism was a Black teenager named Emmett; and no one suffered his loss more deeply than his own mother, Mrs. Mamie Till. Seeing her only child's brutally battered body must have undoubtedly plunged her into the depths of despair. Nevertheless, she somehow found the strength to look past the pain and recognize the importance of letting the people see what many find all too difficult to see. For Mamie Till, Emmett was gone. All that was left there lying in that casket was a visible and visceral manifestation of anti-Black racism. Heeding her call, I made it my mission over the years to "let the people see." Like hers, my mission in doing so was to trouble the conscience in ways that encouraged people to confront the vicious nature of anti-Black racism in its most horrific forms. Tragically, one need not turn to the images and stories of the past to get a visceral sense of the vicious and violent nature of anti-Black racism in American society. Indeed, one need only turn to the day's news to see and hear how scores of Black people are being schematized as suspicious and summarily killed in the streets and in their homes with no care or concern for their humanity. Surely, we've seen too much of this, but let us not turn away from the horror of it. Rather, let us turn to the societal structures and forces that sanction it. Moreover, let us turn to the task of seeing that these structures and forces get radically reconstituted in ways that actively denounce and disrupt this nation's vile and repugnant anti-Black racism.

Acknowledgment: This chapter is in honor of Emmett, who was murdered in his fourteenth year, and on the occasion of my son just entering upon his fourteenth year.

NOTES

1. Mamie Till, *The Murder of Emmett Till*, Directed by Stanley Nelson (2004; Boston, MA; PBS).
2. This and all other quotations that follow are drawn from journal responses to an in-class screening of the documentary. Ordinarily I change the names when referring to students; however, my pride in these particular young people and their earnest desire to exemplify a personal commitment to combating anti-Black racism both demand that I share their true identities. Their quotes and full names are printed with their permission.

BIBLIOGRAPHY

Till, Mamie. *The Murder of Emmett Till*, Directed by Stanley Nelson (2004; Boston, MA; PBS).

Chapter 4

The War on Blackness
Black Men and the State of the Union
Arnold L. Farr

INTRODUCTION: FALLING OF THE SCALES

There comes a time when one has to sit down and reevaluate everything that he once believed. There is a moment when one's raw experience of the world (one that we've been in denial about) overcomes you like a title wave. Even for those of us who have spent our lives examining reality through critical lenses, there comes a time of reckoning. The fact that the United States has racism and hatred of blackness in its DNA has always been clear to me. However, many of us (myself included) have been in denial about the fundamental nature of American racism. That is, the ongoing violence against black and brown people must be described in much stronger terms than mere racism.

In his work, *The German Ideology*, Karl Marx makes the following claim:

> The ideas of the ruling class are in every epoch the ruling ideas: i.e., The class which is the ruling *material* force of society is at the same time its ruling *intellectual* force. The class which has the means of material production at its disposal, consequently also controls the means of mental production, so that the ideas of those who lack the means of mental production are on the whole subject to it.[1]

Although Marx was concerned with economic exploitation and injustice, the main idea in this passage can be applied to an analysis of racism in America. Furthermore, there is a material element to racism that parallels Marx's point. That is, slavery was an economic enterprise insofar as the slave's body (and mind) was a property that was owned by someone. The body of the slave was used to create wealth for his slave master. As the slave existed in a place of powerlessness, the master was able to give shape to the material and intellectual worlds in which slave and master live. The master uses his place of dominance to interpret the world and construct a historical narrative that is designed to control the memory and thought processes of the slave. The narrative constructed by the master and imparted to the slave has such a grip on the slave that the slave conforms to the narrative even after the slave is legally free. However, there may come a moment when the scales of the master narrative will fall from the eyes of the slave. Perhaps that moment is now.

As the scales fall away from our eyes, we find ourselves in a position to discover the truth about our situation. That is, we are in a war that we've been forced to deny. It is fashionable to use terms like white supremacy, racism, bigotry, domination, and so on. However, while those terms are correct when describing the historical attitudes of white people toward black people in America, they convey a certain shallowness in light of an honest assessment of the black situation in America. In light of the ongoing existence of white supremacy in its overt form as well as in its covert form, as in institutionalized white supremacy, I have come to accept the fact that we black people are victims of a war that we've been duped into denying. I find it irresponsible now to suggest that we black people are not prisoners of a war that was waged against black people over 400 years ago. White supremacy in all of its forms has been successful because we have been tricked into denying our own experience. It is now time for the scales to be removed from our eyes so that we may see our situation in America for what it is. American society has its origin in the war on blackness. It continues to flourish as a white supremacist state because of the ongoing war on blackness.

I am sure that there will be quite a bit of resistance to my claim that a 400-year war has been waged on black people. I find it hard to imagine that the invasion of another people's land to kidnap and enslave them is not an act of war. Furthermore, the ongoing forms of dehumanization of black people are ongoing features of this war. There is no room here to list the names of innocent unarmed black people who are killed. It is a regular occurrence in America for white killers of black people to face no consequences. Many may argue that maybe slavery began by an act of war against black people, but we are beyond that now. They would claim that the many killings of innocent unarmed black people are isolated incidents carried out by a few racist individuals. Such a claim is designed to avoid dealing with systemic racism (war) and the anti-black justice system. It is an attempt to avoid dealing with the daily fear with which black people must live, a fear passed on to our children. It is an attempt to ignore the many stages of war as well as its many weapons. The cold-blooded murder of George Floyd is a moment in a war that has never ended and has never been acknowledged as such.

RETHINKING THE STATE OF WAR: IT'S NOT HYPOTHETICAL

One of the dominant views of Thomas Hobbes's theory of the state of nature is that such an idea is merely hypothetical or is a heuristic device used to justify the sovereign power of government. This state of nature is also a state of war, or at least preparedness for war as human individuals compete against each other in a never ending competition for available resources. However, in his classic work, *The Political Theory of Possessive Individualism: Hobbes to Locke*, C. B. Macpherson claims that the Hobbesian theory of the state of nature is much more than hypothetical. Indeed, such a state of nature and the state of humanity as one perpetual preparation for war might be an abstraction from real social relations at the time that Hobbes was writing. Macphereson writes:

> I shall show first that Hobbes's state of nature or 'natural condition of mankind' is not about natural man as opposed to civilized man but is about men whose desires are specifically civilized, that the state of nature is the hypothetical condition in which men as they now are, with natures formed by living in civilized society, would necessarily find themselves if there were no common power able to overawe them all. The evidence for this is contained in Hobbes's description of the state of nature.[2] Macphereson continues: Secondly, I shall examine the claim of deduction from the beginning, and show that the psychological analysis, which begins (or appears to begin) as an analysis of the nature of men in complete abstraction from society, soon becomes an analysis of men in established social relationships; that certain social assumptions have to be made in order to establish that all men in society seek ever more power over others (and even to establish the behavior of men in the hypothetical state of nature), and hence to establish the necessity of the sovereign; and that the necessary social assumptions are valid only for a specific kind of society.[3]

The point is that the image of selfish, self-serving, competitive individuals in a state of nature is derived from or abstracted from the human condition as it is lived in established civilized society. The apparent lawlessness that is to be found in the state of nature is also found in the law-governed civilized society. However, the lawlessness present in civilized society is a well-organized, systematic, systemic, free, democratic lawlessness. Well-organized lawlessness is well-hidden lawlessness. So it is with the perpetual state of war. From this Hobbesian insight, I would like to suggest that what we are seeing in the United States right now are the results of an over four-hundred-year war and a form of organized lawlessness that has succeeded because it has been hidden by social, economic, religious, and political narratives. The United States is also built on a founding murder that has been largely concealed by U.S. identity narratives.

I will discuss the founding murder in the next section. Here I want to elaborate a bit on the idea of the perpetual war in America, that is, the fact that black people in the United States are victims in a 400-year war. It is a war where our ability to fight has been paralyzed by the fact that we have not recognized our situation as one of war. I began this chapter with the quote by Marx because that quote refers to the fact that the ruling class, or in this case, white supremacy in all of its forms have collected for itself all of the weapons so that we have very little to fight with. One of the weapons possessed by white America is its control of the narrative about our situation. They even control the language whereby we speak of our situation.

The black situation in America is similar to, if not worse than, the situation in a Hobbesian state of nature where everyone is in a perpetual state of preparedness for a war of all against all. The difference is that in America it is not a war of all against all, but rather, a war against blackness. It is black and brown people who spend each day of their/our lives anticipating violence directed at us. It is black and brown people who experience the kind of nervousness that one would experience in a completely lawless state of nature. Even in a so-called civilized country, where white people make a lot of noise about law and order, black and brown people live each day outside of the social contract wherein we should be included and protected. The white gaze at the black or brown body automatically criminalizes it so as to transform blackness into the mark of the enemy who must be subdued and/or killed. Hence, black bodies are criminalized by the descendants of those who hunted down, kidnapped, enslaved, and dehumanized our ancestors.

I can hear the majority of my white friends and colleagues suggesting that the use of the idea of war is too strong when applied to the situation of black and brown people in America. However, this is one of the ways in which we have been tricked into denying our situation as one of war. One of the most effective weapons used by white racists is to take away our power to define our own experience. They get to tell us what words to use and what racism "really" means. They have established the ruling ideas, the language, and the narrative whereby we think about and describe our experience. The term war perhaps makes them a bit uncomfortable. It uncovers a reality that they would rather not see. However, why would we call the extreme brutal nature of slavery and the ongoing violence against blacks anything less?

The criminalization of black and brown bodies has led to the creation of spaces that are white and black spaces. The presence of a black body in white space arouses suspicion by white people regarding the presence of the black body. The shooting of Trayvon Martin is an example of this problem. Trayvon appearing suspicious because he was walking through or near white space led to his violent murder. However, the white gaze that passes judgment on the black body for occupying white space does not always end in physical violence. As a black professor, I have had the experience of having my presence questioned on campuses where I taught. On our predominantly white campuses, positions such as professor and administrator are viewed as positions for whites only, while the kitchen and cleaning rooms are deemed black spaces. This carving out of black and white spaces is the result of white supremacist narratives that continue to marginalize blackness.

THE FOUNDING MURDER AND THE WAR ON BLACKNESS

The origins of a society say much about the struggles that will lie waiting in the future of that society. Rene Girard has argued that every society is built on a founding murder. He spent his entire career disclosing this phenomenon in religious texts, myths, and literature. Even if one could find a counterexample to Girard's claim, that is not of concern. It is certainly true that American society is built on a founding murder. The blood of Native Americans and kidnapped Africans cry out from America's soil. If we can imagine anything like a social contract invoked in the founding of America it surely does not include black and brown people. Here I am not interested in exploring Girard's theory of the founding murder. If we consider the violence with which America was founded, the founding murder is not an issue for debate. I am more concerned with the mechanisms of denial. That is, I am more concerned with the social, political, and intellectual mechanisms that are designed to conceal the reality of the founding murder and to trick black and white people into denying the fact that a war has been declared on black people that continues to this day.

One of the most effective mechanisms for putting the reality of the founding murder and the war on blackness under erasure is ritual. However, ritual is also connected to prohibitions. Girard explains:

> There would be no contradiction in intent between prohibitions and rituals; prohibitions attempt to avert the crisis by prohibiting those behaviors that provoke it, and if the crisis recurs nonetheless, or threatens to do so, ritual then attempts to channel it in a direction that would lead to resolution, which means a reconciliation of the community at the expense of what one must suppose to be an arbitrary victim.[4]

If we interpret Girard's theory within the framework of social contract theory, the contract is entered into after a conflict between two or more groups. This contract will include prohibitions that are designed to prohibit behaviors that provoked the crisis that led to violence between the groups. However, Girard ignores the specific features of the American war on blackness. The American war on blackness does not originate with a crisis between people of European descent and those of African descent. Rather, the American situation is one wherein European settlers in America attack, kidnap, and enslave Africans and then set in motion a series of practices, behaviors, laws, and narratives that are designed to put the humanity of black people under erasure. Any prohibitions built into the contract are designed to prohibit violence between whites and retaliation by black people. However, there are no real concrete prohibitions against violence against black people.

Ritual is the mechanism whereby a community reconciles itself while keeping at the margins of the reconciled community a scapegoat that remains the target for hostilities. Going a bit further than Girard would go here, in the American context, ritual also attempts to create the illusion of inclusion of the marginalized scapegoat.

The ritual in the American context is a series of repetitious practices that are rooted in a narrative about American identity that has been solely constructed by white people. The ritual has the narrative function of telling a story and establishing meaning. The problem is that American rituals are attempts to conceal the fact that American society is built on a founding murder and war against blackness, and that the war against blackness has never ended but is still in full force. An example comes from my own childhood. Shortly after I was born, my father expressed to his father the desire to buy a new car. My father had worked hard and had made enough money to buy a brand new car. However, my grandfather talked him into buying a second-hand car because a black man with a new car at that time in South Carolina was perceived by white people as an uppity negro and could be pulled over by the cops to be beaten or killed. A few years later, my second grade teacher made the entire class, every morning, to salute the flag and recite the Pledge of Allegiance and sing My Country 'Tis of Thee. This ritual was designed to produce loyalty to a country that was still engaging in acts of war against my people. My education began by forcing me to lie to myself about my country and my place in it. It is this very lie that people like Colin Kaepernick tried to bring our attention to by kneeling during the National Anthem. It was this attempt to reveal the truth about the war on blackness in America that caused him to lose his job as white America demanded/demands denial about the war that it has waged against us. The all lives matter movement is another attempt to put under erasure the reality of the war against blackness. The universal signifier "all" generalizes in such a way that the particular experience of black people can be completely ignored. Holidays such as the Fourth of July involve the ritualistic celebration of the independence of white people, an independence gained while black people were enslaved. The ritualistic cover-up of this holiday was challenged by Frederick Douglas in his speech, "The Meaning of July Fourth for the Negro."[5] While black people as Americans are expected to participate in the celebration of U.S. independence, there is still the experience of being outsiders. We actually celebrate the independence of white people as we are treated as if our lives do not matter.

GEORGE FLOYD AND THE WAR ON BLACK MEN

After reflecting on the founding murder upon which America was/is built, and on the war on blackness, we may ask: what is the state of the union in the United States today? The answer is that the war on blackness has never missed a beat. We black men are, in some way, all George Floyd. I am George Floyd. My son is George Floyd. My three brothers and my father are all George Floyd. Even though we are still among the living, we are still trying to survive in a war that we have been taught to deny. The nervousness and insecurity that governs the lives of individuals in the Hobbesian state of nature/war governs ours as we must rise from our beds every day hoping that this will not be the day that we lose our lives in the war against blackness. The fact that I have to tell my son not to wear his hoodie when he is walking to a friend's house is my attempt to save him from being a casualty in the war on blackness. After I said to my son not to wear his hoodie, he said to me "but this is a good neighborhood." We live in a predominantly white middle-class neighborhood. I explained to him that that was the problem. There are those who think that he and I do not belong in our neighborhood. It is in our so-called good neighborhood where he is most likely to become a victim in the war on blackness. We have to deal with the fact that at every moment of our lives we may find ourselves like George Floyd, crying for help as this war on black people continues to take our lives.

If on the Hobbesian account the state of nature is also a state of war or a perpetual preparedness for war, it seems clear to me that the situation of black people in America is a state of war insofar as we spend our lives in constant fear for our lives. Black people are killed at will by cops as well as by regular citizens like George Zimmerman. It has become a common occurrence in America for innocent unarmed black people to be killed while the killers are not punished for their crimes. While many white people verbally claim that all lives matter, it is clear from the practices of white America that black lives do not matter to them. The essence of Dr. King's message to white America was that it claimed an identity for itself that it did not live up to. The situation has not changed today. The war on blackness that King fought against is still in full swing today.

The murder of George Floyd is symbolic of the state of the union for black people in America. Of course, the murder of George Floyd is only one of many in white America's ongoing war on blackness. What is unique about it is the national and worldwide response by black people and some of our white allies. This massive outcry may have been due to the fact that more people were on social media during a worldwide pandemic. Nevertheless, this also seems to be the moment when *legitimate* black anger is being unleashed. This chapter does not offer a solution to the war on blackness. At best, it is an attempt to take the power of narrative formation away from white people. This may be the first step toward figuring out a solution. We must empower ourselves to speak about our experience. We can no longer let white people define racism for us. We must no longer let white people paralyze us with their white washed morality. We must no longer allow white people to force us to use their "polite language" to address our situation.

At the merely theoretical and verbal level, white America offers us the language of "inclusion." It offers us an abstract American identity. White America offers us the failed promise of democracy. It offers us universal signifiers such as the "all" in "All Lives Matter." It offers us narratives about being an American while at the same time denying our humanity. It tells us that all lives matter while systematically and perpetually destroying black life. At the practical level of human lived experience, black people are treated as the enemy. We are treated as invaders who don't belong here. Our suffering is ignored for the sake of white theoretical comfort. In the context of real life, every black neck is the potential target of a policeman's knee. Every black body is a target for a bullet from a policeman's gun or the gun of a "good white American citizen" standing his/their ground. This is not a condition of being under law for one's protection. It is a war on blackness that will not end until we recognize it as such and then seek to end it by any means necessary. One of the possible means to ending this war is to acknowledge it for what it is. Acknowledging that we, as black people, are the targets of an ongoing state of war on blackness is one step toward our taking control of our own narrative and experience. The perpetual violence against black people in America deserves to be called nothing less than a war on blackness.

It is my hope that the new wave of activism, since the murder of George Floyd, will launch a new massive movement that will first recognize that we are in a state of war. My second hope is that once we are honest about our predicament that necessary changes will be made. Isolation due to the pandemic gave the murder of George Floyd more visibility that it might not have otherwise had. More descent white people got a view via social media of what black life is like in the United States. They got to see evidence of the war that has been declared on us.

NOTES

1. Karl Marx, *The German Ideology* (Amherst, New York: Prometheus Books, 1998), p. 67.
2. C.B. Macpherson, *The Political Theory of Possessive Individualism: Hobbes to Locke* (Oxford, New York, Toronto, Melbourne: Oxford University Press, 1979), pp. 18–19.
3. Ibid., p. 19.
4. Rene Girard, *Things Hidden Since the Foundation of the World*, translated by Stephen Bann and Michael Metteer (Stanford, CA: Stanford University Press, 1987), p. 25.
5. Charles Mills provides an insightful discussion of this speech in Chapter 8 of his *Blackness Visible: Essays on Philosophy and Race* (Ithaca and London: Cornell University Press, 1998).

BIBLIOGRAPHY

Macpherson, C. B. *The Political Theory of Possessive Individualism: Hobbes to Locke* (Oxford, New York, Toronto, Melbourne: Oxford University Press, 1979).
Marx, Karl. *The German Ideology* (Amherst, New York: Prometheus Books, 1998).

Chapter 5

Blues Sons and Sorrow's Kitchen

Houston A. Baker Jr.

A Prologue

He have a babe that was standing at the station
Waiting for a train.
I ran to the door with my heart in my hand
And all my future plans.
I've gotta catch him if I can.

The present meditation focuses what might be considered family troubles of a distinct kind, namely, mental illness. The heart of the meditation takes its hue and cry from a larger field of race matters in the United States, specifically the troika comprised of murder, myth, and monsters. It was James Baldwin, decades ago, who set the facts of American murder, myth, and monsters in luminous prose. Baldwin wrote:

> I am terrified by the moral apathy, the death of the heart that is happening in this country. These people [whites] have deluded themselves for so long they really don't think I'm human . . . and this means they have become . . . moral monsters[1] (in a brilliant exposition from Nicholas Buccola).

To verify Baldwin's assessment, compare two photographs: Emmitt Till on his departure from Chicago for the South, next—Emmitt Till's body, in open coffin, after he was lynched by white monsters of Dixie, his grotesque remains shipped home to a grief-stricken mother, Mamie Till-Bradley, in Chicago. George Floyd, another beloved son, perished as have so many black citizens in recent decades, under the gaze and bestiality of moral monsters.

What follows is a personal meditation on one black American son (mine and my wife's) who, by grace and family, is still alive.

In dark moments of our son's illness I could not stop thinking of trains. I would listen in Durham, North Carolina, to the long whistle of midnight freights and feel an aching in my soul. One afternoon when I was in a deep funk about our son's hospitalization, I found myself suddenly elated by the rush and clamor of a huge smoking locomotive racing along Durham city tracks that literally paralleled the town's main thoroughfare. In lonesome moments I remembered Delta bluesmen, harmonicas, and guitar licks that were meant to emulate sounds of southern trains in motion.

Trains have always fascinated me. I spent my youth in Louisville, Kentucky, where long freights and plush *L&N* passenger liners rolled all day and with melancholy moans through the night. We had no air-conditioning, so open windows were steamy summer entryways for train whistles that tossed us sleepily on perspiration-soaked sheets.

Trains heading north were a big event during my youth. A train whistle in the night signaled possibility: people going somewhere. Black Pullman Porters were held in high esteem because they were always traveling, and they were paid union wages. I longed for our son, who was born in Charlottesville, Virginia, in 1970, to become—in motion and character—an avatar of those venerable, uniformed Pullman Porters of my Kentucky youth. Pullman Porters sported sharply pressed jackets and blindingly spit shined shoes. They possessed impeccable etiquette. They were organized, precise, and ingenious. They took no guff (at least, not without poised irony) from anybody! James Alan McPherson's short story *Solo Song for Doc* is essential reading for a brilliant portrait of the Pullman Porter.

I dreamed our son would always be on the rails, moving toward wellness and health and big city success. I imagined him as an inspiration for longsufferers in lonesome rooms. I wanted him to be the one whose mere wave from a southern caboose encouraged men and women laboring in fields of "no wages at all" to hope.

Two moments of my adult life have threatened to kill me and mine, and to still the lonesome valley potency of trains. There is no need to grow gruesome or melodramatic here. After all, this is a blues meditation, and the canny critic and novelist Albert Murray succinctly declares that: *In blues, you must be nimble, or not at all!* In the vocabularies of the novelist and anthropologist Zora Neale Hurston, this translates: "I have been in Sorrow's Kitchen, and I have licked out every pot. . . . But still have had the gumption to jump at the sun!"

The blues are strict, but nimble. They are laconic, yet rife with wisdom. Never melodramatic or tragic, never bereft of a bold cool irony, the Blues know a great deal about Sorrow's Kitchen. But, they repeatedly sounded assurance that "the sun's going to shine in my back door some day!"

Sorrow crashed through the flimsy wooden door at the top of our basement stairs on a humid summer evening in 1981. Two men armed with knives and guns invaded our Philadelphia home. My wife, son, and I were at home. The men were black and practiced in cruelty. They were also high on alcohol and drugs. Rape, obscenity, and terror claimed the night. The men burgled everything moveable. Surrounded by policemen on our front porch after the men departed our house, we gave thanks that we were alive. There was little else to be grateful for.

Years later, a telephone call from our son to Philadelphia from Los Angeles brought sorrow back on stage with a vengeance. Our son was panic-stricken. He talked rapidly about things we had no way of understanding: commands from Uranus, dead bodies secretly stowed in his apartment building, invisible men following him. He didn't even know where he was. He had suffered his first crippling psychotic break. He was in Los Angeles, but he might as well have conceded like the bluesman Dwight Yoakam that he was "a thousand miles from nowhere/And there's no place I wanna be/I got heartaches in my pocket/I got echoes in my head." Our son was diagnosed with *Bipolar Disorder Type I with Psychotic Features*. Predictions about his re-stabilization were hopes written in sand.

I think I am talking here more about *sadness* than tragedy. Perhaps I feel this way because sorrow has been ameliorated by time and music. Trains are very much a part of it. "How," I ask myself, "can this be so in an age where Internet hyperspace transects time and space on a daily?" Maybe, I speculate, my old-school fixation on trains has much to do with a retro-nostalgic commitment to blues geographies—those nimble territories of sanity and wholeness inextricable from train whistle guitars and rollicking jukes. Trains and blues signify a cultural hopefulness that serves like a personal trainer, bringing emotional fitness and promising amazing leaps at the sun.

AH'WHOOOOEEEE DE WHOOOOEEEE!!! AH'WHOOOOEEEE DE WHOOOOEEE!!!!

It's after midnight. Trouble in mind melds with express sounds and celebrations of mobility. Time changes . . . at the behest of music and love.

Following his summer call, our son disappeared without a trace for more than a year. When he surprisingly rang our doorbell on a blistering August morning in Philadelphia, he was emaciated, dirty, and trembling. He had burned holes in his retinas trying to outstare God. "I ran to the door with my heart in my hand/And all my future plans."

In the aftermath of rape, madness, silence, and emotional paralysis, my wife and I looked at and held each other as though there was no other support in the universe. And we walked the precincts of our home like blues sentinels. We would not be displaced. We righteously guarded our son and each other from harm. Gwendolyn Brooks writes in "The Mecca": "Guard here. Guns loaded." We were nimble, attuned to train wheels moving rhythmically over track junctures. We knew we had to "be ready or not at all." Red-eyed and weary in our solitude, we looked at each other in the way those boastful black porters might have done when in some backwater nothingness of night, they were called "Nigger" and told by a drunken lout of a passenger that they were *not* children of God. Like them, we grew fierce in blues.

It was not *race* that was at issue in the home invasion, or in that awful telephone call from our son, but something far more metaphysical. A practical question: "When actually is God (if there is one) awake?" Our son was ill. His mother had been repeatedly raped. I had been kicked in the face and bound with telephone cords on the night of the home invasion. Where was our "ride"? *How long, how long, how long had that evening train been gone?* My present meditation is not a New Age salvation narrative. It will never qualify as a recommendation of a *single song* that saved our lives.

After we re-arranged our Philadelphia home into a post-invasion fortress, we still had one small space newly equipped with an inexpensive turntable and amplifier connected to bookcase speakers. We gathered in that space regularly, the three of us. It was immaculate at sunset, recalling, I now know, chattel slavery's *bush arbor prayer spaces*. We listened together to William Dawson's arrangements of sorrow songs: "I Couldn't Hear Nobody Pray" and "There is a Balm in Gilead" as sun set and our vigilance increased for another night of watchfulness. We were on our own. Then later when our son was beset by bipolar disorder, we listened together to Marvin Gaye's brilliant What's *Going On?*

Existentialism and all that jazz to the contrary not withstanding, we are *not* the sum of our choices. Who chooses disaster and loss, rape and madness, tsunami and earthquake? We are, rather, I think, receivers of saving song. We are vessels of recovery. We are all Blues People. We survive by converting sorrow into sun. We have the good sense to know, in the phrasing of Junior Wells: "trouble don't last always." We are capable of listening to sorrow songs and Marvin Gaye and discovering—even in the question mark "what?"—what is *really* going on. We blessedly save ourselves through sound and soundings.

Our son's return to Philadelphia was cacophonous with the whoop, sampling, dash, vulgarity, and wisdom of hardcore and deep bass gangster rap. He strove to pound demons from his head with the raucous "dropped science" of his generation's blues nimbleness. He persevered always at his poetry. He writes now, these many years later, with the fitness of the sun. His mother some intense time ago pushed the "send" on a lyrical recap of matters to do with what she titled *This Fragile Life*, a beautiful and powerful memoir—of our son's and our family's struggle with bipolar disorder. Our son's poetry and prose are interwoven with her words.

What saved my life was the music of my wife and son. Their beauty and expressivity are the essence of the blues. They know, like Marvin, what's really going on. We shared our sorrow and our son's suffering in lonesome acres of the spirit where, at times, we could hear nobody pray. At other times, we have been amply anointed by the very balm of Gilead. In my heart, I know that Marvin's inner-city blues are prophecy and witness of all we must inhabit and understand if we would save our own and the life of our planet. Blues sustainability.

NOTE

1. Nicholas Buccola, *The Fire is Upon Us*: *James Baldwin, William F. Buckley Jr., and the Debate over Race in America* (Princeton University Press, 2019), p. 186.

BIBLIOGRAPHY

Buccola, Nicholas. *The Fire Is upon Us*: *James Baldwin, William F. Buckley Jr., and the Debate over Race in America* (Princeton University Press, 2019).

Chapter 6

Disaggregating Death

George Floyd and the Significance of Black Male Mortality in Police Encounters

Tommy J. Curry

INTRODUCTION

The execution of George Perry Floyd Jr., his public lynching, has been broadcast all over the world. Nine minutes and twenty-nine seconds has become synonymous with Black male death. Nine twenty-nine now represents an epoch of death—the period in which Black life expires and death occurs. In 9 minutes and 29 seconds, Mr. Floyd's living flesh was turned into rotting meat, his body was transformed into a corpse.[1] Derek Chauvin killed Mr. Floyd Jr. in broad daylight on the street in Minneapolis, Minnesota, on May 25, 2020. Chauvin deliberately murdered Mr. Floyd. He was unmoved by the demands of the public to take his knee off the neck of Mr. Floyd and showed little remorse or regard toward Mr. Floyd after his actions lead to Mr. Floyd's death. The Minneapolis police chief, Medaria Arradondo, described Chauvin's killing of Mr. Floyd as murder. However, the brutality and indifference shown to Mr. Floyd suggests that there was a culture of permissibility and violence that allowed the other attending police officers (Tou Thang, Thomas Lane, and J. Kueng) to remain unmoved by the asphyxiation and subsequent death of Mr. Floyd.[2]

No words or philosophical reflection accurately describes the ferity, that most lethal violence generated to enforce dehumanization, behind the act that killed Mr. Floyd. It is not only white racism but the societal-level stigmatization of Black males that permits this repetition of death. The horrors Black men endure in the United States highlight the illusion of racial progress.[3] The lethal violence and oppression Black males suffer in the United States differ by orders of magnitude from that of their female counterparts and whites. America is a slaughterhouse for Black men and boys and attempts, through violence, to remove them from American society. This unbridled assault upon the Black male is enacted by the most grotesque displays of torture and torment. The public exhibitions of power enacted upon Black male bodies inspire wonderment and awe among anticipating American audiences. Their spilled blood, their last breaths, the videos of Black males urinating on themselves or calling for their mother—the murmurs of desperation heard only as last yells of "I Can't Breathe!"—fascinate American observers who yearn for that brief moment where the Black male dies and becomes a corpse. Black males live with death on their minds. Throughout their daily lives, rituals of dehumanization are administered upon their flesh and imposed upon their souls. This violence is of a different kind than that which is often deployed in philosophical and more academic prose. The Black male is the cadaver of white America's sadistic delight. His flesh absorbs the racist paroxysm of the world; he is the object of (non)human experimentation.[4] Because his death serves as an example, his brutalization takes place before the world that assaults him with physical and psychical violence, white rage, and societal disregard. A world where he is trapped by the knowledge that a Black boy only lives to see just how deadly the internecine insouciance toward a Black man can be.

For the last several years I have sought to understand the murder and suffering of Black males in the United States. In 2014, when Michael Brown was executed in broad daylight, I suggested there was a need for a genre study of Black male death and dying in the United States.[5] Since then I have argued that the systematic violence against Black males was the product of sociopolitical forces designed to have population-level effects on Black men and boys.[6] My work culminated in a field of study showing that the lethal violence against Black males is so disproportionate that current race and gender theories throughout American universities were deliberately misrepresenting the conditions of Black men and boys to preserve their political illusions of democracy and maintain the coherence of disciplinary theory. For better or for worse, Black Male Studies has demanded a reexamination of the previous research depicting Black males as beneficiaries of masculinity in white patriarchal societies. Given the misandric aggression of anti-Black racism, the ignored but astronomical rates of sexual violence against Black males, and the demonization of Black men within contemporary gender theory, I argued that the death and dying of Black males called for new study.[7] Expressing outrage at the systemic Phenomenon of Black male death is futile. The removal of Black males from society is purposive, not accidental. It is not an aberration of democracy, but rather programmatic and foundation to the thriving of white society and the social mobility of various racial groups, even other Blacks.

Consequently, my reaction to the death of Mr. George Floyd Jr. looks at the usurpation of Black male death within academic theory, or how the death of Black men and boys is possessed by others as racism, or made generic and conceptualized as a kind of violence that maligns all Black bodies equally. Academic theory and political consensus allow everyone, except Black men and boys, to claim Black male death as their own. This usurpation of Black male death is conceptually numbing. It forces us to elide the evidence of a deliberate program against Black males of which Mr. Floyd fell victim. This brief reflection on the murder of George Floyd attempts to contextualize his murder and then theoretically explore the ramifications his death has for our thinking and resistance against white America.

DISAGGREGATING DEATH BY POLICE: THEORIZING MISANDRIC AGGRESSION AS THE BASIS OF DISPROPORTIONATE MALE KILLINGS

Mr. Floyd's death is the product of misandric social processes used to discipline, debase, and in many cases eliminate Black males from American society. The negative stereotypes whites have about racial groups are more similar to their perception of the men from racial-ethnic groups than of the women.[8] Consequently, the racist caricatures whites have of Black people—the most negative attributes associating the race with violence, promiscuity, and lack of intelligence—are based on their beliefs about Black males.[9] These stigmas against Black males build societal consent for their murder and removal from society, no matter how brutal the means. In racist capitalist patriarchal societies, the criminalization and lethal extermination of outgroup (racialized) males are strategies that maintain social hierarchy and promote societal cohesion. This targeting and elimination of outgroup males by the dominant race due to the biological and cultural threats these men and boys pose to the dominant group is called the subordinate male target hypothesis.

The subordinate male target hypothesis explains why throughout Western capitalist societies tend to socially construct outgroup males as threats to dominant groups and the established order of society. Social dominance theorists argue that outgroup men are the primary targets of arbitrary-set discrimination, while women of subordinate and dominant classes are primarily victims of patriarchal oppression. In other words, the patriarchal violence against women is paternalistic and coercive, not lethal, and exterminatory.[10] The specific type of violence outgroup males disproportionately suffer is called arbitrary-set discrimination. Arbitrary sets are socially constructed and highly salient groups based on characteristics such as race, nation, religion, and so on.[11] While arbitrary-set groups exhibit higher levels of flexibility, arbitrariness, and plasticity compared to age and gender systems, arbitrary sets are associated with the most extreme forms of lethal and genocidal violence in human history.[12] The purpose of such violence is to create as much distance and negative social capital between racialized male groups and the dominant racial group as possible. This means outgroup males will suffer more direct discrimination in the housing market, incarceration, employment, and policing than subordinate and dominant group females within the same society.[13] As Jim Sidanius and Rosemary Veniegas explain,

> The reasoning behind this expectation is that arbitrary-set discrimination is primarily a form of intrasexual competition perpetrated by males and directed against males. As such, arbitrary-set discrimination can also be viewed as a form of low-level warfare directed against outgroup males.[14]

This pattern of discrimination has been conceded by intersectional theorists. Valerie Purdie-Vaughns and Richard Eibach argue that in Western patriarchal societies invisibility protects subordinate females from generally being the direct targets of oppression and lethal violence. However, these authors argue that subordinate males become targets of lethal violence because patriarchal societies value men over women, and that this lethal targeting of subordinate males within patriarchal societies should be interpreted as a kind of androcentrism—or male privilege. As Purdie-Vaughns and Eibach explain:

> The oppression of subordinate group men is the product of psychological dispositions that evolved as males competed for resources in the human ancestral environment. By contrast, [intersectional invisibility] views the oppression of subordinate group men as a reflection of the general tendency in an androcentric society to view all men—both those of dominant groups and those of subordinate groups—as more important than women. It is this marginalization of women in an androcentric society that causes subordinate women to be relatively ignored as direct targets of oppression compared to subordinate men.[15]

The patterns of violence within racist capitalist patriarchal societies have remained stable throughout the twentieth century and mirror the trends found in ethnic conflicts, wars, and genocides.[16] The sex-selective extermination of Black males is an attempt to remove them from America's civil society. The brutality enforced against Black men and boys is not simply psychoanalytic as is often suggested by liberal arts theorists, but a historical pattern of sex-selective violence designed to lessen the population of opposing racial groups.[17] Augusta Del Zotto explains,

> While the black female as threat can be controlled through policies of manipulation, the black male as threat requires the implementation of policies of direct force to keep him at the margins, and policies of containment to ensure that

he does not encroach upon the serenity of growing industrial parks and gated communities.[18]

The United States has adopted sex-specific strategies that focus on the elimination of Black males from society. Previous research going back to the 1970s designated this confluence of lethal violence and the prison industrial complex as a program of institutional decimation.[19] However, contemporary research ignores social scientific and comparative data showing the similarities between racialized groups throughout the world and repetitive strategies of violence. Present theorizations concerning the death of Black people assert intuitive accounts of racial disparity as the basis of generalizable theories. The impression a scholar has about the world, a set of events, or an incident is theorized as fact without any investigation into the processes at work.

The murder of George Floyd is no different. His death has yet to be explained as the product of sociohistorical forces and patterns of violence which anticipate population-level effects. In interactions with the police, the escalation of violence toward Black men is a far too often ignored aspect of police homicide and aggression. For example, a recent study analyzing police stops in Ferguson, Missouri, found sharp gendered disparities in how Black men and women are treated if they question the police.

> [W]hen Black men challenged the police, it proved harmful for them, as they were often handcuffed, jailed, or assaulted. Black women were more likely to question the police than any other tactic during police-citizen encounters. Despite challenging officers' actions, they were generally freed without an adverse outcome.[20]

Black women, even when responding with more verbal aggression, did not cause the same escalation that Black men did. This trend holds even in larger studies tracking life course and police homicides.

Homicide due to police shootings is largely a male phenomenon. The male variable holds across all race/sex groups so much so that men of all races are as high as twenty times more likely to be shot by police than their female counterparts. As such, anti-Black racism simply does not provide the kind of causal relationship to death by police that many theorists assert. Said differently, the overwhelming number of cases where police escalate to lethal violence resulting in death, and their likelihood to escalate are predicated on race and maleness, not race or Blackness alone. There are many male groups, including white men, more likely to be killed than Black and other minority groups of women over their life course.[21] Of these groups, Black males have the highest lifetime risk of being killed by police. According to a recent study by sociologists Frank Edwards, Hedwig Lee, and Michael Esposito, "Among all groups, black men and boys face the highest lifetime risk of being killed by police."[22] The authors explain that roughly 96 per 100,000 Black men will be killed over life course as compared to 5.4 per 100,000 Black women.[23]

> Between the ages of 25 y and 29 y, black men are killed by police at a rate between 2.8 and 4.1 per 100,000. . . . Women's risk of being killed by police use of force is about an order of magnitude lower than men's risk at all ages. Between the ages of 25 y and 29 y, we estimate a median mortality risk of 0.12 per 100,000 for black women.[24]

Contrary to the assertion that anti-Blackness sufficiently explains the racial-racist disparities of police homicide, recent evidence suggests that

> being Black, but more distinctively, being a Black male in America seems to increase dramatically the chances that someone is likely to have an encounter with the police where the civilian ends up dead. Being Black and male also is a robust marker of who is likely to experience unfavorable and unfair outcomes in criminal justice and across other key sectors of American society. . . . Black males are the only group for which legal intervention is a leading cause of death.[25]

The death of George Floyd must be understood as a particular manifestation of these larger group dynamics. Even at the individual level, the evidence suggests that being a Black male is bad for one's health.

Americans are culturally primed to perceive Black males as threats and engage them with lethal force. In a recent study examining the tendency of white undergraduates to shoot raced and gendered subjects, Ashby Plant, Joanna Goplen, and Jonathan Kunstman found that

> the participants tended toward mistakenly shooting the unarmed Black male suspects more often than the unarmed Black female and the unarmed White male and White female suspects. In contrast, when responding to armed suspects, participants were actually more likely to mistakenly not shoot the Black female and White suspects of either gender than the Black male suspects.[26]

So among whites with some college education, unarmed Black men were still perceived as more of a threat than armed women. Following the argument established by social dominance theorists and to some extent intersectional invisibility, the data is clear that when it comes to lethal violence at the hands of police or throughout American society more generally, Black femaleness often offers a more protective identity when compared to that of Black men. A more recent study found that Black boys as young as five years old still led primed white shooters to perceive them as threats while Black girls did not. The authors of the study explained that

> prior work has found that threat-based racial biases are stronger for male than for female adult targets. Furthermore, whereas White perceivers commonly display biases toward shooting unarmed Black men in first-person shooter tasks, they display biases against shooting unarmed Black women. Female gender may thus modulate threat-based racial biases at any age.[27]

Contrary to the popular intersectional accounts of gender which insist that femaleness adds to and magnifies racial biases, this data shows that femaleness can actually deactivate racist stereotypes. Consequently, Black maleness must be understood as the catalyst for the intensification of lethal violence and police homicides. George Floyd's death was not at all accidental. It was part of a dynamic that enables whites to engage Black males with complete disregard for their life or being. The mere notion that Black men and boys are threats warrants their extermination—hearing a name associated with being Black and male creates a fight or flight response in white men.[28] This is a reality that remains empirically substantiated at multiple levels throughout social scientific research but systematically denied within liberal arts fields and disciplines. Studying the disaggregation of groups, not the abstraction of categories, reveals specific relationships and patterns that cannot be identified conceptually.[29]

CONCLUSION: UNTIL THE NEXT TIME THERE IS ANOTHER MR. FLOYD

George Floyd Jr.'s death will continue to be replicated and denied as being a product of the strategies of elimination and subjugation tailored to Black men. The proliferation of images and videos of his execution across the world shows that while there might be outrage toward the acts against him, there is no offense taken by the displaying of his corpse. The display of flaccid Black male bodies has become routine. For some, George Floyd Jr. has become the symbol of a new day, but his death has not stopped the murder of more Black men and boys in the United States. In 2020, 242 Black men and 2 Black woman have been shot by police.[30] Because Mr. Floyd was not killed in a police shooting, his death is not tracked by the Fatal Force database. George Floyd is merely an instance of a system attempting to maintain white demographic and political superiority. Mr. Floyd is merely the expression of the racist Weltanschauung of America. Our remorse, and the large and global political demonstrations over his death, mean nothing in the face of political and legal structures and social organizations that are committed to Black death. Our reliance on the good faith efforts of white individuals who can wield more power than other nonwhite groups has been shown to fail time and time again. Yet, we eulogize Mr. Floyd as the start of something new. Mr. Floyd's death demands clarity and deliberate action against a *system* designed to subjugate and kill Black people through the elimination and removal of Black men in the United States.

While there have been various celebrations and praise for the efforts of Black women-led political organizing and leadership, the reality over the last several years is that Black male death has simply not been affected by such efforts.[31] Out of the 1,195 Black people shot by police between 2015 and 2019, 96 percent were Black males.[32] *National Geographic* recently ran a story depicting young Black men as corpses in their mother's arms.[33] The story, entitled "For America's Black mothers, the Fear of Loss and Trauma is Constant," ignores how Black males come to grips with the likelihood of a violent end. Represented as the corpse to the American public, the lifeless pose is meant to remind America of Mr. Floyd's lifeless body. Rather it conveys how the fear of a Black male's doom is not his own, it does not belong to Mr. Floyd, any more than these young Black boys. It is believed to be possessed by others—their mothers—for whom the world can empathize. The Black male is feared, not relatable. He must be represented as a lifeless absence for a reason and affect to thrive. It is this infuriating truth that explains why we continue to celebrate the symbolic rage and protest around Mr. Floyd even though Black male death has remained unchanged since the founding of Black Lives Matter.

We should not insult Mr. Floyd's memory by appealing to the better selves of whites which have not yet been manifested.[34] His death is not and should not be used as an opportunity to have an audience with our oppressors. When Black men are killed by police, we protest their deaths, but within theory, the recognition of the Black male corpse is said to erase other more human victims such as women. Black men continue to die more than other groups, but their corpses are theorized as obstructions to the recognition of others.[35] Contrary to the popular academic ideologies which masquerade as theory, it is the death of Black men and boys that drive and determine the maladies of Blackness. Black men have the lowest life expectancy, the highest rates of mortality, and the greatest economic downward mobility of any race/sex group in the United States.[36] Despite these deleterious demographic realities, Mr. Floyd is not thought to be the *inevitable* consequence of these systems.

(Anti)Blackness is deployed as a generic causal category within contemporary theory. These theories assert that racism is a phenomenon that affects all Black people by the same degree and with the same intensity across the board. Due in no small part to the influence of intersectionality, these scholars assume that the disadvantage imposed upon Blacks gains specificity as various sexual identities speciate the racial experience. As such, the assumption that Blackness is normatively situated as male assumes privilege and a lessened degree of suffering. Against all available evidence and known facts, these intersectional conceptualizations of Black death and disadvantage deploy a seemingly impenetrable logic that says it is Black males who are privileged and invulnerable to certain forms of violence that are primarily experienced by those who are not Black males.[37] Black men then are thought to only suffer from the general racism that all Black people endure. Such accounts do not start with the violence present in the world, the death of Mr. Floyd, and the hundreds like him, it begins with abstractions of identity used to imagine disadvantage that is quite distinct from what can be observed in the world. A serious theorization of Blackness must account for the ways it functions in the world, not merely how one thinks it can be represented.[38]

Even more radical theoretical orientations such as Afro-pessimism fail to disaggregate racial violence and demographic patterns of death and societal disadvantage. Frank Wilderson, for instance, argues that "the Black position . . . is less a site of subjectification and more a site of desubjectification—a 'species' of absolute dereliction, . . . a body that magnetizes bullets."[39] I would contend that some Black bodies magnetize bullets more than others, and it is these bodies that lack explanation within this framework. What produces racial-sex differentiation under Wilderson's account of Black positionality? Despite Black men being the overwhelming majority of the victims of police killings and hate crimes, Wilderson's analysis describes the overrepresentation of Black male victimization as a property of Blackness, not maleness, while other forms of violence like rape or other gender-based stigmas are specifically linked to Black femininity, Black queerness, or Black trans-bodies. While Black maleness may in fact show greater propensity, if not a causal relation to police killings and white vigilantism, Black maleness has no conceptual mode of vulnerability—it simply is (and remains) synonymous with race. Contrary to the dogmas of contemporary theory, a substantial amount of empirical work in sociology, psychology, and economics has shown that racism is in fact misandric aggression. To say this means that racism and racist acts are primarily designed to punish and isolate Black males from society, and makes their deaths spectacles, deterrents to future protests against America's racial order. There will be more George Floyds and when they die at the hands of whites, they too will lack any real explanation in *theory*.

The inability of Black scholars to think about anti-Black racism sociologically, scientifically, and philosophically dooms any serious efforts to lessen police violence. The refusal to explain the disproportionate number of deaths and the more brutal and lethal violence used against Black men is ideological and merely reproduces the aversion the United States has toward the lives of Black men and boys. Black academics and activists have committed themselves to the deliberate misconstruing of George Floyd's murder and hundreds of Black men and boys in the process.

NOTES

1. Abdul JanMohamed, *The Death-Bound-Subject: Richard Wright's Archaeology of Death* (Durham: Duke University Press, 2005), 10.
2. Amy Forlitti, "Minneapolis police chief says Floyd's death was 'murder,'" Twincities.com, June 23, 2020, https://www.twincities.com/2020/06/23/minneapolis-police-chief-says-floyds-death-was-murder/.
3. Calvin Warren, "Black Nihilism and the Politics of Hope," *CR: The New Centennial Review* 15.1 (2015): 215–248.
4. Calvin Warren, *Ontological Terror: Blackness, Nihilism, and Emancipation* (Durham: Duke University Press, 2018).
5. Tommy J. Curry, "Michael Brown and the Need for a Genre Study of Black Male Death and Dying," in *Being Ethical: Classical and New Voices on Contemporary Issues*, eds. Shari Collins, Bertha Alvarez Manninen, Jacqueline M. Gately, Eric Comerford (Ontario: Broadview Press, 2017), 241–247.
6. Tommy J. Curry, "Killing Boogeymen: Phallicism and the Misandric Mischaracterization of Black Males in Theory," *Res Philosophica* 95.2 (2018): 235–272.
7. Tommy J. Curry, *The Man-Not: Race, Class, Genre, and the Dilemmas of Black Manhood* (Philadelphia: Temple University Press, 2017).
8. Alice H. Eagly & Mary E. Kite, "Are Stereotypes of Nationalities Applied to Both Women and Men?," *Journal of Personality and Social Psychology* 53.3 (1987): 451–462.
9. Corrine McConnaughy, "Black Men, White Women, and Demands from the State: How Race and Gender Jointly Shape Protest Expectations and Legitimate State Response," *International Society of Political Psychology* (2017): unpublished, and Corinne McConnaughy and Ishmael White, "Racial Politics Complicated: The Work of Gendered Race Cues in American Politics," *New Research on Gender in Political Psychology Conference* (2011): unpublished.
10. Jim Sidanius & Felicia Pratto, *Social Dominance: An Intergroup Theory of Social Hierarchy and Oppression* (Cambridge: Cambridge University Press, 1999), 50. Black women do experience lethal violence at rates higher than white women, but at rates and numbers not comparable to any male group in the United States. Consequently, it is more accurate to say that Black women are less safe than white women, generally speaking, but not targeted or endangered at rates or numbers comparable to Black men and other male groups in the United States. Whereas Black men are killed for explicit associations with violent crime and danger, Black women's negative interactions with police are found to be more correlated to economic differences. For an explanation of these national and county-based rates of police homicides, see Shytierra Gaston, April D. Fernandes, & Rashaan A. DeShay, "A Macrolevel Study of Police Killings at the Intersection of Race, Ethnicity, and Gender," *Crime and*

Delinquency 67.8 (2020): 1075–1102. This study again shows an order of magnitude difference in rates of police killings per 100,000. Black men are killed at a rate of 8.7 and 11 per 100,000 at the national and county level, respectively. Black women are killed at a rate of 0.34 and 0.44 at the national and county level, respectively (1,086).

Speciating the kind and degree of violence associated with racism and sexism has been of substantial interest to social dominance theorists as well as social science research into benevolent sexism. For a discussion of protective paternalism and benevolent sexism, see Peter Glick and Susan T. Fiske, "The Ambivalent Sexism Inventory: Differentiating Hostile and Benevolent Sexism," *Journal of Personality and Social Psychology* 70.3 (1996): 491–512; and Jean M. McMahon & Kimberly Barsamian Kahn, "When Sexism Leads to Racism: Threat, Protecting Women, and Racial Bias," *Sex Roles* 78 (2018): 591–605.

11. Ibid., 33.
12. Jim Sidanius and Felecia Pratto, *Social Dominance*, 34.
13. Jim Sidanius and Rosemary Veniegas, "Gender and Race Discrimination: The Interactive Nature of Disadvantage," in *Reducing Prejudice and Race Discrimination*, ed. Stuart Oskamp (Mahwah, NJ: Lawrence Erlbaum Associates, 2000), 47–69, and Melissa McDonald, Carlos D. Navarrete, and Jim Sidanius, "Developing a Theory of Gendered Prejudice: An Evolutionary and Social Dominance Perspective," in *Social Cognition, Social Identity, and Intergroup Relations*, eds. Roderick Kramer, Geoffrey Leonardelli, and Robert Livingston (New York: Psychology Press, 2011), 189–220.
14. Jim Sidanius and Rosemary Veniegas, "Gender and Race Discrimination: The Interactive Nature of Disadvantage," in *Reducing Prejudice and Race Discrimination*, ed. Stuart Oskamp (Mahwah, NJ: Lawrence Erlbaum Associates, 2000), 47–69, 54–55. Also see Melissa McDonald, Carlos D. Navarrete, and Jim Sidanius, "Developing a Theory of Gendered Prejudice: An Evolutionary and Social Dominance Perspective," in *Social Cognition, Social Identity, and Intergroup Relations*, eds. Roderick Kramer, Geoffrey Leonardelli, and Robert Livingston (New York: Psychology Press, 2011), 189–220.
15. Ibid., 383.
16. Adam Jones, "Gendercide and Genocide," *Journal of Genocide Studies* 2.2 (2000): 185–211.
17. Errol Miller, *Marginalization of the Black Male: Insights from the Development of the Teaching Profession* (Barbados: Canoe Publishing, 1994), and "Male Marginalization Revisited," in *Gender in the 21st Century: Caribbean Perspectives, Visions, and Possibilities*, eds. Elsa Leo-Rhynie and Barbara Bailey (Kingston: Ian Randle Publishers, 2004), 99–133; and *Men at Risk* (Kingston: Jamaica Publishing House Ltd, 1991).
18. Augusta C. Del Zotto, "Gendercide in a Historical-Structural Context: The Case of Black Male Gendercide in the United States," in *Gendercide and Genocide*, ed. Adam Jones (Nashville: Vanderbilt University Press, 2004), 157–171.
19. James B. Stewart and Joseph W. Scott, "The Institutional Decimation of Black American Males," *Western Journal of Black Studies* 2.2 (1978): 82–92.
20. Jennifer E. Cobbina, Michael Conteh, and Colin Emrich, "Race, Gender, and Responses to Police Among Ferguson Residents and Protesters," *Race and Justice* 9.3 (2019): 276–303, 296.

21. Jennifer A. Hartfield, Derek M. Griffith, and Marino A. Bruce, "Risk of being killed by police use of force in the United States by Age, Race–Ethnicity, and Sex," *PNAS* 116.34 (2019): 16793–16798, 16794–16795.
22. Ibid., 16793–16798, 16793.
23. Ibid., 16794.
24. Ibid., 16795.
25. Jennifer A. Hartfield, Derek M. Griffith, and Marino A. Bruce, "Gendered Racism is a Key to Explaining and Addressing Police-Involved Shootings of Unarmed Black Men in America," *Inequality, Crime, and Health among African American Males Research in Race and Ethnic Relations* 20 (2019): 155–170.
26. E. Ashby Plant, Joanna Goplen, & Jonathan W. Kunstman, "Selective Responses to Threat: The Roles of Race and Gender in Decisions to Shoot," *Personality and Social Psychology Bulletin* 37.9 (2011): 1274–1281, 1279.
27. Andrew Todd, Kelsy C. Thiem, & Rebecca Neel, "Does Seeing Faces of Young Black Boys Facilitate the Identification of Threatening Stimuli?" *Psychological Science* 27 (2016): 384–393, 391.
28. Colin Holbrook, Daniel Fessler, and Carlos David Navarrete, "Looming Large: Racial Stereotypes Illuminate Dual Adaptations for Representing Threat Versus Prestige as Physical Size," *Evolution and Human Behavior* 37 (2016): 67–78.
29. Tommy J. Curry, "Must there be an Empirical Basis for the Theorization of Racialized Subjects in Race-Gender Theory?" *Proceedings of the Aristotelian Society* 121.1 (2021): 21–44.
30. John Muyskens and Joe Fox, "Fatal Force," *The Washington Post*, October 1, 2020, https://www.washingtonpost.com/graphics/investigations/police-shootings-database/.
31. There is a political discourse and ideology in the United States that says Black female or intersectional leadership should be praised simply because multiple (non-cis Black male) identities are at the fore. This stance has prevented Black academics from making basic observations concerning strategy and representation. For example, Critical Race Theorists have often rejected the idea that reform will change the legal and political structures of American racism, yet numerous academics who hold such a view claim that Black Lives Matter is legally, politically, and socially transformative.
32. John Muyskens and Joe Fox, "Fatal Force." *The Washington Post* Fatal Force database shows that 1,195 Black people were killed between January 2015 and December 2019. Black men were 1,148 of those killed, or roughly 96 percent.
33. Lonnae O'Neal, "For America's Black mothers, the fear of loss and trauma is constant," *National Geographic*, August 27, 2020, https://www.nationalgeographic.com/magazine/2020/10/jon-henrys-stranger-fruit-shows-black-mothers-constant-fear-of-loss-and-trauma/?fbclid=IwAR1NVsdOyGrZQpVkHARhlSwFe2p2K7tdaOyOhpbBfZGECCD9yaqivdCuqtk.
34. Amir Jaima, "Don't Talk to White People: On the Epistemological and Rhetorical Limitations of Conversations with White People for Anti-Racist Purposes: An Essay," *Journal of Black Studies* 52.1 (2021): 77–97.
35. Tommy J. Curry, "He Never Mattered: Poor Black Males and the Dark Logic of Intersectional Invisibility," in *The Movement for Black Lives: Philosophical Perspectives*, eds. Michael Cholbi, Alex Madva, Benjamin Yost, & Brandon Hogan (Oxford: Oxford University Press, 2021).

36. Black men's wages remain practically unchanged from the segregation era, see David Leonhardt, "The Black-white Wage Gap is as Big as It was in 1950," *The New York Times*, June 25, 2020. On the downward mobility of Black males, see Patrick Bayer and Kerwin Kofi Charles, "Divergent Paths: A New Perspective on Earnings Differences between Black and white Men since 1940," *The Quarterly Journal of Economics* 133.3 (2018): 1459–1501; and Raj Chetty et al., "Race and Economic Opportunity in the United States: An Intergenerational Perspective," *The Quarterly Journal of Economics* 135.2 (2020): 711–783. For a discussion of life expectancy, see Sabrina Tavernise, "Black Americans See Gains in Life Expectancy," *The New York Times*, May 8, 2016, https://www.nytimes.com/2016/05/09/health/blacks-see-gains-in-life-expectancy.html?fbclid=IwAR2kzFx2uAQ1tZK2xQ5QTfqNEe8Vu Bqp3brnFFkRAxnE_8xs4-lFzPowk_Y.

37. T. Hasan Johnson, "Challenging the Myth of Black Male Privilege," *Spectrum: A Journal on Black Men* 6.2 (2018): 21–42.

38. See Michael Sawyer, *An Africana Philosophy of Temporality: Homo Liminalis* (New York: Palgrave Macmillan, 2018).

39. Frank Wilderson, *Red, white, and Black: Cinema and the Structure of U.S. Antagonism* (Durham: Duke University Press, 2010), 77.

BIBLIOGRAPHY

Bayer, Patrick and Kerwin Kofi Charles. "Divergent Paths: A New Perspective on Earnings Differences between Black and white Men since 1940," *The Quarterly Journal of Economics* 133.3 (2018): 1459–1501.

Chetty, Raj, Nathaniel Hendren, Maggie R. Jones and Sonya R. Porter. "Race and Economic Opportunity in the United States: An Intergenerational Perspective," *The Quarterly Journal of Economics* 135.2 (2020): 711–783.

Cobbina, Jennifer E., Michael Conteh and Colin Emrich. "Race, Gender, and Responses to Police among Ferguson Residents and Protesters," *Race and Justice* 9.3 (2019): 276–303.

Curry, Tommy J. "Michael Brown and the Need for a Genre Study of Black Male Death and Dying," in *Being Ethical: Classical and New Voices on Contemporary Issues*, eds. Shari Collins, Bertha Alvarez Manninen, Jacqueline M. Gately, Eric Comerford (Ontario: Broadview Press, 2017), 241–247.

Curry, Tommy J. *The Man-Not: Race, Class, Genre, and the Dilemmas of Black Manhood* (Philadelphia: Temple University Press, 2017).

Curry, Tommy J. "Killing Boogeymen: Phallicism and the Misandric Mischaracterization of Black Males in Theory," *Res Philosophica* 95.2 (2018): 235–272.

Curry, Tommy J. "Must there be an Empirical Basis for the Theorization of Racialized Subjects in Race-Gender Theory?" *Proceedings of the Aristotelian Society* 121.1 (2021): 21–44.

Curry, Tommy J. "He Never Mattered: Poor Black Males and the Dark Logic of Intersectional Invisibility," in *The Movement for Black Lives: Philosophical Perspectives*, eds. Michael Cholbi, Alex Madva, Benjamin Yost, and Brandon Hogan (Oxford: Oxford University Press, 2021).

Del Zotto, Augusta C. "Gendercide in a Historical-Structural Context: The Case of Black Male Gendercide in the United States," in *Gendercide and Genocide*, ed. Adam Jones (Nashville: Vanderbilt University Press, 2004), 157–171.

Eagly, Alice H. and Mary E. Kite. "Are Stereotypes of Nationalities Applied to Both Women and Men?," *Journal of Personality and Social Psychology* 53.3 (1987): 451–462.

Edwards, Frank, Hedwig Lee, and Michael Esposito. "Gendered Racism is a Key to Explaining and Addressing Police-Involved Shootings of Unarmed Black Men in America," *Inequality, Crime, and Health among African American Males Research in Race and Ethnic Relations* 20 (2019b): 155–170.

Forlitti, Amy. "Minneapolis police chief says Floyd's death was 'murder,'" Twincities.com, June 23, 2020, https://www.twincities.com/2020/06/23/minneapolis-police-chief-says-floyds-death-was-murder/.

Gaston, Shytierra, April D. Fernandes and Rashaan A. DeShay. "A Macrolevel Study of Police Killings at the Intersection of Race, Ethnicity, and Gender," *Crime and Delinquency* 67.8 (2020): 1075–1102.

Glick, Peter and Susan T. Fiske. "The Ambivalent Sexism Inventory: Differentiating Hostile and Benevolent Sexism," *Journal of Personality and Social Psychology* 70.3 (1996): 491–512.

Hartfield, Jennifer A., Derek M. Griffith and Marino A. Bruce. "Risk of Being Killed by Police Use of Force in the United States by Age, Race–Ethnicity, and Sex," *PNAS* 116.34 (2019a): 16793–16798.

Holbrook, Colin, Daniel Fessler and Carlos David Navarrete. "Looming Large: Racial Stereotypes Illuminate Dual Adaptations for Representing Threat Versus Prestige as Physical Size," *Evolution and Human Behavior* 37 (2016): 67–78.

Jaima, Amir. "Don't Talk to White People: On the Epistemological and Rhetorical Limitations of Conversations with White People for Anti-Racist Purposes: An Essay," *Journal of Black Studies*, 52.1 (2021): 77–97.

JanMohamed, Abdul. *The Death-Bound-Subject: Richard Wright's Archaeology of Death* (Durham: Duke University Press, 2005).

Johnson, T. Hasan. "Challenging the Myth of Black Male Privilege," *Spectrum: A Journal on Black Men* 6.2 (2018): 21–42.

Jones, Adam. "Gendercide and Genocide," *Journal of Genocide Studies* 2.2 (2000): 185–211.

Leonhardt, David. "The Black-White Wage Gap Is As Big As It Was in 1950," *The New York Times*, June 25, 2020.

McConnaughy, Corrine. "Black Men, White Women, and Demands from the State: How Race and Gender Jointly Shape Protest Expectations and Legitimate State Response," *International Society of Political Psychology* (2017): unpublished.

McConnaughy, Corinne and Ishmael White. "Racial Politics Complicated: The Work of Gendered Race Cues in American Politics," *New Research on Gender in Political Psychology Conference* (2011): unpublished.

McDonald, Melissa, Carlos D. Navarrete and Jim Sidanius. "Developing a Theory of Gendered Prejudice: An Evolutionary and Social Dominance Perspective," in *Social Cognition, Social Identity, and Intergroup Relations*, eds. Roderick Kramer,

Geoffrey Leonardelli, and Robert Livingston (New York: Psychology Press, 2011), 189–220.

McMahon, Jean M. and Kimberly Barsamian Kahn. "When Sexism Leads to Racism: Threat, Protecting Women, and Racial Bias," *Sex Roles*, 78 (2018): 591–605.

Miller, Errol. *Marginalization of the Black Male: Insights from the Development of the Teaching Profession* (Barbados: Canoe Publishing, 1994).

Miller, Errol. "Male Marginalization Revisited," in *Gender in the 21st Century: Caribbean Perspectives, Visions, and Possibilities*, eds. Elsa Leo-Rhynie and Barbara Bailey (Kingston: Ian Randle Publishers, 2004), 99–133.

Miller, Errol. *Men at Risk* (Kingston: Jamaica Publishing House Ltd, 1991).

Muyskens, John and Joe Fox. "Fatal Force," *The Washington Post*, October 1, 2020, https://www.washingtonpost.com/graphics/investigations/police-shootings-database/.

O'Neal, Lonnae. "For America's Black Mothers, the Fear of Loss and Trauma Is Constant," *National Geographic*, August 27, 2020, https://www.nationalgeographic.com/magazine/2020/10/jon-henrys-stranger-fruit-shows-black-mothers-constant-fear-of-loss-and-trauma/?fbclid=IwAR1NVsdOyGrZQpVkHARhlSwFe2p2K7tdaOyOhpbBfZGECCD9yaqivdCuqtk.

Plant, E. Ashby, Joanna Goplen and Jonathan W. Kunstman. "Selective Responses to Threat: The Roles of Race and Gender in Decisions to Shoot," *Personality and Social Psychology Bulletin* 37.9 (2011): 1274–1281.

Sawyer, Michael. *An Africana Philosophy of Temporality: Homo Liminalis* (New York: Palgrave Macmillan, 2018).

Sidanius, Jim and Felicia Pratto. *Social Dominance: An Intergroup Theory of Social Hierarchy and Oppression* (Cambridge: Cambridge University Press, 1999).

Sidanius, Jim and Rosemary Veniegas. "Gender and Race Discrimination: The Interactive Nature of Disadvantage," in *Reducing Prejudice and Race Discrimination*, ed. Stuart Oskamp (Mahwah, NJ: Lawrence Erlbaum Associates, 2000), 47–69.

Stewart, James B. and Joseph W. Scott. "The Institutional Decimation of Black American Males," *Western Journal of Black Studies* 2.2 (1978): 82–92.

Tavernise, Sabrina. "Black Americans See Gains in Life Expectancy," *The New York Times*, May 8, 2016, https://www.nytimes.com/2016/05/09/health/blacks-see-gains-in-life-expectancy.html?fbclid=IwAR2kzFx2uAQ1tZK2xQ5QTfqNEe8VuBqp3brnFFkRAxnE_8xs4-lFzPowk_Y.

Todd, Andrew, Kelsy C. Thiem and Rebecca Neel. "Does Seeing Faces of Young Black Boys Facilitate the Identification of Threatening Stimuli?," *Psychological Science* 27 (2016): 384–393.

Warren, Calvin. "Black Nihilism and the Politics of Hope," *CR: The New Centennial Review* 15.1 (2015): 215–248.

Warren, Calvin. *Ontological Terror: Blackness, Nihilism, and Emancipation* (Durham: Duke University Press, 2018).

Wilderson, Frank. *Red, White, and Black: Cinema and the Structure of U.S. Antagonism* (Durham: Duke University Press, 2010).

Chapter 7

Theory, Epistemic Failure, and the Problem of (Hue)Man Suffering

A Phenomenology of Breathlessness

Timothy J. Golden

BLACK MEN AS INHABITANTS OF THE PHILOSOPHICAL PROBLEM OF TRUTH

Immanuel Kant's "Copernican Revolution" in epistemology was grounded on the notion that rather than our consciousness conforming to objects of experience, it is objects of experience that conform to our consciousness. In other words, human beings are not merely passive recipients of sensory information, but instead make a genuine cognitive contribution to experience. In defense of this thesis, Kant advances a series of transcendental arguments designed to refute David Hume's skepticism about the self and its contribution to experience, while likewise refuting René Descartes's naïve psychological realism about the self and its ability to outlive the body. Kant concludes that both Hume and Descartes are correct in what they each affirm, but incorrect in what they each deny: on the one hand, Hume is correct in affirming that our knowledge comes to us from experience, but is incorrect in asserting that there is no part of our knowledge that exists prior to experience, and on the other hand, Descartes is correct in affirming that there is something necessarily and universally true about human knowledge, but is incorrect in claiming that these features of human reason provide access to the *Ding an Sich*, when human knowledge is limited to appearances. Kant, drawing from both of these traditions, synoptically called empiricism (Hume) and rationalism (Descartes), argued that both traditions work together to give a more coherent account of knowledge than either could give alone. So it is that Kant argued that there were such things as synthetic a priori judgments: those sorts of judgments that are both derived from a combination of what is given within the epistemic constraints of a spatiotemporal sensory manifold of intuition and are thus synthetic (refuting Descartes and affirming Hume), and concepts that exist prior to experience and are thus a priori (refuting Hume and affirming Descartes). Synthetic a priori judgments thus become a new and narrow species of knowledge for Kant, so narrow that it leads to Kant's dictum that "thoughts without content are empty, intuitions without concepts are blind."[1] Neither a priori reason nor a posteriori sensibility is sufficient to yield knowledge on its own, which is why synthetic a priori knowledge is possible for Kant only on the appearance of an object of experience (synthetic) that can be brought under a concept (a priori). Although intuitions without concepts do allow for a space of aesthetic creativity according to the faculty of judgment, it is epistemic failure to have an object for which there is no concept present itself to us (this is covered in Kant's *Critique of Judgment*). And it is also epistemic failure to have a concept with no corresponding object. This is Kant's critique of metaphysical speculation: we have conceptions of God, free will, and an immortal soul, but there are no corresponding objects for them. Hence we have, at best, a pseudo-knowledge in speculative metaphysics that is not really knowledge at all, but rather is human reason following its rational impulse far beyond its bounds. Kant was careful to note that his *Critique of Pure Reason* had a positive function, which was to secure mathematical and scientific knowledge on firm ground and to "deny reason in order to make room for faith."[2] Truth, then, for Kant, was a matter of acknowledging its subjective construction on the one hand while restricting its objective reach on the other. Without such restrictions, warned Kant, we run into serious moral problems.

Søren Kierkegaard inherited the Kantian legacy of truth in his ongoing feud with the Danish State Church, who, beguiled by Hegelian theologians, had made truth into a mere article of Christian doctrine, stripping it of its subjective roots in Kant. Turning away from the epistemic restrictions of Kant's transcendental idealism and toward the epistemic liberties of Hegel's absolute idealism, Danish theologians transgressed Aristotelian logic to such a degree that the Incarnation of Christ—what Kierkegaard saw as the ultimate, unresolvable paradox—became a matter of Hegelian dialectical resolution. If there was ever a need for Kantian-styled epistemic limitations that emphasize epistemic failure, they are needed in the case of the Incarnation, the mysterious centerpiece of the Christian faith. But for Danish theologians, epistemic failure was found not in reason extending its boundaries, but rather in failing to consume them within Hegel's absolute idealism. The Incarnation thus became a matter of Jesus Christ as the dialectical resolution (synthesis) of God (thesis) and human (antithesis).[3] Thus made conceptually and metaphysically simple, Christianity lost its way. Kierkegaard saw the passion of first- and second-century Christianity fade under the influence of the Hegelian dialectic, making Christianity a matter of social and cultural ease consistent with the metaphysical ease of its dialectical resolution of the Incarnation. It is in this context that Kierkegaard initiated a complex strategy to communicate with what he saw as a deluded Christendom: he would deploy pseudonyms to communicate indirectly with the Christians of his day because, for Kierkegaard, they needed to be deceived, not into believing what is false, but rather into believing what is true. It was amid this great illusion that Kierkegaard would claim that "it is not truth that rules the world but illusions."[4]

Both Kant and Kierkegaard are interested in moral problems emerging from a failure to adequately interrogate reason. Jewish philosopher Emmanuel Levinas continues this tradition in the twentieth century with his notion of ethical metaphysics. Like Kant and Kierkegaard before him, Levinas is concerned about reason's unchecked intrusions upon moral life. He is especially concerned about these intrusions in philosophical theology, in particular, theodicy. Rather than refraining from theorizations in the interest of appreciating the Other's first-person experience of suffering as "useless," reason imposes itself upon morality and, absorbing evil into a rational, dialectical couplet with good, makes the Other's suffering as useful as a matter of rational justification rather than an impetus for moral action to relieve the suffering. Theodicy thus becomes an evil unto itself, prompting Levinas to write that "for an ethical sensibility . . . the justification of the neighbor's pain is certainly the source of all immorality."[5]

Reason, then, left unchecked, becomes ontologized as matter of law. It becomes what Levinas called a "said": a social order in which a fixed meaning assumes a political dimension, one that is perhaps ontologized as a code or law.[6] Jacques Derrida's contribution to this story of truth is that law is inherently coercive:

> There are, to be sure, laws that are not enforced, but there is no law without enforceability and no applicability or enforceability of the law without force, whether this force be direct or indirect, physical or symbolic, exterior or interior, brutal or subtly discursive—even hermeneutic—coercive or regulative, and so forth.[7]

Kant, Kierkegaard, Levinas, and Derrida, read together, tell us a compelling story about truth as a philosophical problem that has serious moral implications. Kant tells us that truth must be limited to actual objects, and even then such objects may only be known as appearances, not as things-in-themselves. To claim knowledge with concepts and no objects is vacuous. When this vacuity is either under or unexamined, Kierkegaard warns us that epistemic vacuity can become so habitually and wrongly treated as objective knowledge that we have created and abide in a social order ruled, not by truth, but by illusion. Levinas admonishes that morality must precede truth instead of truth preceding morality. Failing to do so, for Levinas, ontologizes truth, authorizing a political dimension in which such truth can become codified as law. And for Derrida, there is no law without force; without coercion, without a forceful application of the law to its subject matter—real or imagined, indeed, as strange as it sounds, even an imaginary ontology.

I am interested in how Black men inhabit this philosophical story of truth insofar as certain "truths" about them exist, despite the Kantian lack of widespread objects (Black men) that correspond to the concepts of "inherently pathological," "rapists," "criminals," nihilists," and so on. Such "truths" have sedimented themselves into a Kierkegaardian culture in which illusion rules, and in which an echo of Levinas is heard that condemns rationalizing the evil of Black male suffering into a dialectical relation to good to such a degree that the pathologizing of Black men has become an article of cultural faith with the coercive force of law as Derrida has described it; laws that are both biological (COVID-19) and political (police killing Black men, often with impunity). Black men thus inhabit a problem not of their own making, but one that nevertheless demands a strong, consistent, and courageous level of resistance. As is usually the case in philosophy, truth—an intellectual problem for white philosophers—is a matter of profound, existential, phenomenological, life-and-death urgency for Black people generally, and, as I argue in this chapter, for Black men in particular. It is with this terrifying sense of urgency, and I hope a courageous sense of resistance that I, a Black male, write these words.

THE BIOLOGICAL, THE POLITICAL, AND BLACK MALE BREATH

The proliferation of social theories about Black men in contemporary philosophical discussions of race and gender damages and distorts their humanity—specifically the Black male body. Recent philosophical research in Black Male Studies has exposed the reiteration of anti-Black, misandric criminological theories about Black men in intersectional feminism that are inconsistent with empirical data, which suggests otherwise about Black men as it relates to intimate partner violence and egalitarian attitudes toward women.[8] And yet despite this epistemic failure, such dangerous theories about Black men persist in abundance. Again, it is as though, in a Kantian sense, there is a form of transcendental illusion: there are concepts, that is, there are racist ideas about Black men as generally violent, predatory, and nihilistic but there are no corresponding objects for those concepts insofar as empirical data does not support such generalities about Black men. The persistence of such theories in the absence of credible evidence is dehumanizing. Such theoretical dehumanization, I submit, leads to a crisis of Black male death by suffocation: a breathlessness that emerges both from a certain sort of law "enforcement" in both the biological condition of COVID-19 and in the ongoing problem of police brutality that so disproportionately affects Black men; a problem that is depicted with the horrifying exclamations of Eric Garner and George Floyd that they "can't breathe."[9]

In this chapter, I argue that contemporary philosophical and gender-based theorizations of Black men—among other anti-Black racist phenomena—sever the would-be, life-preserving epidermal connection of the Black male body to the external world and transform it into a horrifying instrument of Black male alienation and death, creating an existential and phenomenological crisis of asphyxiation. In support of my argument, I begin with a discussion of breathing and a phenomenology of breathlessness. I then discuss the suffocating proliferation of social theory and the problem of epistemic failure as it relates to Black men. Despite the latter, the former abounds. I draw from two biblical texts to show how theory, in the Aristotelian tradition, is idolatrously "divinized" at the expense of Black male humanity, causing an existential crisis of alienation and death worthy of phenomenological attention. I then discuss the nature of the crisis by showing how the biological and the political converge to transform the pulmonary and epidermal functions—functions that support life and connect human beings to the external world—into systems that deprive Black men of life by disconnecting them from the world. Both COVID-19 and corrupt, socially and politically operative semiotic formations of transcendence deprive Black men of breathing—an essential function synonymous with the very notion of human life itself. I conclude the chapter with a discussion of Emmanuel Levinas's moral notion of the "interhuman order" as it relates to the utter uselessness of Black male suffering and with a brief commentary on the need to end harmful theorizing about Black men.

BREATHING AND BREATHLESSNESS

Havi Carel has recently produced important research on the phenomenology of breathing and breathlessness.[10] Here, I draw from her work, applying her phenomenological insights to the plight of Black men who suffer from breathlessness due to the "enforcement" of natural laws in the biology of COVID-19 and the enforcement of politically produced laws, both of which, I will argue, result from their epidermal alienation. Cavel's phenomenology begins by bracketing breathlessness as an objective medical symptom that a patient presents to a physician. The theorizing of the scientific natural attitude thus suspended, Carel identifies breathlessness as a subjective problem that impacts one in ways that are frightening. Carel suggests that the experience of breathlessness is "total and overwhelming to the sufferer."[11]

According to Carel, breathing is fraught with a variety of "tensions and juxtapositions."[12] Breathing is at once continuous and unconscious; we are seldom aware of our own breathing unless we are somehow deprived of it. And when we are so deprived, breathing becomes "the focus of attention, and the experience can be uncomfortable."[13] Carel then makes the following observations about breathing and how it connects us to the world:

> Breathing is also intimately connected to emotion: surprise or horror make us gasp, hearty laughter leaves us gasping for breath, crying involves involuntary short, sharp inhalations. Breathing is richly modulated by emotional experience, be it pleasurable or painful. The lungs are the only bodily site (other than the skin) where interior and exterior spaces are in constant exchange. We breathe in the air and what it contains, extract the oxygen we need, and expel carbon dioxide. The air around us, with its pollutants, odors, humidity, and heat, becomes internalized briefly, connecting us to the environment and exposing our lungs to pollutants, irritants, and potential sources of infection. The lungs are thus vulnerable and open to the external environment in a way that does not occur with other internal organs.[14]

Breathing provides us with a reciprocity between our bodies and the external world. And it is this reciprocity that brings with it a sense of vulnerability because our pulmonary system exposes us to toxins and pathogens in a way that other internal organs, such as the liver and kidneys for example, do not. In addition to the symmetry of breath, Carel points to the metaphorical and literary interpretations of breath as being synonymous with life itself.[15] She then turns to a discussion of breathlessness and distinguishes between normal and pathological breathlessness, indicating that the former results from physical exertion, is healthy, and even enjoyable, while the latter is breathlessness when there is no exertion, resulting from a disease affecting the respiratory system. This is the sort of breathlessness that one experiences from COVID-19, for example. I would add to Carel's account of pathological breathlessness that sort of breathlessness resulting from external trauma to the body, as in the cases of Eric Garner and George Floyd, whose cardiovascular and pulmonary systems are fully operative, but are disrupted and damaged from forces beyond their bodies, such as a chokehold and a knee. I explore this in greater detail below.

Moving away from breathlessness as a mere objective diagnosis and toward a phenomenological account of breathlessness, Carel discusses the experience of breathlessness as involving a breathing that is more laborious but less fruitful. That is, one breathes much harder but takes in a much lesser amount of air.[16] Carel writes that "unlike healthy breathlessness, it does not deliver the required amount of oxygen to support bodily exertion."[17] For the individual experiencing breathlessness, Carel writes that "it is a total and overwhelming experience of loss of control and is acutely unpleasant. It removes the breathless person from the normal course of events and can cause deep anxiety, panic attack, and trauma."[18] So, breathlessness is an acute condition resulting from either normal physical exertion, internal pathology, or external trauma. In the latter two forms of pathological breathlessness, those without breath work harder for less breath and experience great trauma and anxiety in doing so. I will take up this phenomenological account of breathlessness after I discuss how the proliferation of theory despite epistemic failure provides the social and political background for the epidermal-induced internal and external traumatic causes of breathlessness in the Black male body.

THE PROLIFERATION OF THEORY AND EPISTEMIC FAILURE

Viewed as a literary work, the Bible is a repository of narratives which, when carefully considered, yield philosophical insights with far-reaching moral, social, and political implications. Moreover, because of its proximity to notions of divine superiority and its confessional claims of inerrancy, the Bible resonates with the proliferation of theory which I want to interrogate here. For even as the Bible is associated with divinity, so too is the word "theory," which has as its etymological root the Greek word *theos*, meaning God. Greek philosophy associated thought and theorizing with divinity to such a degree that Aristotle would not only declare that thought itself was the best of divine activities, but also that God's thinking was a "thinking on thinking."[19] This association of thought with the divine is so embedded in language that *theos*, the Greek term for God, is not only the etymological root of theory, but also of "thought" and "thinking." I am interested in this etymology and its philosophical connection to notions of divinity because it brings with it an implicit legitimation of theorizing as conceptual compared with an implicit illegitimacy of moral praxis.[20] It is in this way that theory and its implied sense of superiority drive our understanding of one another and how we relate to one another in the world. We often prioritize theory over praxis in the academy because we have retained the Aristotelian inclination toward its apotheosis. That is, we persist, through the proliferation of theory, in the exaltation of theorizing to a superior sort of "divine" status. But I want to consider theory otherwise. Could it be that our theorizations are not as divine as we thought them to be? Is theory divine at all? Or is theory something more sinister clothed in academic regalia and philosophical argument? The last of these questions is not far-fetched, for it is theory and theorizing that led to what Levinas would call "totality," which, he argued, compromises our moral well-being in the interest of ontological certainty and epistemic clarity. Here, I want to problematize theory's "divine" sense of superiority by interrogating its role in philosophical discussions of race and gender: discussions that too often render Black men expendable casualties of theoretical and ideological academic warfare.

With this in mind, I consider two narratives from the Bible. In each of them, there is a theoretical musing generated from what Gottfried Leibniz would discover and call the "principle of sufficient reason." The first is taken from the book of Job and is the beginning of the first speech of one of Job's three friends, Eliphaz, who is visiting Job amid his myriad catastrophes. Beholding Job's misery, he asks Job "Remember, I pray thee, who *ever* perished, being innocent? or where were the righteous cut off?"[21] These two rhetorical questions imply that innocent persons do not suffer; that when someone suffers there is a good reason for it; that the person must have done something morally wrong to deserve it. In other words, because, as Leibniz argues, "nothing happens without reason," Eliphaz concludes that Job must have done something to deserve the tragedies that have befallen him. Moral wrongdoing is, on this ontotheological view, a metaphysical first principle of personal ordeal and tribulation. The second biblical narrative applies a similar line of reasoning. The passage, in its entirety, reads:

> And as Jesus passed by, he saw a man which was blind from his birth. And his disciples asked him, saying, Master, who did sin, this man, or his parents, that he was born blind? Jesus answered, Neither hath this man sinned, nor his parents: but that the works of God should be made manifest in him.[22]

Upon seeing the awful condition of a man who was born blind, the disciples asked Jesus who had sinned, the man or his parents. Again, due to the principle of sufficient reason, the disciples attribute moral wrongdoing to the man born blind because they, like Eliphaz long before them, believed that either the man born blind or his parents must have done something morally wrong that caused his blindness. Again, the need for metaphysical certainty rears its hideous head here by theorizing moral wrongdoing as the first principle of physical disability. In both of these situations there is a devastating sense of dehumanization. In the first, it seems that Job needs comfort and care, not ontotheological condemnation. And in the second, it is almost as if the humanity of the man born blind is buried deep beneath a carapace of one theoretical insight after another, with the disciples' question to Jesus simply representing the latest attempt to "understand" his blindness with reference to some moral wrong that he committed. Eliphaz and the disciples seem to abide in Plato's cave, seated and bound by the chains of an ontotheological tradition that only permits them to see the shadows of their theories cast upon the cave wall rather than the hard realities of Job's and the man born blind's suffering humanity. Again, in both instances, it seems that theory has proliferated not only at the expense of one's humanity but also, due to the rampant speculation about Job's and the man born blind's conditions, theory has proliferated in the absence of epistemic reliability. Those around Job and the man born blind cannot see them as they are, but only as they are theorized. They are, in Edmund Husserl's terms, trapped in a dehumanizing "natural attitude" that demands a radical suspension in order for their humanity to be seen. A phenomenological reduction is thus in order that there may be a revelation of responsibility both to and for Job and the man born blind.

It is, of course, not the case that Eliphaz and Jesus's disciples were knowingly and intentionally doing metaphysical speculation. They certainly were not engaged in the resolution of any cosmological conundrums or intellectual puzzles that demanded the application of philosophical principles that Leibniz would not articulate until centuries later. But that is the nature of the principle of sufficient reason: since Immanuel Kant's interrogation of rational theology, rational cosmology, and rational psychology in the *Critique of Pure Reason*, we are aware that it is a rational principle lying at the very core of metaphysical speculation, and that it is so embedded in human consciousness that the faculty of reason functions unaware of its influence in theoretical cognition. So despite the anachronistic relationship between Leibniz's discovery of the principle of sufficient reason and its use in biblical literature, it is certainly reasonable suggest that long before Leibniz's articulation of it and Kant's critique of it, it was at work in the reasoning of both Eliphaz and the disciples. A fortiori then, the principle of sufficient reason is certainly at work today, long after Leibniz discovered and formalized it as philosophical doctrine.

With this level of theorizing in mind, consider the myriad theories about Black men. From Kimberlé Crenshaw's intersectional feminism to bell hooks's mimetic theory of Black masculinity, Black men occupy the position of Job and the man born blind. That is, their humanity is buried deep beneath layers of specious theory that have little basis in empirical reality, but are nevertheless useful in maintaining a certain racist sort of ideology about Black men that has been recycled from not only first-wave feminism but also from racist criminological and sociological theories of the twentieth century.[23] And despite the discrediting of these theories, they persist, putting Black men in the position of being dehumanized in virtue of their characterization as "criminal," "violent," "patriarchal," "predatory," and "nihilistic."[24]

Indeed, as I will describe below, it is these characterizations that precede their physical appearance in everyday life, keeping Black men dangerously ahead of themselves. They are condemned prior to their appearance, so that upon appearing they cannot be conceived as being worthy of anything other than an insidious neglect in the form of a denial of testimonial credibility in the case of COVID-19, or a homicidal rage in the form of aggressive policing, as in the cases of Eric Garner and George Floyd. In both cases, as I describe below, Black men experience the overwhelming suffering and anxiety of pathological breathlessness from either an internal disease left untreated because of neglect (COVID-19), or because of the external trauma of the chokehold and the knee in the form of social and political oppression.

NATURE OF THE CRISIS AND THE NEED FOR PHENOMENOLOGICAL INTERVENTION

The skin of the Black male body, which, on the one hand, protects it from invading pathogens and connects it to the external world, on the other hand, becomes a marker that signifies the legitimacy of pulmonary oppression that is both biological and political. That is, the highly theorized skin of the Black male body—a theorization that is epistemically unsupported, indeed, an epistemology without an epistemology—scripts it for epistemic injustice as it stands before the white coat and stethoscope of the physician, and social and political injustice as it stands before the gun and the badge of the police officer. In both situations the skin of the Black male body leads to the enforcement of laws that cause suffocation. In the case of the physician, Black male skin, theorized as "criminal," "violent," "nihilistic," and "patriarchal," delegitimizes testimonial credibility, rendering the Black male body's articulation of COVID-19 symptoms unbelievable despite the Black male body's own experience. Thus denied a medical intervention, the Black male body succumbs to the natural law of cause and effect: the unimpeded biological path of the virus, operating consistent with the causal laws of nature, relentlessly attacks the lungs and suffocates the Black male body. Here we consider the case of Gary Fowler, a fifty-six-year-old Black man from Detroit, Michigan, who presented himself with COVID-19 symptoms to three different hospitals and was sent home. His son would later find him, blue and dead from COVID-19 suffocation, sitting in a chair in his bedroom.[25] And in the case of the police officer, the highly theorized but epistemically unsupported skin of the Black male body signifies violence and criminality that justifies deadly force delivered in the form of police—induced suffocation designed to keep it under control. Biologically, socially, and politically, the role of the epidermis is thus transformed from an organ of protection from and connection to the external world into an instrument of alienation and death, leading to a crisis of breathlessness for the Black male body. I am not making any strong causal claim that Gary Fowler, Eric Garner, or George Floyd in each instance died because of a conscious targeting. To be sure, they were targeted, but in a different sense. My much more modest claim is that their theoretical dehumanization is so pervasive and, firmly ensconced in the social consciousness of anti-Black male violence as to incline many to dehumanize Black men without realizing it. In Platonic terms, our traditional but inaccurate theories and beliefs about Black men so shackle us that we only see the shadow of who Black men really are and take it to be reality. This is what makes the theorization so dangerous and puts Black men in crisis. This crisis demands a suspension—indeed a termination—of a certain sort of theorizing in the interest of alleviating what I call "(Hue)Man" suffering: the suffering of those human beings of a certain hue or color, who are both Black and male.

How does one make this phenomenological move? Consider the man born blind. In verse 1 of John, chapter 9, Jesus sees none of the prevailing, popular theories about the man born blind. Indeed, when Jesus saw him, he saw "a man." All that Jesus saw was "a man which was blind from his birth." He also never theorized the man's condition. Instead, Jesus resists the principle of sufficient reason and sees the man simply as he is: a man. Phenomenologically speaking, one may argue that Jesus, in contrast to the disciples, performs an *epoché* of sorts, suspending the theorizations about this man—the "natural attitude" of his day—and accesses his own inner-subjective life, enabling him to see the man born blind not as others have theorized him, but rather to see both his own contribution to the man as his creator (his "transcendental subjectivity") and his intentions toward the man as his healer, neither of which are visible in the natural attitude's endless proliferation of theories about the man. The man born blind becomes the *noema* of a *noesis*, and, no longer an over-theorized object, he is re-created as a human being *imago Dei*. So what Jesus sees is the man whom he loves as he intended him to be and not as society has constructed him. As applied to Black men, a suspension of the theoretical natural attitude demands seeing them as human beings, as "men" who are worthy of an intentionality directed at them for their benefit rather than their detriment. At the end of theorizing, then, there is an opportunity for justice.

AFTER THEORY

Black men have been dehumanized within the American social and political order at least since their arrival to America's shores in Jamestown, Virginia, in 1619, and long before. Since that time, much of the preoccupation has been with securing political freedom and dignity within the confines of Lockean and Rawlsian contractarianism. Scholars such as Charles Mills have gone to great lengths to show the inadequacies of contemporary political theory because the problem of abstraction prevents any reckoning with the myriad injustices inflicted on Black people in the modern West.[26] This is not to say that such efforts within the liberal paradigm are not useful. Indeed they are. But they are not exhaustive and fall far short of the deep moral need to see Black men as human beings, independent of whatever legal protections are secured in the social contract.

Such a deep moral need is met in what Levinas referred to as the "interhuman order." In his essay, "Useless Suffering," Levinas interrogates theodicy, which he argues renders human suffering "useful" as part of a dialectical relation between "evil" and "good" that is itself evil insofar as it justifies the suffering of the Other. It is this criticism of theodicy that resonates with the task of this chapter, which is to point to the proliferation of theory as the source of the invisibility and justification of Black male suffering. For Levinas, at the end of theodicy, there is an "interhuman" order, which

> lies in a non-indifference of one to another, in a responsibility of one for another, but before the reciprocity of this responsibility, which will be inscribed in impersonal laws, comes to be superimposed on the pure altruism of this responsibility inscribed in the ethical position of the *I qua I*. It is prior to any contract that would specify precisely the moment of reciprocity—a point at which altruism and disinterestedness may, to be sure, continue, but at which they may also diminish or die out. The order of politics (post-ethical or pre-ethical) that inaugurates the "social contract" is neither the sufficient condition nor the necessary outcome of ethics. In its ethical position, the *I* is distinct both from the citizen born of the City, and from the individual who precedes all order in his natural egotism, but from whom political philosophy, since Hobbes, has tried to derive—or succeeded in deriving—the social or political order of the City.[27]

Levinas articulates a moral order of the I and the Other that he argues is superior to the symmetry and reciprocity of social contract theory. This is a responsibility that is not derived from a rational, autonomous, self, who legislates universal moral principles. No. This is a self who is always already encumbered and burdened by the demands of the Other: the Other who bellows not to be harmed. Prior to any theory—and, considering this essay, after theory—moral responsibility commands our regard for the Other. Our first task is not to theorize Black men, but rather to recognize that they ought not to be harmed; to recognize that our first move toward Black men must be an ethical move of care and genuine concern rather than a move of epistemic and metaphysical domination. It is thus not until the theory of the sort used to "explain" Black men and justify a certain mistreatment of them is no more that we can have a properly moral view of Black men. In the end, then, it is only through the death of theory, the death of Aristotle's divinized activity that thinks about thinking, that Black men will be morally visible. If theory is equated with divinity, then, in the end, this chapter concludes with a Nietzschean call for the death of a certain "god." For it is the death of this theoretical idol that makes way for the moral sensibilities of what Levinas called the "interhuman order." And it is in the interhuman order that Black men can be given life.

NOTES

1. Immanuel Kant, *Critique of Pure Reason*, trans. Norman Kemp Smith (Boston, MA: Bedford/St. Martin's Press, 1929), A51/B75.
2. Ibid., Bxxx.
3. See Johan Ludvig Heiberg, "A Remark on Logic in Reference to the Right Reverend Bishop Mynster's Treatise on Rationalism and Supernaturalism," and Hans Lassen Martensen, "Rationalism, Supernaturalism, and the *principium exclusi medii*," in *Mynster's "Rationalism, Supernatrualism," and the Debate about Mediation*, ed. and trans. by Jon Stewart (Copenhagen, Denmark: Museum Tusculanum Press, 2009), 111–144.
4. Søren Kierkegaard, *The Point of View*, ed. and trans. by Howard V. and Edna H. Hong (Princeton, NJ: Princeton University Press, 1998), 59.
5. Emmanuel Levinas, "Useless Suffering," *Entre Nous: Thinking-of-the-Other*, trans. by Michael B. Smith and Barbara Harshav (New York, NY: Columbia University Press, 1998), 98–99.
6. Levinas, *Otherwise than Being, or Beyond Essence*, trans. Alphonso Lingis (Pittsburgh, PA: Duquesne University Press), 37–38, 42–43.
7. Jacques Derrida, "Force of Law: The Mystical Foundation of Authority" trans. Mary Quaintance, *Acts of Religion*, ed. Gil Anidjar (New York, NY: Routledge, 2002), 233.
8. See Tommy J. Curry, "De-Colonizing the Intersection: Black Male Studies as a Critique of Intersectionality's Indebtedness to Subculture of Violence Theory," *Critical Psychology Praxis: Psychosocial Non-Alignment to Modernity/Coloniality*, ed. Robert Beshara (New York, NY: Routledge, 2021).
9. According to a *Washington Post* database, police killed 1,195 Black people between January 1, 2015, and December 2019. Of those Black people killed, 1,148 or roughly 96 percent were Black men. See John Muyskens and Joe Fox, "Fatal Force," *Washington Post*.
10. Havi Carel, "Invisible Suffering: The Experience of Breathlessness," *Atmospheres of Breathing: The Respiratory Questions of Philosophy*, eds. Lenart Škof and Petri Berndtson (Albany, NY: State University of New York Press, 2018), 233–245.
11. Ibid., 233.

12. Ibid., 234.
13. Ibid.
14. Ibid.
15. Ibid., 234–235.
16. Ibid., 236.
17. Ibid.
18. Ibid., 237.
19. Aristotle, "Metaphysics," 1074b, 32–34, in *The Complete Works of Aristotle*, ed. Jonathan Barnes, trans. W. D. Ross (Princeton, NJ: Princeton University Press, 1984), 1698.1074b, 32–34.
20. I have written of this problem elsewhere. See "From *Logos* to *Sarx*: Black Philosophy and the Philosophy of Religion" *The Black Scholar*, 43.4 (2013): 94–100 and "From Epistemology to Ethics: Theoretical and Practical Reason in Kant and Douglass" *Journal of Religious Ethics*, 40.4 (2012): 603–628.
21. *Holy Bible*, Job 4:7, King James Version (Nashville, TN: Holman Bible Publishers, 1998).
22. Ibid., John 9:1–3.
23. For a detailed exposition of the racist theories used to describe Black men, see Curry, "De-colonizing the Intersection."
24. See especially Curry's discussion of the Duluth Model in *The Man-Not: Race, Class, Genre, and the Dilemmas of Black Manhood* (Philadelphia, PA: Temple University Press, 2017), 117–120.
25. See McLaughlin, Kelly. "A Detroit Family Says Their Relative Died from COVID-19 after Being Turned Away from 3 ERs." Insider. Insider, April 22, 2020. https://www.insider.com/detroit-family-says-relative-died-covid-19-ers-denied-him-2020-4. Accessed October 22, 2020.
26. See Charles Mills, *The Racial Contract* (Ithaca, NY: Cornell University Press, 1997), and "Rawls on Race/Race in Rawls," *Southern Journal of Philosophy*, 47.51 (2009): 161–184.
27. Levinas, "Useless Suffering," 101.

BIBLIOGRAPHY

Aristotle. "Metaphysics," in *The Complete Works of Aristotle*, ed. Jonathan Barnes, trans. W. D. Ross (Princeton, NJ: Princeton University Press, 1984).

Carel, Havi. "Invisible Suffering: The Experience of Breathlessness," *Atmospheres of Breathing: The Respiratory Questions of Philosophy*, eds. Lenart Škof and Petri Berndtson (Albany, NY: State University of New York Press, 2018), 233–245.

Curry, Tommy J. "De-Colonizing the Intersection: Black Male Studies as a Critique of Intersectionality's Indebtedness to Subculture of Violence Theory," *Critical Psychology Praxis: Psychosocial Non-Alignment to Modernity/Coloniality*, ed. Robert Beshara (New York, NY: Routledge, 2021).

Curry, Tommy J. *The Man-Not: Race, Class, Genre, and the Dilemmas of Black Manhood* (Philadelphia: Temple University Press, 2017).

Derrida, Jacques. "Force of Law: The Mystical Foundation of Authority" trans. Mary Quaintance, *Acts of Religion*, ed. Gil Anidjar (New York, NY: Routledge, 2002).

Golden, Tim. "From *Logos* to *Sarx*: Black Philosophy and the Philosophy of Religion" *The Black Scholar*, *43*(4), (2013): 94–100.

Golden, Tim. "From Epistemology to Ethics: Theoretical and Practical Reason in Kant and Douglass" *Journal of Religious Ethics*, *40*(4), (2012): 603–628.

Heiberg, Johan Ludvig. "A Remark on Logic in Reference to the Right Reverend Bishop Mynster's Treatise on Rationalism and Supernaturalism," in *Mynster's "Rationalism, Supernatrualism," and the Debate about Mediation*, ed. and trans. by Jon Stewart (Copenhagen, Denmark: Museum Tusculanum Press, 2009).

Holy Bible, King James Version (Nashville, TN: Holman Bible Publishers, 1998).

Kant, Immanuel. *Critique of Pure Reason*, trans. Norman Kemp Smith (Boston, MA: Bedford/St. Martin's Press, 1929), A51/B75.

Kierkegaard, Søren. *The Point of View*, ed. and trans. by Howard V. and Edna H. Hong (Princeton, NJ: Princeton University Press, 1998).

Levinas, Emmanuel. "Useless Suffering," *Entre Nous: Thinking-of-the-Other*, trans. by Michael B. Smith and Barbara Harshav (New York, NY: Columbia University Press, 1998).

Martensen, Hans Lassen. "Rationalism, Supernaturalism, and the *principium exclusi medii*," in *Mynster's "Rationalism, Supernatrualism," and the Debate about Mediation*, ed. and trans. by Jon Stewart (Copenhagen, Denmark: Museum Tusculanum Press, 2009).

McLaughlin, Kelly. "A Detroit Family Says Their Relative Died from COVID-19 after Being Turned Away from 3 ERs." Insider. Insider, April 22, 2020. https://www.insider.com/detroit-family-says-relative-died-covid-19-ers-denied-him-2020-4.

Mills, Charles. *The Racial Contract* (Ithaca, NY: Cornell University Press, 1997).

Mills, Charles. "Rawls on Race/Race in Rawls." *The Southern Journal of Philosophy* 47(Supplement), (2009): 161–184.

Muyskens, John and Joe Fox. "Fatal Force," *The Washington Post*, October 1, 2020, https://www.washingtonpost.com/graphics/investigations/police-shootings-database/.

Chapter 8

What's Happening Brother?

Josiah Ulysses Young III

George Floyd's murder in Minneapolis, Minnesota, in 2020 awakened the *world* to how dangerous it has been to be a black male in the United States. The white policeman sadistically jammed his knee into Floyd's neck for over 8 minutes. George called out *"I can't breathe!"*—called on his deceased mother to help him—but the policeman would not relent, and his fellow officers did not make him stop. Outraged people took to the streets all over the world to protest the injustice despite COVID-19's virulence. Many blacks no doubt thought to themselves, *now* everybody *finally* sees *that black males have suffered from the evil attempts to emasculate, criminalize, and incarcerate us, have lost our lives, and have been overcoming these atrocities (while fighting disproportionate unemployment and health disparities) for centuries.*

White supremacy, however, is no respecter of gender, a point Georgetown professor Paul Butler makes cogently in his paper, "Black Male Exceptionalism? The Problems and Potential of Black Male-Focused Interventions."[1] Police shot Breonna Taylor five times in her home, March 13, 2020. *Innocent* of any wrongdoing, she lingered for a while and died before medical help arrived. So, though this chapter reflects my experiences and those of other black males, our pain is but one door to the pain African Americans have endured because of what philosopher Achille Mbembe calls "necropolitics."

NECROPOLITICS

Anchored in "pro-slavery democracy", "necropolitics" surfaces two coexistent orders—"a *community of fellow creatures* governed, at least in principle, by the law of equality, and a *category of nonfellows*, or even of those without part, that is also established by law."[2] In the North American context, *those without part*—those who had "no right to rights"—were enslaved Africans and their progeny governed "by the law of inequality . . . founded on the prejudice of race."[3] And since leopards cannot change their spots, this *law of inequality* has undermined black lives from the time our ancestors fled the plantations at the Civil War's end.

Mbembe argues that "pro-slavery" democracies are historically inseparable from colonialism. I take him to mean that the nations that profited from slavery—principally England and France—profited as well from the Partition of Africa (1885). Playing a major role in undermining the Congo's (now the Democratic Republic of Congo's) fragile independence from Belgium, the United States came relatively late to the colonial manipulation of Africa but made quite a contribution to neocolonialism, especially during the cold war among the United States, the Soviet Union, and China.[4] Mbembe thus points out that colonialism and enslavement "represent democracy's bitter sediment" that "corrupts the body of freedom, driving it ineluctably toward decomposition."[5]

Kwame Ture and Charles Hamilton argue in their book, *Black Power: The Politics of Liberation*, that U.S. black ghettos have functioned as a colony within the United States,[6] an argument echoed recently by journalist Chris Hayes.[7] That makes perfect sense to me, especially since both modes of domination have, as Mbembe puts it,

> always consisted in spatializing and discharging . . . terror by confining its most extreme manifestations in some racially stigmatized third place—the plantation under slavery, the colony, the compound under apartheid, the ghetto, or, as in the present-day United States, the prison.[8]

"Necropolitical power proceeds . . . as if life [were] merely death's medium." Racism, Mbembe argues, drives "the necropolitical principle"[9]—"stands for organized destruction."[10] It thus seems very true to hold that necropolitics in the United States means that its sovereignty "largely resides in the power and capacity to dictate who is able to live and who must die." Forget about live and let live. The too-early deaths of people like George Floyd and Breonna Taylor disclose what is closer to reality: "To kill or to let live" is what necropolitics is all about, and since black lives have scarcely mattered in the United States, the decision to kill us has been par for the course. I am a witness.

BUSHWICK

I grew up in the 1960s on Putnam Avenue between Bushwick and Evergreen Avenues in a section of Brooklyn, New York City, called Bushwick. The neighborhood was "integrated" when my family moved there. Most of our white neighbors moved away soon after my family moved in. The change was so rapid that one might say that Bushwick changed "overnight," and unfortunately it was for the worse. I have come to understand that when middle-class blacks like my family began to move in homes and "pre-war apartment buildings" around 1960, city planners' attitude toward Bushwick changed. They—the guardians of pro-white democracy—did not see hardworking people moving up the social ladder. Instead, they saw the start of a slum, and soon helped turn "Bushwick into a slum worthy of the name."[11] Real estate brokers accelerated white flight, scaring white homeowners into selling their property dirt cheap beginning around 1960. Their tactics included placing ominous messages in whites' mailboxes: "Don't wait until it's too late!"[12] The brokers, or speculators, having bought the empty stock cheaply, sold the properties to "minorities" at greatly inflated prices. Many working-class blacks and Latinxs qualified for Federal Housing Administration (FHA) loans due to "corrupt FHA credit inspectors" who qualified them though they could neither keep up the payments nor the property. When they foreclosed, the FHA paid off the mortgage. The scammers then boarded up the homes and moved on "to the next property."[13] Tenant landlords who wished to cut their losses allowed homes to rot. The die was cast, and the community declined—rapidly.

Bushwick brought out the worst in black males around my age and even younger during this time. Hard drugs—principally heroin—caused many deaths. Many young men were unemployed or moving in and out of the prisons. Sociopolitical factors worked to their detriment. As the authors of *A Plague on Your Houses* point out, communities that are broken or "targeted for destruction" are hornets' nests of discontent and heartbreak. The man-child reacts to this pain in a particularly unconstructive way. He acts out—expresses "in exaggerated ways the hidden feelings of family, friends, and self"—and bonding with others like him, roams the neighborhood with bad intentions. This "kind of behavioral code . . . zips through the core groups" and is "both destructive and self-destructive."[14] But where could the males perishing in Bushwick go? Ghettos like Bushwick have been like internment camps that have kept poor people of color walled in and away from the communities in which whites have enjoyed the best New York City can offer.

BURNING BUSHWICK

The Bushwick community showed its discontent the night Martin Luther King Jr. was assassinated in 1968. Police and fire department sirens signaled that Broadway, where the shops of the community were centered, was burning. People ran frantically toward or away from Broadway, some of them with weapons in their hands. In the aftermath of the riot, storeowners invested in metal shields for their plate glass windows. I found myself on Broadway near Gates Avenue shortly after the riot. I saw a white man dressed all in black pulling down his metal panel to protect his shop. He had a high-powered rifle strapped across his back, and his free hand held the leashes of two large Doberman Pinschers. It seemed that we were at war: the proprietors against the people. After 1968, fires of various kinds became the norm in Bushwick. The scores of buildings that unscrupulous landlords abandoned and sometimes set afire invited other acts of arson. As far as the firebugs were concerned, these houses were easy pickings. Wooden and constructed "with airshafts over the stairwells," "they burned like furnaces."[15] And since these homes shared cocklofts—"the attic space between the roof and the ceiling"—the infernos advanced from building to building.[16]

Mayor John Lindsay's administration and the New York City-Rand Institute implemented a policy called "planned shrinkage" shortly after the King riots. "Planned shrinkage" curtailed fire services to Bushwick, Harlem, and the South Bronx beginning around 1969.[17] Scholars point out that the policy was systemically linked to the ideology of "benign neglect" championed by Nixon adviser Daniel P. Moynihan, who writes:

> The incidence of anti-social behavior among young black males continues to be extraordinarily high. Apart from white racial attitudes, this is the biggest problem black Americans face, and in part it helps shape white racial attitudes. Black Americans injure one another. Because blacks live in de facto segregated neighborhoods, and go to de facto segregated neighborhoods, the socially stable elements of the black population cannot escape the socially pathological ones. Routinely their children get caught up in the anti-social patterns of the others.[18]

Arson, Moynihan reports, evinces the problem: *"Fires,"* he writes, *"are in fact a 'leading indicator' of social pathology for a neighborhood.* They come first. Crime, and the rest, follows." For Moynihan, arsonists exemplify "the types of personalities which slums produce . . . The urban riots of 1965–1968 could be thought of as epidemic conditions of an endemic situation."[19]

According to Moynihan, "The time may have come when the issue of race could benefit from a period of 'benign neglect.'" Black people, he writes, have "been too much talked about. The forum has been too much taken over to hysterics, paranoids, and boodlers on all sides. We may need a period in which Negro progress continues and racial rhetoric fades."[20] Moynihan advises Nixon to tackle this problem by focusing on the plight of "Indians, Mexican Americans and Puerto Ricans." He thought it would be wise "to ignore provocations from groups such as the Black Panthers." (Here

Moynihan alludes to the 1969 murder of Fred Hampton, who is a cultural hero for the African American left.)[21] Planned shrinkage was thus part of a strategy designed to let ghettos like Bushwick wither away in obscurity through a cleanup policy that "actively [looked] for sick neighborhoods and [pulled] services from them to free the resources for healthy neighborhoods."[22]

Reportedly, *four thousand* fires raged in Bushwick from 1975 to 1977.[23] The New York City Blackout occurred in 1977. I was living and working in Manhattan by that time and recall that the entire city lost power. Setting fires and looting, legions of Bushwick's enraged folk converged on Broadway and nearly destroyed it. A local woman called the Police Department in a panic: "They're coming across Broadway like a herd of buffalo."[24] *Thousands* of people were waiting for them on Broadway, "thousands more," Jonathan Mahler writes, "were pouring in from every direction. 'If they had turned on the lights,' one cop remembers, 'it would have looked like the Macy's Thanksgiving Day Parade.'"[25] By that time, by 1977, several of the guys I grew up with on Putnam Avenue had perished from heroin and the deadly criminality that attracted them like moths to a flame. Bushwick was a death camp for those brothers. Something Mbembe writes about colonialism heuristically comes to mind. The racism at work in New York City manufactured "a panoply of suffering" to which privileged whites were by and large immune. What is more—and I saw this with my own eyes—policies such as planned shrinkage and racist ideologies such as "benign neglect," as a species of "colonial violence," maimed the minds and souls of black males in directing them, however subliminally, to "unproductive investments." The powers that be meant to "block [our] desire to live . . . aimed to affect and diminish [our] capacities to consider [ourselves] moral agents."[26] I believe this is why many brothers who perished did not realize what was happening. They were destroyed.

GONE WITH THE ASHES

How did I manage to survive Bushwick—get out alive when others perished? I think of one brother (Marvin)[27] who lived in the middle of the block. He was older than me; he used to babysit for my parents. He was a tall, very dark-skinned brother—handsome like "Shaft" (Richard Roundtree). I saw him change as Bushwick made its way to the ashes. He became super hip, dressed expensively, and seemed suddenly unapproachable. The word was that he was dealing. He was an "entrepreneur." He had income. One summer, about 1964, I think, I heard him say something like this in front of his mother's home where a small crowd had gathered. "Tell him *I* said, 'If you don't like me, *fine*. You ain't got to like me; but if you don't *dig* me—if you don't dig *me—FUCK* YOU!!!'" Someone shot him to death several days later. I didn't go to the viewing at a funeral home on Evergreen Avenue. I heard he was a beautiful corpse. Another brother I knew was but fifteen-year-old when he overdosed around 1965. He lived across the street from me. He was good with his hands (he was a talented boxer). I heard that his weeping baby brother kept screaming his name loudly and desperately at the service and the graveyard, as if he were trying to wake the dead. During my freshman winter break from college (1971), I saw another brother from my block circling around the Gates Avenue bus stop near Bushwick Avenue. He soon swooped down on a young woman carrying bags of Christmas gifts. Slipping on the ice and snow, his nose runny from his jones rather than the cold, he grabbed what he could, nearly knocking down the astonished woman. When I returned to Bushwick that following summer, I learned from my peers that someone had stabbed him to death. I also heard his corpse had been thrown under his bed. Someone shot his brother to death soon thereafter; and another black male, who lived across the street from me, was shot in the head. The word was that he had been dealing, got hooked, and was murdered by those he owed money. I told his brother how sorry I was. Sorrow darkened his face as he nodded his round and uniquely shaped head up and down in some of the most pained grief I have witnessed. So, to repeat the question, how *did* I escape Bushwick's mean, funky streets?

I did not feel the need to prove myself or protect myself by joining a gang or making money by selling dope. Not even the most derisive putdowns I endured—*punk-ass, bitch-ass motherfucker!*—were incentives to risk my life or incarceration. My family was functional; my parents were college graduates. I was literate, in accelerated college-bound classes. I think, though, that the deciding factor in my survival and even success was that my father, a strong figure many of the brothers lacked, and a gifted psychoanalyst, helped me see what was going on in Bushwick even at a very early age. In one of the songs on Marvin Gaye's Motown blockbuster album from the early 1970s, *What's Going On*, a black man who just returned from Vietnam asks,

> What's going on across this land
> ... what's happening brother?[28]

Thanks to my father, I knew what was happening and *why*. From the very beginning of Bushwick's shift toward destruction, dad steered me onto a path of political and spiritual *consciousness*, which few of the guys seemed to experience. I was keenly aware of the civil rights and black power movements and knew what was going on. My father gave me a copy of *The Autobiography of Malcolm X* when it first came out and told me to read it. Minister Malcolm's prophetic narrative was as sacred scripture to me then (and is like holy writ to me now). I knew what was happening in Bushwick: we were waging a struggle for fair treatment in the land of our birth. In some ways, we were getting our asses kicked! Minister Malcolm and Dr. King had been assassinated and the Black Panther Party was fading fast. (In 1969, Chicago police, allegedly in conjunction with the FBI, pummeled Fred Hampton's body with gunshot as he lay in his bed. This brilliant brother, a star of the Black Panther Party, was only twenty-one.)[29] I was politically aware and wanted to learn more and understand more. The good thing is that political consciousness fortified the barrier between me and the negative consequences of life in Bushwick. I learned, however, that political consciousness by itself—though surely necessary—would not be enough. It alone did not save some of us. I knew several politically aware brothers whom Bushwick consumed.

Robbie lived a few blocks over on Jefferson between Bushwick and Evergreen. He was very politically aware, as were two other brothers, Joey who lived beyond Evergreen Avenue, and Donnie who lived near the Greene Avenue ruins. All three brothers were connected to our local United Methodist church. Robbie joined the Air force. During my last year of high school, he came home on leave. The word was that he was found, "drooling at the mouth and 'stank,' slumped in a chair" at one of his friend's home. He overdosed on heroin. The mortician overly powdered his dark face; even his lips and hair seemed ashen. He was in uniform, and someone placed his eyeglasses on his bloated face (perhaps in a desperate attempt to make him look like himself). His remains really shook me up. For weeks, I'd look in the mirror and see his face. I considered him a good friend and sort of looked up to him.

Joey was well-read, politically conscious, and an articulate brother who gave me a copy of Trotskyite George Breitman's book, *The Last Year of Malcolm X*, when it first came out (1970). He would ask me questions about the book to see if I really had read it. He attended Boy's High School where my mother taught English and was a guidance counselor. Joey joined the Nation of Islam, and he and I even visited a temple together in Bedford Stuyvesant. I last saw him on Broadway selling copies of *Muhammad Speaks!* sometime in 1971. I learned of his death when I returned to Bushwick in 1979 to work as a youth minister at my home church while studying at Union Theological Seminary in Manhattan. A dear sister-friend told me in church, "he nodded off in his bathtub—drowned: Ain't that some shit."

Politically astute and hopeful, Donnie was another bright brother. We would talk for hours when I returned to Bushwick. One night, we sat on the curb until after midnight as he told me about his earlier years of being strung out and how *he*—rather than Wall Street and the Great White Way across the Williamsburg Bridge—represented the real New York City. "Josiah, man: People be talking about the *City* and all that *bull*shit. But, Josiah, *man:*

I'm telling you, *brother*. I'm the *real* New York City—*that* ain't no bullshit. That's square, s*quare* business!" AIDS snuffed him out about ten years later. Had he started using again? Was the retrovirus incubating in him in the late 1970s? I don't know. I do know that too many young brothers my age numbed themselves from the racism and poverty that made Bushwick an incinerator for hundreds.

Bushwick got *worse* in the 1980s. According to Steve Malanga's essay, "The Death and Life of Bushwick," "45 percent" of all Bushwick residents were impoverished in the 1980s; "nearly 60 percent of all children were born out of wedlock," and more than "70 percent of female-headed Bushwick families were impoverished." The absence of fathers swelled the ranks of "gang membership and the local high school had one of the worst drop-out rates in the city."[30] Hard drugs were everywhere—especially crack cocaine: Bushwick was "one of New York's centers of drug dealing and abuse." Abandoned buildings—abandoned *blocks!*—became Crackville. According to Steve Malanga, "Bushwick's brand of the crack trade was among Gotham's most vicious." A Bushwick junkie put it this way:

> Out here you see your people livin' on the street. . . . There're like cavemen. . . . If they could eat each other, they would, if it comes down to that. That's how this neighborhood is getting—very thirsty.[31]

"By 1990," Malanga writes, "murders had nearly tripled in Bushwick, reaching a high of 77 that year, one of the worse rates in the city."[32]

Today, Bushwick is being touted as a crown jewel of urban renewal. Upwardly mobile whites for whom Greenwich Village is too expensive are buying up renovated properties in phoenix-like Bushwick. Crime is down so the streets are safer; and though Bushwick's largely Latinx population views the incoming whites apprehensively, certain urban planners speculate that re-gentrification will benefit the people who have managed to endure the infernos. I wonder, though: *Will Bushwick remain a place where black and Latinx Americans are of no concern to the majority of those in power?* Plus ça change, plus c'est la même chose? *Is Bushwick on its way to becoming what it was before the 1960s—a place for middle- and upper-class whites? Will people of color find a viable place in re-gentrified Bushwick when released from prisons like Riker's Island, Sing Sing, and Green Haven? Is there hope for them?* Only the resurrection of the dead in a beautiful city would right the wrongs done to those who died young, some of whom were my brothers: Robbie, Joey, and Donnie. One has no control over putative eschatological events; they are probably mythic; but one can agitate for public policy that is more humane and correct than "planned shrinkage" and the racist ideologies, such as "benign neglect," that prop up such a policy. My grandchildren's generation must not perish from man-made blight in American ghettos. More lyrics from *What's Going On* come to mind:

Save the babies . . .
If you wanna love, you got to save the babies[33]

Davell Garner Jr. was but twenty-two months and in his stroller when gun violence took his baby-boy life in the Bedford Stuyvesant section of Brooklyn, July 12, 2020. Gun violence, another plague in this country, appears to be as indifferent to black life as is COVID-19, which is playing grim reaper in black communities at an alarming rate. Our morbidity problems—the high incidence of diabetes, obesity, cancer, hypertension, which are consequences of centuries of "necropolitics"—have made us easy pickings for this new coronavirus. Service occupations that put food on the table make it difficult, if not impossible, to shelter-in at home where high density living makes social distancing a challenge. As of today, therefore, African Americans are dying from the COVID-19 pandemic at a higher rate than our white counterparts. *Plus ça change, plus c'est la même chose.* That's what's happening in the United States today, brothers and sisters, but the struggle continues (*a luta continua!*). Black lives matter for those of us who envision a truly humane way of living and are dead set against "necropolitics," by any means *necessary*. Amandla . . . ngawethu!

NOTES

1. Paul Butler, "Black Male Exceptionalism? The Problems and Potential of Black Male-Focused Interventions," *Du Bois Review* 10:2, 2013. https://scholarship.law.georgetown.edu/cgi/viewcontent.cgi?article=2323&context=facpub#:~:text=Since%20the%20Ebony%20special%20issue,politically%E2%80%9D%20(Deas%201987). Accessed July 27, 2020.
2. Achille Mbembe, *Necropolitics* (Durham: Duke University Press, 2019), 17.
3. Mbembe, 17.
4. See Ludo De Witte, *The Assassination of Lumumba* (New York: Verso, 2001); and Emmanuel Gerard and Bruce Kuklick, *Death in the Congo. Murdering Patrice Lumumba* (Cambridge: Harvard University Press, 2015).
5. Mbembe, 20.
6. Kwame Ture and Charles Hamilton, *Black Power: The Politics of Liberation* (New York: Vintage Books/Random House, 1992), 2–32.
7. Chris Hayes, *A Colony in a Nation* (New York: W.W. Norton and Company, 2017).
8. Mbembe, 34.
9. Mbembe, 38.

10. Mbembe, 38.
11. Deborah Wallace and Roderick Wallace, *A Plague on Your Houses. How New York was Burned Down and National Public Health Crumbled* (New York: Verso, 1998), 26.
12. Steve Malanga, "The Death and Life of Bushwick," *City Journal*, Spring 2008. http://www.city-journal.org/2008/18_2_bushwick.html. Accessed July 24, 2020.
13. Jonathan Mahler, *Ladies and Gentlemen, The Bronx Is Burning. 1977, Baseball, Politics, and the Battle for the Soul of a City* (New York: Picador/Farrar, Straus and Giroux, 2005), 212–213.
14. Wallace and Wallace, 144.
15. Mahler, 211.
16. Mahler, 211.
17. Wallace and Wallace, 38–39.
18. Daniel Patrick Moynihan, "Memorandum for the President," 4. https://www.nixonlibrary.gov/sites/default/files/virtuallibrary/documents/jul10/53.pdf. Accessed July 27, 2020
19. Moynihan, 5.
20. Moynihan, 7.
21. Moynihan, 7
22. Wallace and Wallace, 26.
23. Mahler, 211.
24. Mahler, 181.
25. Mahler, 191.
26. Mbembe, 5.
27. I use pseudonyms for those who perished out of respect for the dead and their families.
28. Gaye, *What's Going On*, Motown Records, 1971.
29. See Jeffrey Haas, *The Assassination of Fred Hampton: How the FBI and the Chicago Police Murdered a Black Panther* (Chicago Lawrence Hill Books, 2010).
30. Malanga, "The Death and Life of Bushwick."
31. Malanga, "The Death and Life of Bushwick."
32. Malanga, "The Death and Life of Bushwick."
33. Gaye, *What's Going On*, Motown Records, 1971.

BIBLIOGRAPHY

Butler, Paul. "Black Male Exceptionalism? The Problems and Potential of Black Male-Focused Interventions," *Du Bois Review* 10:2, 2013. https://scholarship.law.georgetown.edu/cgi/viewcontent.cgi?article=2323&context=facpub#:~:text=Since%20the%20Ebony%20special%20issue,politically%E2%80%9D%20(Deas%201987). Accessed July 27, 2020.

Gaye, Marvin. *What's Going On*, Motown Records, 1971.

Gerard, Emmanuel and Bruce Kuklick, *Death in the Congo. Murdering Patrice Lumumba* (Cambridge: Harvard University Press, 2015).

Haas, Jeffrey. *The Assassination of Fred Hampton: How the FBI and the Chicago Police Murdered a Black Panther* (Chicago Lawrence Hill Books, 2010).

Hayes, Chris. *A Colony in a Nation* (New York: W.W. Norton and Company, 2017).

Mahler, Jonathan. *Ladies and Gentlemen, The Bronx Is Burning. 1977, Baseball, Politics, and the Battle for the Soul of a City* (New York: Picator/Farrar, Straus and Giroux, 2005).

Malanga, Steve. "The Death and Life of Bushwick," *City Journal*, Spring 2008. http://www.city-journal.org/2008/18_2_bushwick.html. Accessed July 24, 2020.

Mbembe, Achille. *Necropolitics* (Durham: Duke University Press, 2019).

Moynihan, Daniel Patrick. "Memorandum for the President," 4. https://www.nixonlibrary.gov/sites/default/files/virtuallibrary/documents/jul10/53.pdf. Accessed July 27, 2020.

Ture, Kwame and Charles Hamilton. *Black Power: The Politics of Liberation* (New York: Vintage Books/Random House, 1992).

Wallace, Deborah and Roderick Wallace. *A Plague on Your Houses. How New York was Burned Down and National Public Health Crumbled* (New York: Verso, 1998).

Witte, Ludo De. *The Assassination of Lumumba* (New York: Verso, 2001).

Chapter 9

To be Overdetermined from Without

Negotiating White Supremacy from Corporeal Blackness

Linden F. Lewis

The world stands at a critical conjuncture, in which a public health crisis, COVID-19, coincides with a renewed and reawakening consciousness of racism. Both of these historical moments have exercised much of our contemporary waking moments. Part of this coincidence of crisis is the symbiosis of occurrence. Indeed, the public health crisis has unmasked health disparities in the United States and around the world and social inequity among different racial groups. This is no mere inflection point; the convergence of crises did not happen by chance. In fact, these problems of race and health disparities are a *fundamental* part of American capitalism. It is how the system works, but is, on the contrary, accorded the misnomer of "exceptionalism."

The most dramatic zeitgeist was, of course, the death of George Floyd, which exponentially energized the Black Lives Matter movement. The manner of Floyd's killing, the spectral quality of the end of his life, generated a global moral outrage. Perhaps, the entering of the macabre into our living rooms through our television sets or on social media jolted our complacency. However, disregard and dehumanization of black life historically had long been rehearsed on the sugar plantations of the Caribbean and South America, and on the cotton and sugar plantations in the United States. This dehumanization was central to the process of lynching in the United States, where the event and location were advertised, and white people scrambled for mementos after the event, and where the event was memorialized on postcards. This history alone should silence many Americans of the contemporary racial "innocence," which now pours forth from many people, and from some of the least expected places. In all this, there are of course hopeful signs. More people have raised their voices in opposition to racism, bigotry, and economic marginalization. Social movements have been energized and resistant voices amplified. We can only hope that such changes are sustainable and that we are not doomed to repeat a familiar history.

Perhaps the most appropriate place to begin a reflection on the corporeality of blackness is by addressing two related issues immediately. First, this point should be intuitive, but failure to acknowledge it is to behave as though men who experience racial anguish do so without regard for the suffering of women. In recent times, the Kimberlé Crenshaw *#SayHerName* initiative has forced us to come to terms with all victims of systematic violence, not just the violence meted out on black male bodies. Racial animus harbors no distinction between men and women. However, capitalism in conjunction with the practice of white supremacy will seize on differences between genders for its own strategic purposes. We, as black men, face a daunting system of structural racism and inequality, but we should not be distracted by the modalities of its expression into thinking that our suffering is more morally righteous or socially debilitating than the suffering of Black women. In short, our experience of racial injury embodies no more moral value than the racial injustice meted out to Black women.

Second, do the experiences that many of us in this book seek to analyze in "masculine" terms simply come from the color of our skins, or are they the product of a particular history fashioned in the crucible of society? If we could modify the question raised by Cornelius Castoriadis[1] several years ago, we might ask: Can there be human experience without history? Do these experiences that we share as men take place in a vacuum? "Should we then say that history, in the proper sense, is the product of societies?"[2] Castoriadis went on to argue: "History does not happen to society: history is the self-deployment of society."[3] If therefore Castoriadis's position is an appropriate point of departure, the idea of being overdetermined from without is not merely a reading off of our worth from the color of our skins, but rather a more complex reading of our experiences based on a long and tortured history of institutional fashioning of our being, of the devaluing of our labor, the circumscribing of our citizenship, and the blocking of available opportunities. The racial anguish, anxiety, and alienation that we experience is not simply the product of our color, as alluded to earlier, it is rooted in the material base of society and the way it is organized. Our task therefore is not only to describe our experiences but also to be cognizant of social and economic relations that undergird such experiences. Understanding these relations helps us to appreciate Walter Rodney's observation about poverty when he argues:

> There is nothing with which poverty coincides so absolutely as with the color black—small or larger population, hot or cold climates, rich or poor in natural resources—poverty cuts across all of these factors in order to find black people.[4]

Lest there be any misunderstanding about this relationship between skin color and poverty, Rodney adds the following:

> That association of wealth with whites and poverty with blacks is not accidental. It is the nature of the imperialist relationship that enriches the metropolis at the expense of the colony, i.e., it makes the whites richer and the blacks poorer.[5]

It is also in this context that we must locate the famous reflection of Frantz Fanon about his feeling of objectification:

> I came into the world imbued with the will to find a meaning in things, my spirit filled with the desire to attain to the source of the world, and then I found that I was an object in the midst of other objects.[6]

This observation represents the crushing alienation that we experience on a daily basis, but it does not descend on us out of thin air, it is rooted in the way society has socialized others to view and treat us, and for us to view ourselves. The task then for us is not simply to understand these relationships, but ultimately to change them. The question then is how do we, as black men, seek to transcend this iron cage of race and racial relations in our everyday lives?

At the personal and individual levels, some of us have employed a number of survival strategies for dealing with the dominance of white supremacy. Indeed, many of us fall in line with what W. E. B. Du Bois called the legacy of our spiritual striving,[7] that is, we place all confidence in the transforming power of education. The belief is that once we acquire more education, we would become more respected, more acceptable. Of course, this did not happen in Du Bois's day, and it has not changed a great deal today—case in point, we had one of the most brilliant presidents in recent history, but the level of disrespect and contempt for him was astounding, and this was the case because in the end, he was a black man. Sadly, education on its own does not make that much of a difference, it is not a panacea. I am reminded of the great John Henrik Clarke who during a television interview once noted that there is nothing more dangerous than an educated bigot.

Others have settled for thinking that proper deportment, affability or even fame, would save us from being a stimulus to anxiety—Fanon's negrophobogenesis.[8] Ultimately, these strategies all have their limitations, even if at times they serve as a mitigating factor temporarily. As black professors, we live with the evaluation from students that we are intimidating. I used to think that this was a singular definition affixed to me because of my height and size, but in conversation with other men, and some black women, I have learned that this description is widely used to apply to black professors generally. I have on occasion used humor as a pedagogical tool to allay fears about my presence in this supposedly democratic space of the classroom. At best, such measures result in a modified comment: "Professor Lewis is intellectually intimidating," or sometimes the comment is more ambiguous: "The professor is funny, but sometimes he is intimidating." Perhaps at some deeper level, however, these comments mask a deeper concern, namely, that of reconciling decades of socialization that characterize the black man or woman as ignorant and incapable of producing knowledge. Yet, in our classrooms, white students come face to face with a black man or woman, in an academic context, obviously confounding such stereotypes embodied in the personage of a learned and articulate, black professor. For some then, the classroom becomes a site where negotiating difference represents a steep learning curve. The question must now be raised, does this moment of racial reckoning provide more room to explore such anxieties or does it dry up like a raisin in the sun?

How do black men attempt to mitigate the fear and intimidation that others experience in our presence? At times we resort to self-censorship. We chose other courses of action that are less likely to elicit fear in others: not walking into a restaurant, store, or bank, as a group of black men, or making sure that in a car full of black men, we follow all traffic laws. For others, another option is self-deprecation, but this mode is plagued by the possibility of descending into a debilitating obsequiousness that few black people would want to recreate in the twenty-first century. These daily concerns faced by black men and women provide us with some insights as to the extent of the burdens and constraints imposed on black people by the pervasiveness of structural racism. We are, as Fanon reminded us, not simply judged for our individual actions but for our bodies, race, and our ancestors, simultaneously.

EMBODYING CRIMINALITY

Any black man or boy learns very early on that not only is he marked racially, but that he also embodies a particular notion of criminality by many whites, and also by some blacks who, wittingly or unwittingly, participate in their own oppression in concert with white supremacy. It is a peculiar experience to be overdetermined from without, to be cognizant that people become convinced that they "know you," your intentions, your personality, or your capabilities just by looking at you, or, more specifically, by a determination based upon your somatic features. It is this "certitude" of others that imposes self-constraints on black men in certain situations.

When I served as the chair of my department, on many occasions during the days that we hosted prospective students, several white parents, with their children, would simply move pass me to ask one of my junior colleagues questions about the department's offerings and programs. My colleagues would have to inform the parents that I, whom they had totally discounted, was the chair of the department and they should raise certain questions with me. Others would come to the table, if I were alone at the time, observe the materials laid out, but not ask any questions, even when invited to do so by me. In other words, racism does not always operate as an overt frontal altercation. Many times, it operates through the modality of the daily visitation of sleights.

At the university where I have taught for many years, I was involved in a case of racial profiling, which I found very revealing. I became interested in a particular model car. I anticipated buying the car. Upon leaving my office one day, I saw the same model car that I had anticipated buying. I moved in the direction of the car to get a closer look. As I approached the car, I noticed that the windows were halfway down. Being sensitive to the idea of embodying criminality as a black man, I stepped away from the car, thinking that seeing me approach this open car, someone might think that I was about to hotwire it and execute a carjacking, a scenario which only a black man in a predominantly white space could possibly conjure. I was reminded of Fanon's meditation: "I move slowly in the world, accustomed now to seek no longer for upheaval."[9] I recalled thinking to myself that I should not have to act so defensively given my innocent interest in this car, but I was aware of how others might have read the situation, and in effect imposed constraints on my own behavior and my interest in the vehicle by moving away to avoid the appearance of criminality.

A day or so later, as I am leaving my office once again, I see the same vehicle, parked in the same spot, but this time with the windows closed. I moved toward the car, thinking that all was well. As I moved near the vehicle, I noticed a member of the public safety staff in his car. He waved at me, and I returned his wave. He turned in the opposite direction from where I was standing just beside the car I was observing. However, now, he drove more slowly. I assumed that he thought the car I was close to was mine, but on seeing that I did not open the door and enter the vehicle, it seemed to have given him some cause for pause. The friendly gesture offered initially seemed to dissipate into concern. He proceeded in his public safety vehicle to another parking lot from where he could view my actions clearly. As this point, I became very uncomfortable with the evolving situation, and moved away from the car I was observing to my own vehicle. As I drove out of the parking lot, in the direction of the public safety vehicle, I noticed that it was at that point that the public safety driver decided to move from his stationary position. In other words, when he was satisfied that I had no apparent criminal intent he felt that it was safe for him to move on. I was disturbed by these actions, especially as a long-standing member of that community, so I complained about it publicly.

There was an outpouring of concern from many of my colleagues. Indeed, some were incensed by what I had experienced and offered commiserations. However, one administrator asked another colleague if he thought that what I had described had actually happened, or presumably, that it was just my imagination running away with me. Though slightly annoyed at hearing about this query, it did not strike me as particularly significant at the time. Among the issues that subsequently began to irritate me were the Director of Public Safety, who sought to assure me that there was no policy of racial profiling at that university. Now that bit of information astounded me, for surely there would be no need to develop such a policy and it would never be shared outside of public safety circles. Indeed, such a policy is so ingrained in policing circles that it would be unnecessary to develop a training model. Then came a series of disavowals from my colleagues. One white colleague said that she had a "similar" incident in which a public safety official she had summoned to open up her office, because she had temporarily misplaced her key, began to interrogate her about the whereabouts of the key. His fear seemed to have been that the key could end up in someone else's hands and be used illegitimately. Moreover, he apparently was questioning her with his hand on his gun. Another white colleague said that he had read my complaint with sympathy, but then explained how on one Saturday afternoon, he came up to the building in which he teaches, and where his office was located. His wife and child had accompanied him. As soon as he got out of his car, he explained that a public safety vehicle began circling the building he had gone into and hung around until he came back out and left with his family.

In both of these situations, my colleagues, as well as the public safety official, were attempting to tell me, not so subtly, that my interpretation of what I had experienced as *racial* profiling might have been a misinterpretation based on my "sensitivity" to the issue of racial discrimination. By implication they were making a case for alert public safety policing, not some type of action that was directed toward me because of my race. George Yancy describes this type of disavowal as "epistemic denial."[10] I have little doubt that my colleagues did not intend to indicate that I had fabricated a story. My sense is that it was their attempt to say that what I believe had happened to me was not unique to me, but generally happens to *everybody* (regardless of race) because of overzealous policing. This brings me back to my earlier point about history. As a black man, I was acutely aware of the history of such profiling people who looked like me on campus. Many of my African American and Latino students had on several occasions told me of similar run-ins with public safety and the issue of racial profiling. They in turn had reported such incidents to administrators; this was not a one-off affair. My colleagues did not share this long history of profiling and discrimination.

Even if they were actually scrutinized by public safety officials, it was not because they were white. I, on the other hand, was keenly observed precisely because I was black. It did not matter how I was dressed, it did not matter that I was a fairly well-known professor at the institution. I was presumed to be doing something suspicious. "The evidence was there, unalterable. My blackness was there, dark and unarguable. And it tormented me, pursued me, disturbed me, angered me."[11]

EVEN THE DOG IS BETTER RECOGNIZED

At my current institution, I once went to the financial office to ascertain some information. I was familiar with the woman who fielded my questions. She was a heavy smoker, whom I had seen on many occasions outside of her office building having a smoke, irrespective of the freezing temperature at the time. Often, we would exchange perfunctory greetings. I assumed she knew me, as I believed I was at least acquainted with her. When I approached her in her office, she greeted me warmly and said: "I know you." I smiled because I thought this was in recognition of our chance encounters outside of her office building. She continued: "You are that guy who stands outside of the CVS with that big dog." I was flummoxed! How could I be so misidentified? I too had seen the guy who waited for his wife or girlfriend standing outside of the CVS with a huge dog. My guess is that this man was taller than I, and he wore his hair in locks. I have never worn locks, and I am too busy to stand outside the CVS Pharmacy. I own no dog, big or small. I assured this lady that she was mistaken and that I had never stood outside of CVS awaiting anyone. A year later, I had occasion to interact with the same office employee. This next greeting proceeded in racial textbook fashion like the first. When she referenced the dog again, I turned to her, and, somewhat exasperatedly, said: "You know what is remarkable to me? It is that you actually remembered the dog and not the man." My sarcasm went completely over her head, or at least she chose to appear not to get the point I was trying to convey. Her response, with a warm smile to me, was: "Yes, I like dogs," at which point, she began showing me the pictures of her dogs on her desk. I left her presence in haste. This scenario represents the quintessential contradiction of blackness; it is so visible in the context of social opprobrium, yet so invisible in terms of social recognition. This encounter points to the fact that it is not always the explicit frontal assault of racism that is demoralizing, but the cumulative effect of unconscious bias that wears you down. Lest the reader believes that there is a universal blackness, the following section seeks to unpack the lived experience of this racial category.

IS BEING AFRICAN CARIBBEAN THE SAME AS BEING BLACK?

Does blackness reside in the cauldron of the American experience exclusively? How universal is the color black? Granted there is a rigid system of racial stratification in the United States that brooks no quarter with racial nuance. One is black or one is white; there are no somatic variations in between. However, what happens when there is simply no room for ambiguity? Is the non-African American insufficiently black because he or she has not experienced American slavery? Was Caribbean slavery so fundamentally and qualitatively different? Were there not more Africans sent via the Middle Passage to South America and the Caribbean than to the United States? Was there not a similar transatlantic experience—a horrifying Middle Passage for people en route to the Caribbean and the United States? For some, one only qualifies as black and/or African American when one has parents who were born in the United States. This criterion of course would pose some very awkward problems of identity for some of the most beloved black American leaders, many of whom have one or both parents from the Caribbean or Africa. It would be absurd to think of W. E. B. Du Bois as not being African American because his father was Haitian, or to think of Malcolm X as any less an African American because his mother was from Grenada. Do we put an asterisk next to the names of Kareem Abdul Jabbar because he was born in Trinidad, as was the militant, Civil Rights leader and Black Power advocate, Kwame Touré (Stokely Carmichael)? Then how do we embrace Barack Obama as black with a Kenyan father and white mother? The list of black people who fall into this category with ancestry from the Caribbean is extensive and includes among others such names as Prentice Hall, Harry Belafonte, Sidney Poitier, Colin Powell, Eric Holder, one of hip hop's founding fathers, Grandmaster Flash, and of course all the countless, enslaved Africans banished from the Caribbean to the United States between 1736 and 1737 because of their recalcitrance. One of my colleagues in making the nationalist distinction between us, admittedly in jest, notwithstanding the fact that so much angst finds an outlet in humor, described me as "one of them island niggers." Another colleague characterized me as an "honorary white." When aggrieved students went to an erstwhile African American colleague for some assistance on a series of racial issues, she told them: "If you need someone to fight for you, you need to go to one of those Caribbean Negroes on campus." The reference in this instance was to me and two other African Caribbean male professors who were on faculty at the time.

My point above is not intended to flatten out differences; surely there are historical, cultural, and economic differences between African Caribbean and African Americans. Rather the objective here is to suggest that given the historical ties between these two groups of people—the experience of slavery and the Middle Passage, the preponderance of Barbadians in South Carolina from as early as 1671, the solidarity of struggles, particularly in the Jim Crow era and during the Civil Rights struggle, the involvement of the Caribbean-based Harlem activists in the Scottsboro Boys' case and Marcus Garvey's Universal Negro Improvement Association, or the struggle for working-class women's rights and the rights of domestic workers by the Trinidad-born Claudia Jones, and the subjection to police surveillance, brutality, profiling—it would seem to be more productive to forge better relations between these two groups of people, than to magnify differences. It is the rejection of such narrow nationalism that prompted Paul Robeson to note that "when he spoke of the Negro he meant American Negroes as well as West Indians and Africans."[12] Only a narrow, Black Nationalist orientation would celebrate what appears to be a black essentialist position over who qualifies as being black. Why is this point important? It is significant because white supremacy thrives on such divisions. The specificity of the black experience in America cannot be overlooked. However, that specificity is part of a broader vision of the problem that would allow us to understand why the killing of George Floyd resonated in the Netherlands, France, Italy, Germany, Spain, the Caribbean, and Latin America. It is a testimony to the fact that all black lives matter and a change in the status of one group of oppressed blacks in one country has implications for other blacks in the Diaspora. Beyond this point, we are also beginning to recognize the synergies being created among the wretched of the earth so that building on the Black Lives Matter movement, we are simultaneously drawing attention to the important struggles of the lives of Native American and other indigenous people in the United States, Canada, Australia, New Zealand, and in Latin America, and this recognition is also being tied to the lives of the LGBTQ community, immigrant lives, and impoverished workers all over the world. We can never hope to transcend our present situation without recognizing the extent to which our solidarity can be so easily splintered.

CONCLUSION

Being black and male requires us to think carefully about how we negotiate the rapids of a structure dominated by white supremacy. The experience of black maleness is not merely a matter of being perceived as a problem, but of being already knowable in advance *as a problem*. It requires a delicate balance of walking the tightrope of the lived experience. On the one hand, we do benefit from the patriarchal dividend of privilege, though not to the same extent as more powerful, white men of course, but we do benefit as men nevertheless. On the other hand, we are socially marked as aggressive (dare I say "intimidating"), sexually profligate, irresponsible parents, and generally hedonistic. A careful examination of these features would reveal, however, that these are mostly not personal character flaws, but the results of deeper structural issues of inequality and unequal power. The widely read article by Ta-Nehisi Coates[13] on reparations makes a very important point. It brings us back to a consideration of the material base of inequality and the unequal distribution of power in this society. It is at this site that we ought to begin the work of transformation, not merely on the surface of our skins.

NOTES

1. Cornelius Castoriadis, *Philosophy, Politics, Autonomy: Essays in Political Philosophy* (New York and Oxford: Oxford University Press, 1991).
2. Ibid., p. 33.
3. Ibid., p. 34.
4. Walter Rodney, *The Groundings with My Brothers* (London: Bogle-L'Ouverture Publications, Ltd., 1975): 19.
5. Ibid., p. 19.
6. Frantz Fanon, *Black Skin, White Masks* (New York: Grove Press, 1967): 109.
7. W. E. B. Du Bois, *The Souls of Black Folk* (New York: A Signet Classic, 1995): 43–53.
8. *Black Skin, White Masks*, ibid.
9. *Black Skin, White Masks*, p. 116.
10. Personal communication, the American Philosophical Association Conference, Central Division, Kansas City Sheraton, Missouri, March 4, 2017. Permission granted to use.
11. Ibid., p. 117.
12. Paul Robeson, *Paul Robeson: The Artist as Revolutionary* by Gerald Horne (London: Pluto Press, 2016): 103.
13. Ta-Nehisi Coates, "The Case for Reparations," in *The Atlantic, 313*(5), (June 2014): 54–71.

BIBLIOGRAPHY

Castoriadis, Cornelius. *Philosophy, Politics, Autonomy: Essays in Political Philosophy* (New York and Oxford: Oxford University Press, 1991).
Coates, Ta-Nehisi. "The Case for Reparations," in *The Atlantic, 313*(5), (June 2014): 54–71.
Du Bois, W.E.B. *The Souls of Black Folk* (New York: A Signet Classic, 1995).
Fanon, Frantz. *Black Skin, White Masks* (New York: Grove Press, 1967).
Robeson, Paul. *Paul Robeson: The Artist as Revolutionary* by Gerald Horne (London: Pluto Press, 2016).
Rodney, Walter. *The Groundings with My Brothers* (London: Bogle-L'Ouverture Publications, Ltd., 1975).

Chapter 10

Navigating the Aguala

Blackness, Shamans, and Drag Queens

Sterlin Mosley

There are at least five of me in here, maybe more depending on the minute; shifting selves, each one more transient than the next. The "real" me, however, is none of these, but an elegant weaving of aspects of myself known and unknown into a tapestry we could call a human being. The only stable thing is that which watches these shifts, that is, consciousness itself. In the Western world we require labels, definitions, classifications, and structure so we can organize our experiences. So, since I am attempting to communicate in the confines of the West, we could classify me as a cisgender black, queer, academic, poet, teacher, friend, and, most importantly, in my mind, a mystic. The intersectionality of my existence mimics a familiar tradition for people like me who have, due to the very ingredients of their identity, been othered. I continue to traverse the shifting landscapes of my identity because I can't not. My existence is my activism. After settling into the stark realization that for me there was no way to avoid the inevitable alienation of intersectionality, I endeavored to traverse the liminal world as an act of active protest against a world that craves structure, order, borders, and assimilation. Of course, I'm not the only one, and we find ourselves at a phenomenological apex of identity as the spaces and lines between this and that are challenged. Suffering and discontent tend to evoke change whether we're ready for it or not. As black and brown people, and their allies, find themselves thrust yet again into the seemingly perennial struggle for liberty, freedom, and dignity, the call to spiritual and embodied activism stirs for a new generation.

Unlike the Civil War and the Civil Rights Era of the 1950s and 1960s, our awareness of the intersectionality and ambiguity of various activists are at the forefront of the current movement. We owe this advancement in great part to the strong, albeit at times problematic, work of the second wave feminists and the co-occurring LGBTQ movement of the 1960s and 1970s occurring alongside the black power and post Jim Crow era civil rights activists. With the third and fourth wave of feminism, the emphasis shifted to the centrality of identity as an important aspect of activism and its philosophical and intellectual presumptions. Words like "queer," trans," "gender non-conforming," and the use of "they/them/theirs" pronouns illustrate a general adjustment in the cultural zeitgeist to encompass greater variance outside the Western binaries (man/woman, gay/straight, white/nonwhite). As we recognize the necessity of "coloring outside the lines," there are two relics of Western duality that remain triumphant and stubbornly rigid: race and gender. Whatever shifts occur inside of me minute by minute or however transformative or monumental my subjective experiences are at any given moment, they are often overshadowed by my blackness. My activism—no matter how transcendent in form, emotionally or spiritually poignant, insightful, talented or genuinely bereft and lost I may have been—always risks being ignored, ridiculed, scrutinized, or rejected as "racially motivated" or "black" stuff. Sometimes "black stuff" was contending with the veiled insults of my high school band director who couldn't tell me and the other quiet effeminate black kid in the band apart from one another (we looked nothing alike). At other times, the "black stuff" was blissfully bypassed and whitewashed as I found in the New Age spiritual circles I ran in during my mid-twenties. Well-meaning but ignorant white women who found the "chip on my shoulder" off-putting and objectionable often shared their belief that the primary "spiritual obstacle" which I needed to overcome, in order to "transcend my ego" and live on my true plane of consciousness, was to recognize that race was an illusion because, of course, they didn't see me as black. Indeed, the "black stuff" was always a thing. My body was inscribed long before my birth with the etchings of a painful historical, anthropological, and cultural narrative that depended on the reductionism of my life and its problems and triumphs to the black stuff.

I could be ten thousand things, each more fascinating, grotesque, or bland and still only remain black in the eyes of the conditioned colonized gaze. Because my body and its performance in the world communicate a variety of signifiers embedded in my cells, I must carry with me the history of my ancestors who fought and died to be more than "the black stuff." This is a genetic history ripe with a variety of inherited scars replicated in the form of generational alcoholism, depression, hypertension, PTSD, glaucoma, diabetes, lupus, and obesity. It is also a narrative rich with symbolism that can be traced to Ancient Egyptian traditions that heralded sophisticated spiritual philosophies and technologies that long predate the Western world by thousands of years.

So how does one traverse the subtle and delicate terrain of embodied spiritual activism in a world where being black or brown could quite simply get you killed? How does someone like me seek greater heights (or depths) of spiritual profundity in a culture that has positioned my sexual identity as "wrong," "bad," and "evil"? A sexuality that at one time in my ancestral lineage was a marker of spiritual wisdom and an honor among my ancestors. A sexuality that, propagated and strengthened by the bigotry of subverted Judeo-Christian doctrines, was passed onto my people and turned into a sin rather than a point of distinction. In the face of these conditions, the lofty mysticism of identity shifting and *naguala*[1] would seem less important when at times the business of the day seems to be to stay alive. Abraham Maslow, one of the great fathers of American psychology, especially humanistic psychology, and a definitive yet brilliant hegemonic philosopher, identified some important features endemic to surviving in the West. Maslow stated that one must first feel a sense of physical safety, then be properly nourished and satiated and feel free from impending threat to one's life force in order to begin to develop emotional or spiritual depth or awareness.[2] But Maslow had not spent time in the slave quarters of a seventeenth-century plantation, where the threat of death was imminent, but where, nevertheless, the spiritual connection, love, and the magic of emotional expression were ample food for growth because there was nothing else that was safe to which to cling.

SNUFFING OUT THE MAGIC: WESTERN HEGEMONY AND THE COLONIZATION OF IDENTITY

Western hegemony and its children—racism, sexism, scientism, ableism, homonegativity, and bigotry—were intended to siphon the magic of the spirit. Indeed, the magic itself was the enemy: a "disgusting" remnant of heathens who deserved to be conquered, punished, and reformed in order to be redeemed in the arms of a loving yet rational and fair yet punitive God(s) made in the Western man's image. The magic must be beat out of you in order to survive in a dualistic world where up is always up, men are better than women, white people are superior, time is linear, and money is power. There is no place for magic where time is money and money is life. Magic is a reminder of the Western man's lost sense of a mystery world prior to his deadening, which had to be driven deeper into the subconscious. However, magic still exists in the shapes and symbols of our dreams and unconscious musings and imaginations, but is best left for children or the pages of fantasy novels and the colorful scenes of superhero movies.

Insistence on essentializing identificatory structures, anchored in a scientific model that deifies the body, the colonialization of identity was perpetuated beyond the mighty slave ships that sailed to the Americas. As is well evidenced in the history of the Western world, black and brown people were beaten for performing the "savage," "barbaric" rituals and religious ceremonies of their homelands. Their spiritual tools, artifacts, and mythologies were made profane and became fearsome reminders of the colonizers' disowned anxiety of the mysterious. The bludgeoning of Western religious dogma on African, indigenous, and Latinx peoples in the United States resulted in a silent but equally devastating identificatory massacre that resulted in the "Great American melting pot." The desire to bury the unacceptable, uncertain, or complicated aspects of a perpetrator's psyche, through the sadistic exploitation and denigration of the victim, is a key feature of most abusive relationships. The Other[3] was not only literally murdered but figuratively annihilated by the gauntlet of colonial ideology, which seeks to stifle the natural process of creation for its own ends.

Western hegemony's reign of ideological terror began with the essentializing philosophies of Aristotle, who doled out both moral and scientific classifications and delineations to his students in order to elucidate virtuous Greek life. Man, light, consciousness, the heavens, logic, reason, and rhetoric were positioned as the highest of virtues (aka as "truth"), while women, darkness, the unconscious, the underworld, emotion, intuition, and sensuality were positioned as illogical (aka "becoming truth"). For Aristotle, that which had not yet become truth had an opportunity to be converted to truth, hence his distinction of "becoming" truth. His belief in the conversion of what was untrue to virtuous laid the groundwork for the conversion of the savage tribal lands surrounding the Greek city states. And so began a 2,300-year-old love affair with the binary universe. However, the binary itself isn't necessarily the problem. Undoubtedly, there are instances where classifications, essentializing, and logic are helpful (as is the case with some Western medicine, advancements in sanitation, and creation of the other Western scientific technologies that enhance and strengthen human quality of life). It is the moral conditions upon which he positioned the various components of his binary universe that are problematic. Living as a privileged and educated Greek man, the barbarous nature of the neighboring North African tribes and their ancient symbolism, goddesses, and nature-centric philosophies and emotional and sensual expressions threatened the increasingly restrained "civility" of the Greek metropolis and were believed to need subjugation and education. Women, who harkened to the mysterious impulses of the underworld due to their menstruation, ability to give birth, heightened intuition, and emotional fluidity, were also positioned as dangerous. Women were in need of strong logical tempering and of course a good dose of a strong, logical husband in order to be worthy of the Heavens. Taking a page from Aristotle's proverbial book, many subsequent philosophies, political systems, and Western social structures further solidified the fate of the Other. The Western obsession with classification and taxonomy is tantamount to a desire to contain the existential anxiety of the liminal world. Science was constructed as a bastion against uncertainty and a bulwark against the inevitability of death. Rhetoric became the primary weapon of war and proved far mightier than the sword in the long run. Wars were fought in the name of ideological dominance and the victor was given not only control over the conquered bodies but, perhaps more importantly, how those bodies (and the consciousness which inhabits them) experience themselves. In a gross and fundamental distortion of emancipation, slave labor, torture, and even extermination are sold as necessary conditions for the Other to find freedom from their unvirtuous existences: *Abreit mach frei*.[4]

There have been many iterations of Western philosophy, each seeking to deal with the anxiety of existence and the longing to find (or strip) meaning from humankind and "make sense" of our experience. In the twenty-first century, identity has taken a decisively postmodern (and materialistic) turn, in which the lived experience of an individual cannot exist outside their sociopolitical contexts. Identity is heavily contingent upon the political, racial, economic, and gendered conditions through which one performs that identity and is developed primarily in relation to the whims of those conditions. We have Karl Marx and his predecessors to thank for this spiritually bereft reductionism, his well-intentioned desire to free the disenfranchised from their shackles notwithstanding. Most social change movements, post-Marx, relied upon his suppositions for activism and took the pragmatic (if radical) approach that one can only navigate and challenge unfair power and elitism if one is aware of the structures themselves. According to Marx and Friedrich Engels, in *The Communist Manifesto* (published in 1848), transformation is best achieved when the individual can join with other like-minded, similarly classed people, to create a movement to shift the structures of power and control the means and modes of production. Because this conception of the subjective experience was conceived within the confines of the Western paradigm, it inevitably contains little magic and minimizes the role of emotion, spirit, and the value of the unknown. It is, for me, just as flat and static as the materialistic or idealistic Western philosophical visions of identity.[5]

The human soul was meant to travel between the spaces of what is clear and discernible. Most spiritual traditions in their mystical forms acknowledge the value of the undefined as fodder for personal growth. However, the discomfort that arises from the liminal is not for the faint of heart. The Western world and its philosophical hegemony have been undoubtedly successful at ensuring its growth, but that growth was secured through the brute strength of its desire to survive. Charles Darwin, another decisively materialistic Western philosopher, observed, in his *The Origins of Species*, that only the fittest survive, and that fitness was contingent upon the development of either clever or ruthless adaptive mechanisms that could defeat potential usurpers and ensure its propagation and replication.

There is an audacious strength (and arrogance) in the capturing of foreign lands and the enslavement of its natives for one's own economic power. There is an undeniable vicious cleverness in the indoctrination of one's own ideals into those same natives for whom you've just stolen from and slaughtered. The very idea to travel to another foreign land—attacking, capturing, and enslaving your captors to build upon their backs—is predicated upon one's vision of absolute power. Slavery is an ancient concept, but the Portuguese, Spanish, Italian, and British slavers who industrialized slavery was something new in human history. Survival of the fittest indeed. However, behind the clever adeptness of hegemonic control lies the fear of loss and uncertainty and the subsequent cruelty and malice enacted to prevent the loss of control. When fitness is only measured in physical strength, cleverness, and survivalist instincts, it leaves little room for the development of more subtle faculties like empathy, emotional intelligence, creativity, or compassion.

The insidious prison of the colonized gaze is designed to choke out our very life force but is also eating the West from the inside. The great Western experiment has come at a steep price for all but a few. Nuclear war, disease, economic anxiety, poverty, widespread depression, and anxiety have a crushing effect on all human beings and are representative of the cancerous overgrowth of the Western obsession with form, power, and progress. The Other, which frankly now includes more of us than not, are forced to focus on what can be dealt with in the physical realm: trained to function in the world that Aristotle built, in a game for which we are often powerless to change the rules. We must then challenge the system: protest for health reforms, police reforms, voting rights, marriage rights, reproductive rights, religious rights, and protest against gun violence, health disparities, incarceration, drug abuse. Indeed, we must fight for human rights! At times we have to break a few windows and set a few fires, because the loudest language is one that threatens form. We have been conditioned by the colonizer to seek safety first (survival of the fittest), and deal in the tangible currency of Western duality in order to survive the landscape of hegemony. The irony is that safety is, and will always be, fleeting for the Other. The game was designed that way.

For the Other, our identities, bodies, and spirits are stuck in the loop of a rigid and abusive dialectical relationship with Western hegemony that must maintain its balance in order to not upset the established power structures. We have been engaged in the dynamic yet painful cycle of fear and struggle as a means of keeping us engaged in the game itself. The very scaffolding of America was quite literally built on the backs of slaves, migrant Mexican and Central American workers, and indigenous people; the foundation of the American dream has been cemented over with fear, pain, and domination. Yet hope springs eternal.

GROWTH THROUGH ALIENATION

Through fear and pain, spiritual fortitude and freedom flourish. They provide even the most downtrodden among us with the potential to soar. Because we have so often been thrust into a liminal abyss through the trauma and abuse of our past, we have been forced to traverse the darkness of the liminal and find meaning in the darkest of places. Whether in the cotton fields, the trail of tears, ICE camps, prison cells, inner-city ghettos, or Japanese or German concentration camps, the pulse of the Other's spirit has always been fit to survive. While the normal pain and trauma of the human condition is an expected part of the life cycle, trauma inflicted at the hands of the cruel and misguided is harder to transform but ripe and perhaps provides an enriched nutrient for wisdom. Edouard Glissant beautifully describes this process in the *Poetics of Relation*:

> Experience of the abyss lies inside and outside the abyss. The torment of those who never escaped it: straight from the belly of the slave ship into the violet belly of the ocean depths they went. But their ordeal did not die [once they arrived]; it quickened into this discontinuous/discontinuous thing: the panic of the new land, the haunting of the former land, finally the alliance with the imposed land, suffered and redeemed . . . thus the absolute unknown projected by the abyss and bearing into eternity the womb abyss and the infinite abyss, in the end became knowledge.[6]

The potential for growth in extreme pain can enact a sort of transmogrification that forces one to expand the concept of their identity beyond or outside of the confines of the skin.

Historically, it has always been the shamans, witches, wizards, seekers, mystics, and prophets that are cast out of the "normal world," tasked with traversing the unseen world in order to provide wisdom to the whole. We are all now given the option to take the path of the mystic, to harness the power of the shaman and inhabit the spirit of the magical warrior as we reach a turning point in the history of the Western world. Indeed, the West has fallen before. Rome saw its demise through a series of foolish emperors' drunk with power and imbued with malice and madness. However, what survived the destruction of the mighty colosseum, always lurking beneath the surface and ready to regrow, as the very idea of duality; the lure of power and the fear of the unknown. Thus, structures are rebuilt, its buildings changed, borders redrawn, governments reappointed, money reprinted, slaves recaptured, and the promise of progress marches ever forward.

In order to shift into the world of *naguala*, we must unlearn many of the precepts of the Western ideological structure, which is a job easier said than done. Of course, there is always the way of pain and trauma, but we are well acquainted with that path. The other is the path of *nepantla*,[7] but its rules are less rigid, more quantum, purposely unbounded, and filled with the powerful magic of our ancestors (whatever color they may be). The outer world, with its restrictions and corresponding duality, is always local, ruthlessly dialectic, bounded, and filled with limited magic. It is and will continue to be subject to gunfire, torture, enslavement, and death by natural and unnatural means. The underworld, however, is unclear, murky, liquid, and tenuous. For many, that evokes existential terror. We have been conditioned to be intolerant of ambiguity and disdainful of the uncertain because in the West, as we've seen, this meant death. Delving into the underworld, we believe, will thrust us into epic battles with monsters, demons, and unspeakable horrors, and indeed if those exist, they are fueled by the fearful gaze through which we've been conditioned to view them. However, as mythologist Joseph Campbell notes, the underworld is filled mostly with our own monstrous projections and to slay them is to march headfirst into the darkness of our own proverbial caves.

NEPANTLA: DRAG, IDENTITIVE ACTIVISM, AND BLACKNESS

Latinx queer theorist Gloria Anzaldúa provides an adept framework for understanding the navigation of the liminal world. In order to fully embark upon the path of *nepantla*, within the confines of the Western experience, we must first decentralize the concept of identity. For Anzaldúa, the experience of *naguala* is happening inside everyone and particularly within those who, out of necessity, walk between two worlds: the shapeshifters who must inhabit two or more spaces simultaneously (black and queer, deaf and Latinx, trans and native, etc.). For these everyday shapeshifters, the body is the tool through which their identitive magic can manifest and, in the underworld, these shifts allow for various kinds of practical, emotional, psychological, and spiritual work to be administered for the community and the self. This is the tradition of the seer, the healer, and the mystic. For the shapeshifter, the body and its sensual experiences are merely tools for living in the outer world, a medium with which to navigate identities, not the world itself. Pleasure, sensation, and pain are all portals into a wellspring of emotional and spiritual power that pulses in every human spirit. The shapeshifter does not run away from, repress or depress these energies, but rather welcomes them as transient guests in the home of the body. Pain for the shapeshifter comes only when the body and others' experience of the body cannot shift and flow or when the pressures of the sociocultural shackles become too tight.

For the majority (those non-Others), *Nepantla* happens against one's will when something jolts one out of the familiar and into something unknown. Non-Others may reel against this kind of shift because it is imposed rather than chosen. However, for the Other, these identitive shifts happen out of pure necessity. For the Compounded Other,[8] these shifts are survival mechanisms for maintaining one's connection to the complexity of their gender, sexual, cultural, or ethnic identity and the practical need to navigate the outer world safely. Some succeed in adaptation, others do not and are raped, killed, stoned, buried alive, mutilated, or exploited for their inability or unwillingness to adapt to the prison rules.

As a communication scholar, it was drilled into me repeatedly that our communicative competence comes from our ability to expertly negotiate identitive performances in the social world. Never did we discuss the intrapersonal communication of multiple identities within the self and how those identifications shift, or whether they even can. Anzaldúa writes about her own process of navigating multiple identities: "I had to gather, I had to look at all these walls, divisions, gradations of being other other other, and determine where they all belonged. It was an energy of refocusing and bringing it all back together."[9] For Others the journey of shifting selves is treacherous and can only be mapped by crafting a straight-line through one's cultural and societal scripts.

As a Black man, the identities that I'm allowed to inhabit are limited, at least in performance. My *naguala* tendencies are policed because my body is policed. The political implications of my skin institute a strict code of performative standards and assumptions. I can feel as gentle as a wood fairy while walking to my car wearing a hoodie at night, but to the white gaze I am as insidious as a loaded nine-millimeter gun. I can express that my romantic orientation is not bounded to sex, but all the Western ear hears is, "I'm gay." Black men, and particularly queer black men, are a walking representation of the uncomfortable *nepantla* state at its apex. We are in essence a breathing expression of liminality that reminds the outer world of its inevitable transition into darkness. We are danger personified. It is no mistake that the Black form has come to represent simultaneous desire and fear for the Western psyche.

The black body signifies both the brilliant power of aggressive action and the sensual lure of pleasure through repetitive media tropes. The menacing voodoo shaman, the thug, the Nubian prince, the "well-spoken" negro, and the fierce queen are all representations and reminders of the liminality of the Black male form. Out of all of the aforementioned tropes, the fierce queen archetype has the most illuminating potential to navigate the *naguala* consciousness. The Black male queen is an identitive representation of the exhilarating danger and beautiful expression of the liminality of the shapeshifter.

International performer and entrepreneur RuPaul is a recognizable and ample expression of the *nepantla* state. By observing the enduring and popular archetype of the drag queen (particularly in the context of brown skin), we can begin to understand the fascination and hazard of navigating shifting identities, and the performance of those identities in the outer world. RuPaul (RuPaul Andrew Charles) is undeniably a black man outside of his drag persona. Standing at 6'4" and born into a black household where he was subjected to the indignities and homonegative rejections that often accompanied being reared in a traditionally black Christian household in the 1970s. However, his aptitude for shifting identitive spaces (and considerable marketing savvy) has afforded him a prosperous career and the adoration of both queer and mainstream audiences despite the bullying and abuse endemic to being queer in America. RuPaul, like many queer men, exhibited a childhood desire to explore the fierce feminine archetypes pulsing in his psyche which serve a multitude of positive psychological purposes. The first of which was to mitigate the vulnerability of his marginalized type-cast role as a gay man, and the other was a creative discursive act of performativity to contrast parental and familial expectations of traditional black male masculinity. "RuPaul" was unearthed within his psycho-spiritual underworld which involved an opportunity to move outside of his body-cage role.

The drag queens/kings are a manifestation of the *nepantla* state in performative art. They personify the space between two poles, and their ability to shift between the two both fascinates and confuses. It is at once desirable and repulsive. Drag artists are the pop art equivalent of the shapeshifting shaman who morphs themselves into other animals or beings in order to facilitate transformation for other people. Just as the shaman transforms into the hawk to deliver a message to the neighboring village, the queen shifts from male to female to deliver a message to the collective psyche of the community. The queen's message is one that only otherness can communicate: *be all of your selves*. In a 2013 interview with *Rolling Stone*, RuPaul acknowledged that the drag performer is "the shaman, . . . [the] witch doctor, and the court jester whose job it is to remind the culture: This is all facade. Don't take it too seriously."[10]

The drag queen and the shaman call for us to recognize the liminality of our own identities. To finally face the transient nature of all that we deem stable and solid. There is no such thing as stability, except when we enact it through the rigid performative politics of our bodily performance. The color of our skin reminds us where each body is *supposed* to be positioned in space and time. However, these identifiers are no more than our collective attempt to create order in a world of what seems like terrifying chaos. The drag queen, and particularly the Black drag queen, is a virulent personification of that chaos. The inherent spirituality of drag performance is an expression of compounded otherness and exemplifies the nature of the spiritual journey through the underworld; a journey all humans must take at some point. It is the performance of their Otherness that forces the queen into the role of spiritual seeker because the identitive borders, the liminal nature of their very selfhood creates a need to lift the veils of duality so that all aspects of the self can be expressed. Liminality affords the queens who walk between identitive borders the visionary gifts of the shaman to remind us: "this is all a fucking hoax [. . . be] willing to go deeper" and ponder "what's really going on here?" (RuPaul, *Rolling Stone* interview 2013).[11] Anzaldúa notes that the sexual, emotional, and transient/uncertain parts of the self we seek to bury underneath the identitive performances of our "stable" body identities express themselves in surprising and sometimes violent ways. This is why most of that content *stays* in the underworld, unearthed only through crisis or calamity, the way Western ideology ordained it. The pull to maintain the stable "I" prevents the shifting "I's" from bubbling to the surface. Behind the walls of the socially constructed identity of race, gender, and sexuality there is much more to be "tried on" and manipulated as the queen manipulates her wigs, makeups, and costumes to consciously create an illusion.

NOTES

1. Naguala is the indigenous Nahuatl word for "shapeshifter" or shapeshifting.
2. Abraham Maslow and Robert Frager. *Motivation and Personality*. New Delhi: Pearson Education, 1987.
3. Refers to anyone outside the confines of the hegemonic Western ideal of straight, cisgender, male, able-bodied, white, affluent, educated, literate, and so on.
4. "Abreit mach frei" translates to "work sets you free" are famously printed on the gates leading to the German concentration camp, Auschwitz.
5. The materialist views the body and the senses as central to identity, postulating that once sensory experience ends so too does identity. The idealist views identity only in terms of its nonlocal or spiritual state, the original "state of grace" and thus denies the body in favor of transcendental identitive stability.
6. Glissant, Édouard, and Betsy Wing. *Poetics of Relation*. Ann Arbor: University of Michigan Press, 1997.
7. "Nepantla is the Nahuatl word for an in-between state, that uncertain terrain one crosses when moving from one place to another, when changing from one class, race, or sexual position to another, when traveling from the present identity to a new identity" (Anzaldúa and Keating).
8. The Compounded Other can identify with a combination of racial, gendered, sexual, physical able-bodiedness, economic, religious, ethnic, or nationalities. For example, a Black, Jewish paraplegic from Iraq.
9. Anzaldúa, Gloria, and AnaLouise Keating. *The Gloria Anzaldúa Reader*. Durham: Duke University Press, 2009.

10. McClelland, Mac. "RuPaul: The King of Queens." *Rolling Stone*, September 26, 2013. http://www.rollingstone.com/movies/news/rupaul-the-king-of-queens-20131004?page=2 (accessed September 1, 2014).

11. Ibid.

BIBLIOGRAPHY

Anzaldúa, Gloria, and AnaLouise Keating. *The Gloria Anzaldúa reader*. Durham: Duke University Press, 2009.

Darwin, Charles. *The Origin of Species, 1876*. London: William Pickering, 1988.

Glissant, Édouard, and Betsy Wing. *Poetics of Relation*. Ann Arbor: University of Michigan Press, 1997.

Marx, Karl, & Engels, Friedrich. *The Communist Manifesto*. Singapore: Origami Books, 2020.

Maslow, Abraham H., & Frager, Robert. *Motivation and Personality*. New Delhi: Pearson Education, 1987.

McClelland, Mac. "RuPaul: The King of Queens." *Rolling Stone*, September 26, 2013. http://www.rollingstone.com/movies/news/rupaul-the-king-of-queens-20131004?page=2 (accessed September 1, 2014).

Chapter 11

Power, Divorce, and Trauma

Law and Loss

Floyd W. Hayes III

INTRODUCTION

In the present insurgency of antiblack racism in this place called America, these times compel us to reflect on the impact of the systematic murder of unarmed black people by murderous urban police. When, on March 25, 2020, Minneapolis killer kop Derek Chauvin pressed his knee down on the neck of unarmed George Floyd and murdered him, Chauvin—and the other kops who stood by and watched—carried on a long-standing white tradition of brutalizing and killing defenseless black Americans. What is significant about these historic assaults is the white objective and practice of always stifling black security and survival by ripping apart black families.

The contradictions and dilemmas of being black in America have their origins in the traumas of chattel slavery and the collective memory associated with that experience. The Atlantic Slave Trade and chattel enslavement of captured Africans gave rise to a further dehumanization process that totally disrupted the life experiences of African-descended Americans. The prominent black writer Richard Wright encapsulated the devastating impact in deeply personal terms:

> Captivity under Christendom blasted our lives, disrupted our families, reached down into the personalities of each one of us and destroyed the very images and symbols which had guided our minds and feelings in the effort to live. Our folkways and folk tales, which had once given meaning and sanction to our actions, faded from consciousness. Our gods were dead and answered us no more. *The trauma of leaving our African home, the suffering of the long middle passage, the thirst, the hunger, the horrors of the slave ship*—all those hollowed us out,

numbed us, stripped us, and left only physiological urges, the feelings of fear and fatigue.[1] (my emphasis)

Although the victims of slave trading came from regions throughout the West Coast of Africa—from Morocco in the North to the Old Congo Kingdom in the South—the culturally dehumanizing process of enslavement served as the violent and traumatic experience that totally transformed African identities. That is, through the cultural process of trauma, mediated through numerous institutional practices, multitudes of different precolonial African nationalities and ethnicities were coerced into becoming a singular people in America.[2] Slave owners sought to suppress African humanity, identities, and languages. Through the violence, dehumanization, and trauma of the long nightmare of enslavement, whites dominated the consciousness of captured African slaves. These social and historical dynamics produced a new people, American-born Africans.[3]

Slavery and its aftermath served as the matrix of forces that shaped the being and representation of black American males. In order to justify their economic exploitation and cultural domination of black people, white people employed racist notions to emasculate and criminalize black men. Hence, black males came to be represented as subhumans, savage beasts, rapists, and sexual threats to white society. Yet, in white patriarchal America, black men were characterized as inferior to white males, perhaps scarcely men at all. As the targets of racial and sexualized hatred, black men experienced the humiliating practices of white violence, terror, and subjugation. Hence, to be black and male in America has meant to exist in the historical and contemporary context of condemnation and the resultant threat of death and dying. This reality is what constitutes the trauma of black male existence in the United States.[4]

What does a black man do with a painful past that cannot be simply willed to disappear yet is a source of enormous difficulties in the present? For the black man in the United States, existence often is like Frantz Fanon's concept of a "zone of nonbeing" in which he is the problematic construction of whiteness.[5] Within this context, he cannot merely be a man; he is a *black* man who has been constructed as the most hated and feared figure in the white imagination. He is the target of a complex structure of white domination: white ideas, white institutions, and white laws. Chattel slavery constituted the horrendous genealogical situation—of an overwhelming, chaotic, and disruptive experience of catastrophic events—that subjected the great mass of black people to general or cultural trauma.[6] Indeed, chattel slavery served as the traumatizing "social death" that entrapped the early black experience in the United States.[7] Equally significant is the often peculiar and paradoxical experience of existential trauma for the individual. Existential trauma involves intense personal suffering and humiliation. What is important about this phenomenon is that the constant memory of past suffering lives on in the present, becoming an experience of perpetual memory.[8]

In the present chapter, I focus on the pain, anguish, and resentment that resulted from the matrix of traumatic forces surrounding my own divorce, child support, alimony, and alienation from my older children. I hope that my personal account will serve as a message to other black men who may find themselves before judges—and a larger antiblack juridical system—who will decide their fate. Perhaps this chapter may help them deal with their own situations as they face the American (in)justice system, even if it means being prepared to face a reality that is far from fair to black men. Perhaps there is strength to be found in facing such realism and "perhaps" this strength might breed a collective vision of legal transformation. Although the laws related to divorce have changed, black men largely remain the victims of an (il) legal system which sees them always already guilty of something. This is the legacy of antiblack laws from America's slave past. Hence, how can black men avoid mistakes in seeking to handle their cases? How may they avoid the emotional, financial, and political devastation of traumatic divorce?

Although this chapter focuses on the personal experiences of trauma, it needs to be understood that the personal always exists, and needs to be interrogated, in the context of the social. For as George Yancy informs:

> The self is always already linked to a web of significant and meaningful contingent relations that precede its constitution. Hence the self is created vis-à-vis the experience of others. The self is shaped within a dynamic, transactional space of alterity. In short, then, exploring the self inevitably involves exploring the self-with others.[9]

I explore in three parts the deeply social and existential situation of my own traumatic divorce in the mid-1970s. First, I discuss the (il)legal system, divorce, and trauma. Here I want to reflect on the philosophical implications of racist-legal entrapment and humiliation that can give birth to palpable trauma. Second, I describe existential trauma—how the physical aspects of trauma occupy and are transformed in my mind. I lost my children for ten years and was rendered financially incapacitated. As a result, I became deeply depressed and suicidal, and I developed an absolute resentment and hatred of the U.S. (il)legal system—lawyers, judges, and laws. Third, I comment on the sensorium of humiliation, resentment, and memory, and how these traumatic experiences and struggles have shaped my philosophy of personal conduct and intellectual vision. Although I am deeply critical regarding my ex-wife's actions, my critical observations should not be interpreted as antifemale or placing black women under erasure; for I am well aware of the historical and contemporary negative characterizations of black women and the extent to which they are often the victims of legal oppression in the United States.[10]

FAMILY BREAK UP AND EXISTENTIAL ANGUISH

In the mid-1970s, I was involved in a traumatic divorce. I was an only child who valued marriage and children; indeed, I struggled mightily to maintain my family. I was reared in a traditional two-parent home in which both my mother and father set for me the parameters of rules and regulations that I learned to take seriously. From childhood to my mid-teenage years, my parents taught me the importance, value, and sanctity of family, along with the history of our particular family. I was given my paternal grandfather's name; he was an affectionate, strong, and a proud man, who had a great sense of humor. Significantly, I actually looked forward to being married and jointly rearing children with my wife. I used to dream of rearing my children largely similar to the way my parents had reared me, but with less rigidity. However, after a ten-year marriage and three children (a son and two daughters), it was apparent that the dissolution of the marriage between their mother and me was the only alternative. It became obvious that my children's mother and I were just not compatible. There was no problem of infidelity; we just could not get along. We had come from totally different worlds. As a result, I moved from our West Baltimore apartment to a much cheaper apartment in East Baltimore. I continued to support my children and their mother, paying all of their bills and expenses, as if I were still living with them. Contrary to the racist stereotype that all black fathers are lazy and irresponsible vis-à-vis their children, I did not run away, disappear, or evade my responsibilities to my family. Importantly, as we separated, my ex-wife informed me that she did not want our children; she just wanted money—more of it! I was employed as a young instructor at the University of Maryland, Baltimore County (UMBC), and studying for a doctorate in government and politics at the University of Maryland at College Park. Hence, I had very little money.

Significantly, following our separation, my ex-wife sought to prevent my relationship with our children. She consistently denied me regular visits with them. Often, just as I was preparing to drive across town to pick them up for the weekend, she would call and say that something had come up and that I could not see my children. There was an occasion when I had our children for the weekend and attempted to return them to her *on time*, but she was nowhere to be found when we arrived. Unable to locate her, I drove them back to my apartment. Returning late at night, my ex-wife called and angrily demanded the children; of course, I returned them. The next morning, she called her attorney and told him that I had not returned our children on time and that I should not have the right to spend time with them again. When my lawyer called me with this information, I told him what actually happened. Yet, he never raised the truth of the situation in count, and, by extension, her vicious behavior in court was left unchallenged. This reality of loss and law—of losing a significant relationship with my children and the failure of the law to deal with this matter—sent me into the heights of despair and anguish.

Moreover, my ex-wife undertook a series of nasty practices calculated to totally disrupt my employment. On a regular basis, she would call my office in the morning just before my first class met; she screamed an assortment of obscenities and irrationalities! Her desire was designed to interrupt my concentration and preparation for my class. In fact, she had a pattern of calling the chancellor's office, shouting a series of irrational claims and demanding that I be fired. I learned of this practice, one day, when the secretary of UMBC's chancellor called and asked me to come to her office. On the phone was my ex-wife, screaming like a mad woman that I had left her and demanding that I be fired. The secretary informed me that my ex-wife had been making these calls and demands for weeks! Her behavior was illogical, for if I were fired, I would not have been able to support my family!

THE DIALECTICS OF (IL)LEGAL HUMILIATION

Seeking more money, my ex-wife filed for divorce. In what could only be characterized as the dialectics of racist-capitalist domination and corruption, I found myself entrapped in the clutches of an (il)legal system that knew nothing of truth, justice, or fairness.[11] That is, I became the victim of a social institution that had been designed to stifle black people's existence since the historical moment of chattel slavery.[12] The American (in)justice system, its rules of law, is based upon the structure of social control and power relations. Created by and in the interest of white ruling elites, the "law" in the United States reflects and reinforces the powerful dynamics of racism, classism, and sexism. I'm talking about a tyrannical institution that historically was designed to legitimize the domination, exploitation, and dehumanization of the great multitude of black people.[13]

From beginning to end, my courtroom experiences were overwhelmingly degrading, repressive, painful, and disruptive, forcing me to exist between depression and anger. The divorce decree ordered me to pay child support and alimony in an amount far beyond my means as a young college instructor. Literally, I could not pay the judge's order! The lawyer who claimed to be representing me advised that I sign the decree, promising that right after the divorce, he would have the amount lowered. Afterward, I could never get in touch with him; he would not respond to my frantic calls or letters.

Additionally, he did not inform me that in order to reduce the amount ordered by the original judge, I would have had to change my income status by earning less money! I was locked into a vice that others controlled.

Hence, a pattern developed in which my ex-wife began demanding my presence in court for nonsupport. This meant that I was in constant search of lawyer after lawyer, seeking assistance in my struggle against (il)legal tyranny. These lawyers seemed incapable of challenging the rogue judges I faced. After all, judges and lawyers studied the same "white law"; hence, they all were comrades in my debasement and exploitation. At each appearance in court, my existence was dehumanized and tortured, and I was made aware that my life amounted to nothing. I was constantly degraded and insulted! I encountered judges whose courtroom behavior and pronouncements were calculated to debase and reduce me to a position of nonbeing. There were numerous examples. I will cite a few here. On one occasion, a judge asked me what I desired as an outcome of the case. I stood and said: "Your honor, I love my children and . . ." He interrupted, screaming at me to "SIT DOWN AND SHUT UP!" On another occasion, my ex-wife brought her sister to court. In the middle of the proceedings, when I was being grilled by a judge, my ex-wife and her sister began laughing out loud in court; the judge neither looked their way nor said anything to them about their behavior! And then there was a time when I had clear and certain evidence that my ex-wife had perjured herself in a previous court hearing. She had said that she was staying with the man whom she would later marry in order to take care of his child. I later learned from his ex-wife that this was not true. I wanted to present that evidence, but my so-called lawyer didn't appear with me, and the judge refused even to accept the evidence. Finally, on a day that I was to appear before a black judge, a friend told me this judge would listen to my case. Indeed, the judge did listen, and then viciously announced that I pay an additional amount per week in child support! What was so deeply disappointing and disgusting was that my lawyers—to whom I paid thousands of dollars seeking legal assistance—never actually assisted me. Even so, they all seemed quite comfortable extracting my money. Therefore, the divorce decree and later social dynamics of legal repression reduced me to financial, emotional, and personal chaos and despair. Significantly, my encounter with the law, within the context of divorce, had nothing to do with justice, fairness, or the search for truth. These illusions represented the workings of white racist power. Over the years, I felt the subtle erasure of my core self—the cancellation of my being. Tortured and tormented like a prisoner of war, I was a man whose life had become a sign of great disequilibrium. In his recent book, *Trauma and Forgiveness: Consequences and Communities*, political philosopher C. Fred Alford described my condition well:

Trauma undermines our confidence in the stability of the world. Not just the external world, but the inner world. Our trust in the world is violated; frequently our ability to trust in the world is ruined. Trauma is a deeply personal experience; and trauma makes no sense unless it is seen in this way. At the same time, traumatizing experiences do not occur in a political vacuum. They are often the outcome of forces set in motion by human beings.[14]

AN AWAKENING TO (IL)LEGAL DECADENCE

At the edge of suicide, I serendipitously met an older lawyer who told me about the dynamics and outcome of my divorce. He told me that he had assisted my ex-wife's attorney because of his battle with my lawyer. The older attorney said that I was the resultant pawn in the struggle between the opposing lawyers. He noted that they all knew—judges and lawyers—that I could not afford to pay the price of that ticket! Indeed, the drastically high amount was set, the older attorney revealed to me, so that I would be in financial limbo and emotional distress for many years to come. As soon as I walked out of the courtroom, he explained, the despicable goal was to put me in arrears! Hence, the older attorney informed me, this arrangement was designed to allow, and even encourage, my ex-wife to haul me back into court anytime she wanted to do so. Significantly, although my ex-wife had remarried, I was still forced to pay alimony to her. That was the original divorce decree, and I was not able to get it changed. Moreover, my previous and ongoing attempts to gain custody of my children went nowhere. Finally, one of the numerous lawyers from whom I sought assistance and representation announced to me that since Maryland was a common-law state, I would never gain custody of my children unless I proved that their mother was unfit. I knew she was unfit—she scarcely cared for our children and she did not want them—but I could not prove it to a bankrupt court of American (in)justice. I was defeated, insulted, and humiliated. My family was ripped apart and there was nothing I could do about it; I did not see my children for ten years. I had lost everything that mattered to me. I trusted no one. In the face of such a monument of legal hypocrisy, I became an angry man, a desperate man, and a dangerous man. Perhaps this is what interrupted thoughts of suicide.

LAWLESSNESS AND LOSS

Within months after the 1976 divorce, my ex-wife married a UMBC professor who had obtained a well-paying position at Brown University. Without my knowledge, they all moved to Providence, Rhode Island, where our children grew up. Their failure to notify me, as my children's biological father, was an immoral and lawless act, but the law never protected my so-called rights as a father. I did not know that their mother had taken our children out of Maryland until I received my habitual summons to report to court for insufficient child support and alimony; my ex-wife consistently employed the long arm of the law. When I actually learned that our children had been taken out of Maryland, I was devastated. As a result, from the late 1970s to the early 1990s, I existed as a man in deep depression and despair, haunted by traumatic experiences with the decadent (il)legal system and the loss of my children. My world was consumed by law and loss.

I did not see my children for ten years—from 1976 to 1985! By the time I saw them again, my son was graduating from high school, my oldest daughter was fourteen, and my middle daughter was eleven. I was also remarried with an infant child. My daughters later told me that their mother scarcely cared for any of them—they had to fend for themselves—and that the man their mother married had proven to be mentally unstable and had molested them! My daughters said that sometime in the late 1970s he had to leave their home and ultimately committed suicide in Florida. This news of their molestation left me pained for my daughters. Yet, I sought to conceal from them my outrage and anger toward their mother and the decadent U.S. (il)legal system; in my mind, the law and my ex-wife had set the stage for my older children's harrowing and traumatic childhood experiences.

TRAUMA, DEGRADATION, AND MEMORY: TRANSFORMING THE SELF

By the early 1990s, my wife, young daughter, and I relocated from San Diego, California, to West Lafayette, Indiana. By this time, my older children and I had begun to communicate on a regular basis. It had taken many years to accomplish the reconciliation. Because of my renewed relationship with my older children, their mother began making demands for more money, as my arrearages had mounted dramatically! Through legal negotiations, our attorneys developed an arrangement that included a huge payoff to my ex-wife, which precluded her from demanding any more money from me, as our children were now grown. To settle this matter, I had to borrow an enormous amount of money from my mother; it took a number of years to pay her back. I learned later from my oldest daughter that, following reception of the large settlement, they lost the house and had to move. Significantly, in the last years of my ex-wife's life, she was living in a small apartment in inner-city Providence, Rhode Island. Although she had utilized the law and sought remarriage in order to have an opulent lifestyle, both of these veils of illusion evaded this increasingly bitter woman. In some ways, she was as much a victim of the (il)legal system as I, for she won Pyrrhic victories, at best.

As might be imagined, this entire affair—the dynamics of divorce and its atrocious aftermath—has been traumatic. The dialectics of legal humiliation and repression transformed my consciousness and social outlook. My existential trauma, which was accompanied by years of depression from the 1980s through the early 1990s, left me broken and suicidal. Yet, at my very worst, when my world seemed teetering on the brink of collapse, I underwent an existential transformation that rendered me angry, outraged, resentful, and critical. My world was totally unhinged, dislodged, and uprooted. From the 1990s to the early 2000s, I became a desperate man, a horrible man, who trusted no one! Married to a wonderful woman and with a lovely daughter, I was haunted by memories of the pain, anguish, and outrage of having lost my older children as a result of a bankrupt and corrupt (in)justice system that had allowed and even encouraged my ex-wife to (il)legally harass, dehumanize, and degrade me for decades. On one occasion, the overwhelming disruption and fissuring of my consciousness was clearly evident when, in front of my wife and young daughter, I introduced myself to someone by saying that my wife and I were divorced and that I had three children. I failed to include my youngest daughter or even mention my current marriage, which severely and understandably upset my wife, who witnessed this spectacle. I could not move beyond the memory of law and loss. My everyday consciousness centered on past atrocities of legal humiliation and the loss of my older children, even as I was reconstructing and repairing a relationship with them. In my deepest of despair, I again confronted creeping thoughts of suicide. Because I had to take responsibility for the cruel choices I made in regard to a horrible first marriage, I encountered a good bit of self-loathing. Often, I hated myself for having been naïve enough to marry my ex-wife in the first place! Decades of pain, suffering, and degradation had subjected me to a world of personal disaster and disbelief. I was no longer my former self—naïve and believing in the basic goodness of people and the world. I trusted no one; nothing mattered anymore. It became difficult to live with the vision and meaning of the world given to me by my parents. Indeed, I rejected the philosophic vision of optimism, along with its self-satisfactions of the past and present. Richard Wright's ideas opened my vision to the reality of freethinking skepticism.[15] Along with Wright, Friedrich Nietzsche's concept of nihilism made more sense to me and, therefore, helped me to understand and reshape my worldview.

> Nihilism appears at that point, not that the displeasure at existence has become greater than before, but because one has come to mistrust any "meaning" in suffering, indeed in existence. One interpretation has collapsed; but because it was

considered *the* interpretation it now seems as if there were no meaning at all in existence, as if everything were in vain.[16]

In this meditation, I have sought to discover the meaning of my own experience of existential trauma as a black man in the United States. The United States is a cruel, hostile, and indifferent society, characterized by historic contradiction and monumental hypocrisy. From childhood, one is taught that America is a democracy and that the law is about justice, fairness, reason, and truth. However, U.S. law is a veil of illusion that scarcely characterizes reality. Rather, the law is a product of and mirrors a social order that is scarcely democratic, but riddled with racist, sexist, and cultural domination. The law is a social institution that is based upon power, social control, and economic exploitation, that is, its so-called rules of law merely serve to legitimize institutional racism and other forms of insidious discrimination, causing severe catastrophe in the lives of its victims. As a seventy-eight-year-old black man, I have grown increasingly cynical about the United States; this nation lacks the will to overcome its deeply imbedded lies and disjunctions. Many years ago, Derrick Bell emphatically declared: "Racism lies at the center, not the periphery; in the permanent, not in the fleeting; in the real lives of black and white people, not in the sentimental caverns of the mind."[17]

For me, law and loss—facing a decadent (il)legal system and the resultant loss of my children for ten years—destroyed my innocence in the world and shattered my beliefs and convictions about good and evil, which proved inadequate to cope with the deeper forces that literally overwhelmed my well-being. In the process, I learned that law in the United States is a world where morality does not exist. It is a matter of power and its abuse! As a result, I came to regard my past moral political attitudes as lamentable and unforgivably naïve. I became and remain consumed by a wounded resentment, anger, and outrage; and the prolongation of my ex-wife's actions and the (il)legalized terrorism of my existence. I am plagued by the memory of the overwhelming experience in which everything I held dear was taken from me in a seeming instant. What is remarkable is that I continue to live the history of that traumatic subjection. In a penetrating account of trauma, Ruth Leys argues: "The experience of the trauma, fixed or frozen in time, refuses to be represented as past, but is perpetually re-experienced in a painful, dissociated, traumatic present."[18] Ultimately, my entire family was victimized! I have felt that there is no healing from existential trauma; the memory of this experience continues to be a source of torment, anger, and resentment. Equally significant, I felt, and continue to feel, nothing but absolute contempt and disgust toward every aspect of the corrupt and bankrupt system of U.S. (in)justice—its "white law."

History moves, and a thing can turn into its opposite. Realizing how naïve I was with respect to my social outlook and worldview, I had to change my philosophy of life. I needed to develop an ethics of political and intellectual dissent that went far beyond the optimistic veils of illusion that characterized contemporary ideologies of optimism. Modern conceptions of law, truth, reason, justice, and fairness have no value outside of the context of power and its abuse. I sought to enlarge my philosophical vision so that I could think on a broader basis than the limited contradiction between romantic optimism and liberal hopelessness.[19] By means of extensive reading and study, I developed a fiercely critical view of an increasingly decadent and crisis-ridden U.S. social order and its social institutions, especially the system of (in)justice.

CONCLUSION: DECADENCE AND DISILLUSIONMENT IN THE AGE OF AMERICAN CATASTROPHE

In this meditation, it has been my purpose to lay bare the manner in which the circumstances surrounding my divorce disrupted and overwhelmed my existence as a black man in the United States. Through an examination of my own situation as a black man facing the American (in)justice system, I hope that I have shown that I was the victim of white laws that proved to be humiliating, debilitating, and oppressive. Exploited in the most profound manner, I lost everything I cherished—with horrible consequences. The condition of law and loss dominated my consciousness for years. Significantly, I lost my older children for ten years, I became economically unstable, I experienced years of deep depression, and I became suicidal. As a result, I became fiercely angry, seeing no value or meaning in my own existence or in the world. Yet, with the assistance of others, I fought to refashion myself, and I also developed a more critical view of America and the world. I had to recall and embrace James Baldwin's admonition that to be conscious and black in the United States is to be constantly angry.[20] This is the existential and intellectual terrain that has come to map my philosophically sardonic outlook. Indeed, I remain consumed by a complex of perspectives that will not allow me to forget about a despairing past; yet, it is this anxiety that fires my critique of the meaning and practice of American evil.

Writing in the age of disaster, disbelief, and even trauma, one cannot overlook the reality of U.S. contradictions and dilemmas. The dominant culture preaches to the mass public and to the world the values of freedom, justice, equality, and even the sanctity of human life. Yet, at home and abroad, Americans historically have devalued and inverted those values by employing powerful systems of oppression, injustice, inequality, and mass destruction *since the founding of the American polity*. The cruel dimensions of the

U.S. social order become ever present as white Americans engage in domestic and international terrorism. Urban killer kops murder unarmed black people at will. Importantly, white children increasingly commit mass murders in suburban schools throughout America. In Afghanistan and Iraq, the U.S. government has sought mass destruction and death. The self-satisfaction of safety and security no longer characterize the American social order, whose president and political regime rule by confusion, disinformation, and corruption. Rather, a nihilistic threat to the United States is substantial, and it is deepening.

Twenty-first-century America is engulfed in a rising tide of social pessimism, cultural nihilism, and political cynicism; it is a cancer of the national spirit. Suspicion is mounting; trust is declining. There is a growing sense of despair about the modern culture of progress that the United States is supposed to embody. Mounting proportions of Americans are skeptical about whether the social institutions of progress are viable and beneficial: the (in)justice system, political leadership, bureaucracies, business corporations, public schools, religious organizations, the mass media, and even the family. Popular discontent and protest are becoming more comprehensive, penetrating, and corrosive.[21] These dynamics signify the culture of decay and disarray in a declining American empire. Plagued by an intensification of white supremacy, economic crises, social anarchy, and moral nihilism, American civilization is culturally exhausted and sliding down the slippery slope of self-annihilation. Its racist culture and capitalist contradictions render the nation beyond redemption. This is most evident in the breakdown of a decadent (in)justice system, especially in the law of divorce. Destroying people's lives, the United States has no sense of evil or shame.[22] An awareness of moral chaos and cultural death increasingly haunts the soul of American civilization. When all the current reasons—moral, aesthetic, religious, social, political, and so on—no longer guide the people's lives, how can they sustain life without succumbing to cynical disillusionment?

NOTES

1. Richard Wright, *12 Million Black Voices* (New York: Thunder's Mouth Press, 1988).

2. Gwendolyn M. Hall, *Slavery and African Ethnicities in the Americas* (Chapel Hill: University of North Carolina Press, 2007).

3. Robin Blackburn, *The Making of New World Slavery: From the Baroque to the Modern, 1492–1800* (New York: Verso, 1997); John W. Blassingame, *The Slave Community: Plantation Life in the Ante-Bellum South* (New York: Oxford University Press, 1972); David B. Davis, *Human Bondage: The Rise and Fall of Slavery in the*

New World (New York: Oxford University Press, 2006); Saidiya V. Hartman, *Scenes of Subjection: Terror, Slavery, and Self-Making in Nineteenth-Century America* (New York: Oxford University Press, 1997); Orlando Patterson, *Slavery and Social Death: A Comparative Study* (Cambridge: Harvard University Press, 1982); Kenneth Stampp, *The Peculiar Institution: Slavery in the Ante-Bellum South* (New York: Vintage Books, 1956).

4. For a thought-provoking and fearless examination of the racist oppression of black men in America, see Tommy Curry, *Man-Not: Race, Class, Genre, and the Dilemma of Black Manhood* (Philadelphia: Temple University Press, 2017).

5. Frantz Fanon, *Black Skin, White Masks* (New York: Grove Press, 1967).

6. Ron Eyerman, *Cultural Trauma: Slavery and the Formation of African-American Identity* (New York: Cambridge University Press, 2001); Eyerman, "Cultural Trauma: Slavery and the Formation of African American Identity," In *Cultural Trauma and Collective Identity*. Eds. Jeffrey C. Alexander, Ron Eyerman, Bernard Giesen, Neil Smelser, and Piotr Sztompka (Berkeley: University of California Press, 2004): 60–111.

7. See Orlando Patterson, *Slavery and Social Death: Comparative Study* (Cambridge: Harvard University Press, 1982).

8. See Cathy Caruth, *Unclaimed Experience: Trauma, Narrative, and History* (Baltimore: Johns Hopkins University Press, 1996); Kai Erikson, "Notes on Trauma and Community," In *Trauma: Explorations in Memory*. Ed. Cathy Caruth (Baltimore: Johns Hopkins University Press, 1993): 183–199; Dominick LaCapra, *Writing History, Writing Trauma. Baltimore* (Johns Hopkins Press, 2001); Michael Roth, *Memory, Trauma, and History: Essays on Living with the Past* (New York: Columbia University Press, 2012).

9. George Yancy, Introduction, *The Philosophical I: Personal Reflections on Life in Philosophy* (Lanham: Rowman & Littlefield, 2002): xiii.

10. I discuss the negative literary construction of black women in Floyd W. Hayes III, "Womanizing Richard Wright: Constructing the Black Feminine in *The Outsider*," *Spectrum: A Journal on Black Men* 1 (2012): 47–69. On marginalized black women's encounter with the power of U.S. law and the (in)justice system, see Beth E. Richie, *Arrested Justice: Black Women, Violence, and America's Prison Nation* (New York: New York University Press, 2012).

11. John Rawls is the well-known philosopher who argues that the principle of fairness is the main ingredient in justice. See Rawls, *A Theory of Justice* (Cambridge: Harvard University Press, 1971). For a radical critique of this perspective, see Bob Fine, *Democracy and the Rule of Law: Marx's Critique of Legal Form* (Caldwell: The Blackburn Press, 2002); Raymond Guess, *Philosophy and Real Politics* (Princeton: Princeton University Press, 2008); David Kairys, Ed. *The Politics of Law: A Progressive Critique* (New York: Pantheon Books, 1982); Jeffry H. Reiman, *The Rich Get Richer and the Poor Get Prison: Ideology, Class, and Criminal Justice* (New York: John Wiley & Sons, 1979); Richard Quinney, *Class, State & Crime* (New York: Longman Inc., 1977).

12. The nexus between antiblack racism and the U.S. (il)legal system is well documented. Richard Wright often referred to U.S. law as a "veil of illusion" and as "white

law," which was intended to annihilate black development. See Wright, *12 Million Black Voices* (New York: Thunder's Mouth Press, 1941); Wright, *The Outsider* (New York: Harper & Row Publishers, 1953). See also Issac D. Balbus, *The Dialectics of Legal Repression: Black Rebel and the American Criminal Courts* (New Brunswick: Transaction Books, 1973); W. Haywood Burns, "Race Discrimination: Law and Race in America," in *The Politics of Law: A Progressive Critique.* Ed. David Kairys, (New York: Pantheon Press, 1982): 89–95; Michael Tonry, *Malign Neglect: Race, Crime, and Punishment in America* (New York: Oxford University Press, 1995).

13. See Kimberle Crenshaw, Neil Gotanda, Gary Peller, and Kendall Thomas, Eds. *Critical Race Theory: Key Writings that Formed the Movement* (New York: The New Press, 1995); Richard Delgado, Ed. *Critical Race Theory: The Cutting Edge* (Philadelphia: Temple University Press, 1995).

14. C. Fred Alford, *Trauma and Forgiveness: Consequences and Communities* (New York: Cambridge University Press, 2013): 45.

15. See especially, Wright, *Native Son* (New York: Harper & Brothers Publishers, 1940); Wright, *12 Million Black Voices* (New York: Thunder's Mouth Press, 1941); Wright, *American Hunger* (New York: Harper & Row Publishers, 1944); Wright, *Black Boy* (New York: Harper & Brothers Publishers, 1945); Wright, *The Outsider* (New York: Harper & Row Publishers, 1953); Wright, *White Man, Listen!* (New York: Doubleday & Company, Inc., 1957).

16. Friedrich Nietzsche, *The Will to Power* (New York: Random House, 1967) note 55: 35.

17. Derrick Bell, *Faces at the Bottom of the Well: The Permanence of Racism* (New York: Basic Books, 1992): 198.

18. Ruth Leys, *Trauma: A Genealogy* (Chicago: The University of Chicago Press, 2000): 2.

19. See Floyd W. Hayes III, "The Paradox of the Ethical Criminal in Richard Wright's Novel" *The Outsider. The American Philosophical Association/Newsletter on Philosophy and the Black Experience* 11 (Fall) (2011): 16–22; Hayes, "Hope and Disappointment in Martin Luther King, Jr.'s Political Theology: Eclipse of the Liberal Spirit," in *The Liberatory Thought of Martin Luther King, Jr.: Critical Essays on the Philosopher King.* Ed. Robert Birt (Lanham: Lexington Books, 2012): 299–319. In many ways, I developed a philosophy of personal conduct and philosophical vision that became energized and liberating, as it helped to fortify me against the illusions of modern optimistic consciousness. Most helpful in this project have been Frantz Fanon, *The Wretched of the Earth* (New York: Grove Press, 1965); Richard Wright, *The Outsider* (New York: Harper & Brothers, 1953). Also important are E. M. Cioran, *On the Heights of Despair.* Trans. Ilinca Zarifopol-Johnston (Chicago: The University of Chicago Press, 1992); Joshua F. Dienstag, *Pessimism: Philosophy, Ethic, Spirit* (Princeton: Princeton University Press, 2006).

20. James Baldwin, *The Fire Next Time* (New York: Dell Publishing Co., Inc., 1962).

21. See Jeffrey C. Goldfarb, *The Cynical Society: The Culture of Politics and the Politics of Culture in American Life* (Chicago: The University of Chicago Press, 1991); Donald L. Kanter and Philip H. Mirvis, *The Cynical Americans: Living*

and Working in an Age of Discontent and Disillusion (San Francisco: Jossey-Bass Publishers, 1989); Keith A. Pearson and Diane Morgan, Eds. *Nihilism Now!: Monsters of Energy* (New York: St. Martin's Press, Inc., 2000).

22. Andrew Delbanco, *The Death of Satan: How Americans Have Lost the Sense of Evil* (New York: Farrar, Straus and Giroux, 1995).

BIBLIOGRAPHY

Alford, C. Fred. *Trauma and Forgiveness: Consequences and Communities* (New York: Cambridge University Press, 2013).

Balbus, Issac D. *The Dialectics of Legal Repression: Black Rebel and the American Criminal Courts* (New Brunswick: Transaction Books, 1973).

Baldwin, James. *The Fire Next Time* (New York: Dell Publishing Co., Inc., 1962).

Bell, Derrick. *Faces at the Bottom of the Well: The Permanence of Racism* (New York: Basic Books, 1992).

Blackburn, Robin. *The Making of New World Slavery: From the Baroque to the Modern, 1492–1800* (New York: Verso, 1997).

Blassingame, John W. *The Slave Community: Plantation Life in the Ante-Bellum South* (New York: Oxford University Press, 1972).

Burns, W. Haywood. "Race Discrimination: Law and Race in America," in *The Politics of Law: A Progressive Critique*. Ed. David Kairys (New York: Pantheon Press, 1982): 89–95.

Caruth, Cathy. *Unclaimed Experience: Trauma, Narrative, and History* (Baltimore: Johns Hopkins University Press, 1996).

Cioran, E. M. *On the Heights of Despair*. Trans. Ilinca Zarifopol-Johnston (Chicago: The University of Chicago Press, 1992).

Crenshaw, Kimberle, Neil Gotanda, Gary Peller, and Kendall Thomas, Eds. *Critical Race Theory: Key Writings that Formed the Movement* (New York: The New Press, 1995).

Curry, Tommy J. *Man-Not: Race, Class, Genre, and the Dilemma of Black Manhood* (Philadelphia: Temple University Press, 2017).

Davis, David B. *Human Bondage: The Rise and Fall of Slavery in the New World* (New York: Oxford University Press, 2006).

Delbanco, Andrew. *The Death of Satan: How Americans Have Lost the Sense of Evil* (New York: Farrar, Straus and Giroux, 1995).

Delgado, Richard. (Ed). *Critical Race Theory: The Cutting Edge* (Philadelphia: Temple University Press, 1995).

Dienstag, Joshua F. *Pessimism: Philosophy, Ethic, Spirit* (Princeton: Princeton University Press, 2006).

Erikson, Kai. "Notes on Trauma and Community," In *Trauma: Explorations in Memory*. Ed. Cathy Caruth (Baltimore: Johns Hopkins University Press, 1993).

Eyerman, Ron. *Cultural Trauma: Slavery and the Formation of African-American Identity* (New York: Cambridge University Press, 2001).

Eyerman, Ron. "Cultural Trauma: Slavery and the Formation of African American Identity," In *Cultural Trauma and Collective Identity*. Eds. Jeffrey C. Alexander, Ron Eyerman, Bernard Giesen, Neil Smelser, and Piotr Sztompka (Berkeley: University of California Press, 2004): 60–111.

Fanon, Frantz. *Black Skin, White Masks* (New York: Grove Press, 1967).

Fanon, Frantz. *The Wretched of the Earth* (New York: Grove Press, 1965).

Fine, Bob. *Democracy and the Rule of Law: Marx's Critique of Legal Form* (Caldwell: The Blackburn Press, 2002).

Goldfarb, Jeffrey C. *The Cynical Society: The Culture of Politics and the Politics of Culture in American Life* (Chicago: The University of Chicago Press, 1991).

Geuss, Raymond. *Philosophy and Real Politics* (Princeton: Princeton University Press, 2008).

Hall, Gwendolyn M. *Slavery and African Ethnicities in the Americas* (Chapel Hill: University of North Carolina Press, 2007).

Hartman, Saidiya V. *Scenes of Subjection: Terror, Slavery, and Self-Making in Nineteenth-Century America* (New York: Oxford University Press, 1997).

Hayes, Floyd W., III, "Womanizing Richard Wright: Constructing the Black Feminine in *The Outsider*," *Spectrum: A Journal on Black Men* 1 (2012): 47–69.

Hayes, Floyd W., III, "The Paradox of the Ethical Criminal in Richard Wright's Novel" *The Outsider*. *The American Philosophical Association/Newsletter on Philosophy and the Black Experience* 11 (Fall) (2011): 16–22.

Hayes, Floyd W., III, "Hope and Disappointment in Martin Luther King, Jr.'s Political Theology: Eclipse of the Liberal Spirit," in *The Liberatory Thought of Martin Luther King, Jr.: Critical Essays on the Philosopher King*, ed. Robert Birt (Lanham: Lexington Books, 2012).

Kairys, David. (Ed). *The Politics of Law: A Progressive Critique* (New York: Pantheon Books, 1982).

Kanter Donald L. and Philip H. Mirvis, *The Cynical Americans: Living and Working in an Age of Discontent and Disillusion* (San Francisco: Jossey-Bass Publishers, 1989).

LaCapra, Dominick. *Writing History, Writing Trauma* (Baltimore: Johns Hopkins Press, 2001).

Patterson, Orlando. *Slavery and Social Death: A Comparative Study* (Cambridge: Harvard University Press, 1982).

Leys, Ruth. *Trauma: A Genealogy* (Chicago: The University of Chicago Press, 2000).

Nietzsche, Friedrich. *The Will to Power* (New York: Random House, 1967).

Pearson, Keith A. and Diane Morgan, Eds. *Nihilism Now!: Monsters of Energy* (New York: St. Martin's Press, Inc., 2000).

Quinney, Richard. *Class, State & Crime* (New York: Longman Inc., 1977).

Rawls, John. *A Theory of Justice* (Cambridge: Harvard University Press, 1971).

Reiman, Jeffry H. *The Rich Get Richer and the Poor Get Prison: Ideology, Class, and Criminal Justice* (New York: John Wiley & Sons, 1979).

Richie, Beth E. *Arrested Justice: Black Women, Violence, and America's Prison Nation* (New York: New York University Press, 2012).

Roth, Michael. *Memory, Trauma, and History: Essays on Living with the Past* (New York: Columbia University Press, 2012).
Stampp, Kenneth. *The Peculiar Institution: Slavery in the Ante-Bellum South* (New York: Vintage Books, 1956).
Tonry, Michael. *Malign Neglect: Race, Crime, and Punishment in America* (New York: Oxford University Press, 1995).
Wright, Richard. *12 Million Black Voices* (New York: Thunder's Mouth Press, 1988).
Wright, Richard, *The Outsider* (New York: Harper & Row Publishers, 1953).
Wright, Richard. *Native Son* (New York: Harper & Brothers Publishers, 1940).
Wright, Richard. *American Hunger* (New York: Harper & Row Publishers, 1944).
Wright, Richard. *Black Boy* (New York: Harper & Brothers Publishers, 1945).
Wright, Richard. *White Man, Listen!* (New York: Doubleday & Company, Inc., 1957).
Yancy, George. *The Philosophical I: Personal Reflections on Life in Philosophy* (Lanham: Rowman & Littlefield, 2002).

Chapter 12

Black Subversive Memory and a Black Progressive Leadership as Resources for Black Male Engagement in Prolonged Resistance against White Power Structures

Joseph L. Smith

In 1972, amid the Black Panther Party's struggle against various white power structures comprising the "post-civil-rights" urban color line,[1] Huey P. Newton diagnosed a major obstacle in organizing Black males to engage in sustained and prolonged political struggle to dismantle it, namely, what he called reactionary suicide.[2] In his autobiography *Revolutionary Suicide*, Newton theorized reactionary suicide as a spiritual death in which some Black men were crushed by white, anti-Black oppressive forces: forces that included police brutality and murder of Black individuals, State repression of Black-led urban rebellions, and the social production of urban Black ghettos.[3] As a result of white, anti-Black oppressive forces, the primary feature of reactionary suicide was an internalized disposition of hopelessness in the struggle and resistance against white power structures.[4] Newton concluded that the response of reactionary suicide led some Black men to submit and cease resisting white, anti-Black oppressive forces, and thus, this response condemned them to a living death in various, self-destructive ways.[5] In light of this, one of the questions for Newton was: What are some of the necessary resources for Black men to ward off hopelessness in order to engage in prolonged political struggle despite the crushing forces of white, anti-Black oppression?

With the horrendous murder of George Floyd within the decentered, urban, "black" ghetto in Minneapolis, Minnesota,[6] and the ensuing national social movements to dismantle contemporary forms of white, anti-Black structural violence and oppression, we must once again take up Newton's question.

However, due to the shift of white, anti-Black oppressive forces faced by Black men from 1972 to today, we will turn from Newton's analysis of reactionary suicide, and prescription of revolutionary suicide, to Cornel West.[7] We will selectively turn to West's works *Race Matters*, *Democracy Matters*, and *Keeping Faith*. The scope of our use of West's work is confined to his analysis of *nihilism* and his prescription of a *politics of conversion*.

Given the current social context in which local police departments, Black conservatives, and the lingering anti-Black ethos of President Trump and his administration's demonization, criminalization, and pathologization of urban, Black men as tools to justify State murder against Black men in urban spaces such as George Floyd, and repression of Black-led protests,[8] we must engage criticisms that allege West's conception of nihilism within Black America reproduces white intellectual, anti-Black binary logics linked to discourses on the "culture of poverty" prevalent between 1970s and 2000s.[9] As Union Theological Seminary Social Ethics Professor Gary Dorrien points out, intellectuals such as cultural critic Nick De Genova, political scientist "Floyd W. Hayes III, Black studies scholars Lewis Gordon, and Peniel E. Joseph, and philosophers Charles Mils, and Clevis Headley, concurred that West's critique of Afro-nihilism was hard to distinguish from blame-the-victim conservatism."[10] For our purposes, we will focus on examining the kernel of Nick De Genova's article, "Gangster Rap and Nihilism in Black America: Some Questions on Life and Death." Why? Simply stated, if we can show that West's diagnosis of nihilism functions neither as a discursive production of the pathologization of Black men nor as a support of white power structures, then we can explore West's analysis of and prescription for nihilism as providing conceptual tools for our contemporary struggle against white power structures.

My thesis is that West's analysis of nihilism in Black America and his prescription of a *politics of conversion* provide us with some of the necessary conceptual skills and tools needed for Black men to engage in prolonged political struggle despite the crushing forces of white power structures that are constitutive along with the nihilistic threat. In order to advance this objective, we will pursue the following lines of investigation: (1) explicate West's notion of nihilism in Black America, (2) critically evaluate De Genova's criticism of West, and (3) engage West's notion of a politics of conversion as a useful resource for a Black progressive leadership to engage in and work with Black men who embody the response of nihilism to white, anti-Black forces.

West situates nihilism in Black America within the context of historical and contemporary white, anti-Black power structures that continue to devalue, destroy, oppress, and assault the lives of Black individuals and urban communities. Additionally, West contextualizes nihilism within the social history of white people employing ontological, discursive, physical, economic, and

State violence as tools of white power that function to socially condition Black people to internalize such nihilism in the form of self-contempt, self-hatred, and loss of hope and meaning in the possibility of overcoming oppression.[11] It is within this context that West theorizes nihilism. West states,

> Nihilism is to be understood here not as a philosophic doctrine that there are no rational grounds for legitimate standards or authority; it is, far more, the lived experience of coping with a life of horrifying meaninglessness, hopelessness, and (most important) lovelessness.[12]

According to West, the embodied consequence of nihilism is a devaluation of the self that leads to "a numbing detachment from others and a self-destructive disposition toward the world."[13] Furthermore, West asserts that this response to white power structures lends itself to Black individuals violently destroying themselves and others.[14] Thus, nihilism is a threat to Black existence because the embodiment of the loss of hope, meaning, and love rejects the possibility of hope in meaningful forms of personal and collective struggles that seek to dismantle and possibly overcome white, anti-Black forces. Therefore, West's conception of nihilism indexes a devastating exposure to white, anti-Black power structures (in the forms of institutional, spiritual, and psychic violence).[15] On this score, according to West, nihilism is internalized by Black bodies, which threatens Black existence in that it gets played out in the world as a self-destructive outlook: an outlook that does not support effective and prolonged Black struggle and resistance to dismantle white power structures.[16]

West asserts that nihilism in Black America is not new but rather constitutive of the Black experience in the "discovered" land of North America. In light of this, West makes a strong historical claim that "the major enemy of black survival in America has been and is neither oppression nor exploitation but rather the nihilist threat—that is, loss of hope and absence of meaning."[17] Despite white, anti-Black forces, and the nihilistic threat, West posits that, prior to the 1970s, Black folks have been able to create various cultural structures of meaning for Black individuals and communities to survive, and also, for sustaining Black religious and civic institutions to engage in prolonged Black-led freedom struggles.

Specifically, West is referring to what he calls *subversive memory* that is shaped and empowered by the Black freedom struggle and the Black musical traditions. Both of these sites function as two primary resources. Historically, these two grand traditions provide Black people with nonmarket, cultural structures that function as embodied cultural buffers to ward off the nihilistic threat. These buffers consist of cultural structures such as "embodied values of service and sacrifice, love and care, discipline and excellence," and courageous truth telling (speaking truth to power), that sustained forms of collective action to dismantle white power structures by putting bodies and lives on the line for justice, freedom, and deeper democracy.[18]

However, West believes that since the 1970s, the cultural structures of meaning that have historically sustained Black survival and freedom struggles "against the pulverizing force of anti-blackness"[19] have been on the attack and mitigated by "strong market forces and vicious white supremacist . . . stereotypes that disproportionately shape black perceptions and practice,"[20] and thus, they have weakened the necessary cultural armor of subversive memory which previously provided Black America with the capacity to hold the nihilistic threat at bay, especially within urban, black, working and poor communities. For West, corporate market forces (tied to neoliberal policies) dominate and overwhelmingly influence our most powerful social institutions and culture. Market institutions are guided by a market culture based on gangster mentalities and self-destructive wantonness that are primarily motivated by making profits by "any means necessary" (at the expense of the common good) from a consumer culture (corporate institutions that cultivate consumer bases) that thrives on instant gratification and pleasure.[21] Pleasure is best understood in American culture as "comfort, convenience, and sexual stimulation" that stigmatizes "others as objects for personal pleasure or bodily stimulation."[22] Since profits are the end goal of corporate market institutions, the public is bombarded daily with seductive advertised images that encourage the market way of life over all others, and thereby help to create an environment "ruled by a cutthroat market morality," that undermines nonmarket moralities, such as subversive memory.

West asserts that the Black freedom struggle and the Black musical traditions have been hijacked by oligarchs in the media industry by their profit-driven marketization of white supremacist stereotypes of Black people on the Internet, TV, and radio, especially in peddling visual and linguistic representations of the urban, Black, male, hyper-criminal, and hypersexual, *underclass*.[23] Specifically, West is referring to the visual and linguistic representations that show Black men as "depraved, lawless, and pathological," who reside in the "no-go areas" of urban cites,[24] and who pursue the goals of capitalist market institutions (money, power, and conspicuous consumption) by embodying market culture, that is, a gangster mentality.[25] West links the production and distribution of white supremacist stereotypes of Black men to a direct attack of Black subversive memory. I quote West at length in order to demonstrate more fully this important point:

> The wholesale neoliberal attempt to sabotage and hijack the best of the Black freedom struggle and musical tradition is glaring. Spectacle triumphs over spiritual substance, image over moral imagination, money over political mission,

career over sacrificial calling, profession over visionary vocation, and success over genuine greatness. . . . This ugly assault on the Black musical tradition is a form of neoliberal spiritual warfare, a market-driven attack on the very soul of Black folk. The common message of the neoliberal regimes' politics, culture or soulcraft is this: sell your soul for a mess of pottage (spectacle, image, money, status), then pose and posture as if you are or stand for sacrificial love and genuine freedom.[26]

For West, as major sources of the attack and weakening of subversive memory, market forces and white supremacist stereotypes have had a devastating impact on urban, working and poor communities, especially Black men within such communities.

In the first edition of *Race Matters* (1993), West makes explicit that his analysis of nihilism in urban, working and poor Black communities cannot be reduced to a cultural analysis tied to his conception of market forces and white supremacist stereotypes. Rather, West's conception of market forces and white supremacist stereotypes must be understood in relation to the larger social history of the dynamics of white supremacist practices that have socially produced urban, Black traditional ghettos in the early part of the twentieth century.[27] In light of this, West's exploration of market forces and white supremacist stereotypes have to be understood as pointing to the aftermath of the implosion of traditional ghettos and the emergence of contemporary "black" ghettos as features of (1) housing policies that have realigned urban, Black, ghettos based on race and class; (2) neoliberal policies that have shifted urban labor markets from industrial centers to a post-Fordist economy; (3) the neoconservative backlash of racial justice gains; (4) the State use of law enforcement as the front line to violently contain, detain, and control "criminal," "pathological," Black men; and (5) the neoliberal divestment of public goods and services in Black communities, especially in providing decent housing, child care, health care, and education.[28] According to West, within urban, working and poor Black communities, this has resulted in wealth inequality, utter violence directed at Black men by law enforcement agencies, unemployment, hunger, homelessness, and sickness. In other words, West asserts that any cultural analysis of nihilism must be linked to historical and social analyses that examine the life-denying dynamics of how Black people have been victimized, "though not reduced to this victimization,"[29] by white supremacist power structures.

West asserts that the above-mentioned context has resulted in the social production of unique conditions for the possible triumph of nihilism in urban, Black working and poor communities, especially for Black men. For West, since the 1970s, too many urban, Black working and poor communities have been transformed into "hoods" in which Black urban dwellers are denuded of the necessary cultural resources (including Black-led institutions) for warding off nihilism, and thus, being crushed by white, anti-Black forces.[30] In light of this, some urban, Black men residing in Black working and poor communities internalize and embody market culture and white supremacist stereotypes in the form of gangster character types who seek to acquire "pleasure, property, and power by any means necessary," which include a set of market-driven norms and social practices that result in everyday violence.[31] Thus, West's point is that the cumulative effects of life-denying, white power structures that have resulted in the embodiment of nihilism, for too many urban, Black, men, cannot be overcome by the violent, gangster mentalities and self-destructive wantonness of corporate market-based culture and corporate white supremacist stereotypes. In fact, he claims that the predominance of the market-inspired way of life among urban, Black, men "living in poverty-ridden conditions . . . results in the possible triumph of the nihilist threat in black America."[32] Although West makes explicit the context of his analysis of nihilism, within urban, working and poor communities, some of his statements provide theoretical space for appeals to pathological Blackness.

For example, Genova argues that West's analysis of nihilism reinvents "the familiar pathology inherent in the notion of a 'culture of poverty,'"[33] associated with the discursive production of the urban, Black *underclass* within the human sciences.[34] Genova provides two primary examples to support his claim. First, although he acknowledges West's historical and social analysis, Genova claims that West "reduces the majority of African Americans to a subhuman status"[35] when he claims that nihilism, and not exploitation and oppression, is the greater threat to Black survival and social well-being. Second, although Genova highlights West's analysis of market culture in eroding Black subversive memory, he claims West's analysis of violence in the everyday life of Black men assumes the status of a "result" or "consequence" of a pathological condition within Black culture itself.[36]

While I agree that West's language in the above-mentioned examples leaves the door open for the explanatory force of the pathological, Black *underclass*, and the attending "culture of poverty" in explaining the plight of urban, Black, working and poor communities, Genova mischaracterizes and conveniently reduces West's analysis of nihilism to a framework that supposedly discloses the "deficient" and "defective" cultural traits inherent in Black America. For example, West's claim that contrary "to the superficial claims of conservative behaviorist, these jungles are not primarily the result of pathological behavior"[37] clearly leaves open the possibility of the explanatory force of pathological Blackness. However, the force of West's analysis of nihilism in urban, Black, working and poor communities is to show how white, anti-Black forces, as well as market forces, have eroded Black cultural modes of being that enable individual and collective action for prolonged struggle and resistance against it. In other words, West's emphasis on nihilism, as well as the embodiment of market values by urban, Black men, is to demonstrate how the cumulative effects of white power structures have battered and crushed the identities of Black men. Thus, West's analysis of nihilism neither reinvents pathological Blackness nor supports white power structures, but rather attempts to evoke Black America to lean on cultural resources that may ward off nihilism, and potentially sustain prolonged Black-led freedom struggles to dismantle white power structures.

At this point, we must ask: What is to be done to ward off the nihilist threat in Black America? West calls for new models of collective Black progressive leadership that employ what he calls a politics of conversion in working with Black men within local and community institutions as a vital resource against nihilism. Although West realizes that it is individual Black males who must face nihilism and "turn his soul," this turning must be encouraged and given energy by an embodied caring and loving partnership or community. As West states, "a turning of one's soul . . . is done through one's own affirmation of one's self worth—an affirmation fueled by the concern of others."[38] For this reason, West asserts that a politics of conversion must be centered on a love ethic that has the following features: (1) aims to empower individuals through caring relationships that help create new hopes and shared meaning; (2) seeks to increase self-valuation through cultivating modes of self-love and love of others; (3) links self-love and love of others to social movements of Black-led collective political resistance to white, anti-Black forces; and (4) seeks to cultivate and encourage collective political actions, including transracial coalitions. In other words, West's proposal of a politics of conversion proposes a new model of collective Black progressive leadership which aims to work directly with urban, Black men, within transformative communities, that act to support and nourish the positive fostering of their individual potentialities based on a love ethic.

The idea of transformative communities seeks to replace those social patterns that enable and perpetuate nihilism, as expressed by West, with notions of the undeniable value of the uniqueness and preciousness of each individual Black male within face-to-face communities as well as larger social contexts, and with a hope-based transformative ideal (an end-in-view).[39] There are two principles that are vital for transformative communities for facilitating both urban, Black men and urban Black communities to move through nihilism: growth and reconciliation. First, the principle of growth critically engages the inner and outer dimensions of the lived experiences and life of individuals that attempts to move individuals from a disposition of nihilism toward a hopeful direction, which also demands the cooperation and growth of institutions in helping to further foster the development of Black individuals and communities. Second, a principle of reconciliation that focuses on healing and (re)connecting Black men to their individual selves and others. In this sense, West's proposal of a politics of conversion seeks to fulfill a necessary condition to ward off nihilism, namely, by calling for a collective Black progressive leadership to provide some of the social institutional space to collaborate with urban, Black males for the positive fostering of their individual potentialities that includes self-love, love of others, and political resistance.

Moreover, West proposes that a politics of conversion must be grounded within Black subversive memory, especially to ground self-love, love of others, and political resistance. He proposes a model of Black *subversive memory* based on Toni Morrison's novel, *Beloved*. West describes *Beloved*

> as bringing together the loving yet critical affirmation of black humanity found in the best of black nationalist movements, the perennial hope against hope for trans-racial coalition in progressive movements, and the painful struggle for self-affirming sanity in a history in which the nihilistic treat seems insurmountable.[40]

In other words, West proposes the use of Black subversive memory to support the creation of a Black critical consciousness.

In short, if new models of collective Black progressive leadership are to offer effective personal and social transformative models for urban, Black males, then it is necessary to develop a Black critical consciousness that relies on analytical frameworks and resistance strategies found within the Black freedom struggle and the Black musical traditions. Some of the main functions of a Black critical consciousness are the following: (1) understanding the historical and social development of contemporary white power structures in order to put forth analyses of what justice requires and how white, anti-Black racism functions in our present moment;[41] (2) understanding the historical and social dynamics of the internalized aspects of self-hate and self-contempt linked to nihilism in order to provide and nurture individual Black men to develop skills to clearly give voice to their unique guttural cry and to analyze the sources of their pain; and (3) understanding the successes and failures of past transracial coalitions which serves to guide Black community institutions in their efforts to forge contemporary transracial coalitions for progressive social movements. Thus, West's hopes in a politics of conversion are twofold. First, that this new leadership can generate enough love and care so that shattered individuals internalize this love ethic themselves, and thereby empower Black men to feel their own preciousness. Second, that a new meaning of political struggle can be created out of Black subversive memory that can sustain prolonged political resistance.

In conclusion, West's conception of nihilism in Black America, and prescription of a politics of conversion, offers us some of the necessary tools for a Black progressive leadership to use Black subversive memory as a resource in attempting to cooperatively nurture and support the individual growth of urban, Black men that seeks to stimulate hope, love, and meaning linked with Black-led progressive social movements to dismantle white, anti-Black forces in which the possibility of democratic flourishing replaces alienating misery and life-denying forces. West's analysis and proposal becomes even more urgent in our current context in which white power forces seek to crush Black-led social movements and to dismantle them. As such, it is crucial that we attempt to create the necessary tools for urban, Black men to engage in prolonged political struggle and resistance.

NOTES

1. Here I am making reference to the historical emergence of the forced ghettoization of Black people within urban cities. The larger story of the emergence of urban Black ghettos involves the social history of the first Great Migration from 1916 to 1930 and the second Great Migration from 1940 to 1970, during which it is approximated that 6 million Black Americans left the South as landless peasants to become urbanized and proletarianized in industrial cities in the Northeast, Midwest, and West coast of the United States (Gates). Within this social history, specific white power structures emerged as features of the urban color line which sought to social produce Black men as inferior *others*. Please see the following: (1) St. Clair Drake and Horace Cayton, *Black Metropolis: A Study of Negro Life in a Northern City* (New York: Harcourt, Brace and Company, 1945), 755; and (2) Cf. Henry Louis Gates, "The African-American Migration Story," at http://www.pbs.org/wnet/african-americans-many-rivers-to-cross/history/on-african-american-migrations/.

2. For an introduction into Newton's political philosophy, please see: Huey P. Newton, *To Die for the People: The Writings of Huey P. Newton* (New York: Vintage Books, 1972).

3. See Part Two and Part Three in Huey P. Newton, *Revolutionary Suicide*, Ibooks Edition (New York: Penguin Books, 2009). Joshua Bloom and Waldo E. Martin, Jr., *Black Against Empire: The History and Politics of the Black Panther Party* (Berkeley: University of California Press, 2013), 23–30, 50–57, 82–91.

4. Newton's claim is not that *reactionary suicide* is bereft of all hope in the struggle against white, anti-Black oppressive forces. However, it is only Black individuals and organizations that take up the disposition of *revolutionary suicide*, as exemplified by Newton and the BPP as explained in his autobiography, that takes consistent and sustained action to dismantle white, anti-Black oppressive forces. See "Revolutionary Suicide: The Way of Liberation," and "The Defection of Eldridge and Reactionary Suicide," in Newton, *Revolutionary Suicide*.

5. Ibid.

6. See the Mapping Prejudice project, which has detailed restrictive covenants in Minneapolis as a feature of the urban color line faced by Black men. Please refer to *Mapping Prejudice* at https://www.mappingprejudice.org/ in regards to a

visual geographical mapping of the continuation of the color line of urban space in Minneapolis, Minnesota. Also Kirsten Delegard and Kevin Ehrman-Solberg. "'Playground of the People'? Mapping Racial Covenants in Twentieth-century Minneapolis." *Open Rivers: Rethinking The Mississippi*, no. 6 (2017), http://editions.lib.umn.edu/openrivers/article/mapping-racial-covenants-in-twentieth-century-minneapolis/.

7. The white power structures Newton theorized as contributing to the response of *reactionary suicide*, for Black men, have shifted in three primary ways. First, traditional Black ghettos have shifted from functioning as spatial containers for the majority of Black populations within specific cities to the hyperghettoization of the Black working and lower classes. One of the consequences of this is the disappearance of Black institutions that provided cultural resources for Black individuals and communities to sustain the struggle against white power structures. Second, initiated in the 1980s, the "War on Drugs" was a catalyst for the mass incarceration of Black men. As a result, urban, lower-class, Black men are disproportionately incarcerated. Third, beginning in the 1980s, neoliberal economic policies led to the deregulated market and privatization of public goods within urban cities. This resulted in the bifurcation of urban labor markets in which poverty and joblessness rates increased for urban, Black, male, lower classes. (Wacquant, 44–53, 70–74). For an example of the shift from traditional Black ghettos to hyperghettos, please see: (1) St. Clair Drake and Horace Cayton, *Black Metropolis: A Study of Negro Life in a Northern City* (New York: Harcourt, Brace and Company, 1945); and (2) Loic Wacquant, *Urban Outcasts: A Comparative Sociology of Advanced Marginality* (Malden: Polity Press, 2008). For the sociological profile of the mass incarceration of Black men see: (1) Michelle Alexander, *The New Jim Crow: Mass Incarceration in the Age of Colorblindness* (New York: The New Press, 2010); (2) Bruce Western, *Punishment and Inequality in America* (New York: Russell Sage Foundation, 2006); and (3) Gottschalk, Marie. *Caught: The Prison State and the Lock Down of American Politics* (Princeton: Princeton University Press, 2015). For example of the impact of neoliberal policies in urban cities, please see: David Harvey, *A Brief History of Neoliberalism* (New York: Oxford University Press, 2005).

8. See the following: (1) https://nypost.com/2020/06/02/george-floyd-had-violent-criminal-history-minneapolis-union-chief/; (2) https://www.huffpost.com/entry/trump-minneapolis-thugs-george-floyd_n_5ed0a6cac5b6ebd583bed6be; and (3) https://www.youtube.com/watch?v=JtPfoEvNJ74.

9. For examples of white, male proponents of the culture of poverty, please see: (1) Edward C. Banfield, *The Unheavenly City: The Nature and the Future of Our Urban Crisis* (Boston: Little Brown Publishing, 1970); (2) Charles Murray, *Losing Ground: American Social Policy, 1950–1980* (New York: Basic Books, 1984); (3) James Q. Wilson, *Thinking About Crime* (New York: Basic Books, 1975), and (4) Michael B. Katz, editor, *The "Underclass" Debate: Views from History* (Princeton: Princeton University Press, 1993).

10. Gary Dorrien, *Economy, Difference, Empire: Social Ethics for Social Justice* (New York: Columbia University Press, 2010), 324.

11. See "Race Matters in Twenty-First Century America," and "Nihilism in Black America," in Cornel West, *Race Matters* (Boston, Beacon Press, 2017).

12. Cornel West, *Race Matters* (New York: Vintage Books, 1994), 22.
13. Ibid., 23.
14. Ibid.
15. Calvin L. Warren, "Black Nihilism and the Politics of Hope," *The New Centennial Review* 15, no. 1 (2015), 225.
16. See "Introduction," and "Nihilism in Black America," in *Race Matters* (New York: Vintage Books, 1994).
17. West, *Race Matters* (1994), 23.
18. Ibid., 23. Also see, "Race Matters in Twenty-First Century America," in West, *Race Matters* (Boston, Beacon Press: 2017).
19. Warren, "Black Nihilism and the Politics of Hope," 225.
20. See "Preface 2001: Democracy Matters in Race Matters," in West, *Race Matters*, (2017).
21. See "Preface 2001: Democracy Matters in Race Matters," "Race Matters in Twenty-First Century America," and "Introduction: Race Matters," in West, *Race Matters* (2017).
22. Cornel West, *Race Matters* (New York: Vintage Books, 1994), 27.
23. See "Race Matters in Twenty-First Century America," in *Race Matters* (2017). Also see the following for an historical overview of the pathologization of Black men: (1) George Fredrickson, *The Black Image in the White Mind: The Debate on Afro-American Character and Destiny, 1817–1914* (Hanover: Wesleyan University Press, 1971); and (2) Khalil Gibran Muhammad, *The Condemnation of Blackness: Race, Crime, and the Making of Modern Urban America* (Cambridge: Harvard University Press, 2010). Please see note 8 for examples of the "post-civil-rights" discursive production of the *underclass*.
24. Loic Wacquant, *Urban Outcasts: A Comparative Sociology of Advanced Marginality* (Cambridge: Polity Press, 2008), 29, 70–74.
25. See "The Necessary Engagement With Youth Culture," in Cornel West, *Democracy Matters: Winning the Fight Against Imperialism* (New York: Penguin, 2004).
26. See "Race Matters in Twenty-First Century America," in *Race Matters* (2017).
27. Please see the following for examples of the emergence of urban, Black ghettos: (1) Allan Spear, *Black Chicago: The Making of a Negro Ghetto* (Chicago: The University of Chicago Press, 1967); and (2) Kenneth Kusmer, *A Ghetto Takes Shape: Black Cleveland, 1870–1930* (Urbana: University of Illinois Press, 1978).
28. In West's "Introduction: Race Matters," and "Nihilism in Black America," he provides a brief account of the white, anti-Black structural constraints that function to shape the life chances of Black folks. I have combined his comments in order to comprise this list. See West, *Race Matters* (2017).
29. West, *Race Matters* (1994), 19–21.
30. See "Preface 2001: Democracy Matters in Race Matters," and "Introduction: Race Matters," in West, *Race Matters* (2017).
31. See "Introduction: Race Matters," in West, *Race Matters* (2017).
32. West, *Race Matters* (1994), 27.
33. Nick De Genova, "Gangster Rap and Nihilism in Black America: Some Questions of Life and Death," *Social Text*, no. 43 (1995), 92.

34. See note 21.

35. Genova, "Gangster Rap and Nihilism in Black America: Some Questions of Life and Death," 92.

36. Ibid., 93.

37. West, *Race Matters* (1994), 25.

38. Ibid., 29.

39. Here, I am referring to West's engagement with Malcolm X's transformative guide for Black people. See "Malcolm X and Black Rage," in West, *Race Matters* (1994).

40. West, *Race Matters* (1994), 29–30.

41. Cornel West, *Keeping Faith* (New York: Routledge, 1993), 4.

BIBLIOGRAPHY

Alexander, Michelle. *The New Jim Crow: Mass Incarceration in the Age of Colorblindness*, (New York: The New Press, 2010).

Banfield, Edward C. *The Unheavenly City: The Nature and the Future of Our Urban Crisis*, (Boston: Little Brown Publishing, 1970).

Bloom, Joshua and Waldo E. Martin, Jr. *Black Against Empire: The History and Politics of the Black Panther Party* (Berkeley: University of California Press, 2013).

Delegard, Kirsten and Kevin Ehrman-Solberg. "'Playground of the People'? Mapping Racial Covenants in Twentieth-century Minneapolis." *Open Rivers: Rethinking The Mississippi*, no. 6 (2017), http://editions.lib.umn.edu/openrivers/article/mapping-racial-covenants-in-twentieth-century-minneapolis/.

Dorrien, Gary. *Economy, Difference, Empire: Social Ethics for Social Justice* (New York: Columbia University Press, 2010).

Drake, St. Clair. and Horace Cayton, *Black Metropolis: A Study of Negro Life in a Northern City* (New York: Harcourt, Brace and Company, 1945).

Fredrickson, George. *The Black Image in the White Mind: The Debate on Afro-American Character and Destiny, 1817–1914* (Hanover: Wesleyan University Press, 1971).

Gates, Henry Louis. "The African-American Migration Story," at http://www.pbs.org/wnet/african-americans-many-rivers-to-cross/history/on-african-american-migrations/.

Genova, Nick De. "Gangster Rap and Nihilism in Black America: Some Questions of Life and Death," *Social Text*, no. 43 (1995), 92.

Gottschalk, Marie. *Caught: The Prison State and the Lock Down of American Politics* (Princeton: Princeton University Press, 2015).

Harvey, David. *A Brief History of Neoliberalism* (New York: Oxford University Press, 2005). Michael B. Katz, editor, *The "Underclass" Debate: Views from History* (Princeton: Princeton University Press, 1993).

Kusmer, Kenneth. *A Ghetto Takes Shape: Black Cleveland, 1870–1930* (Urbana: University of Illinois Press, 1978).

Mapping Prejudice at https://www.mappingprejudice.org/.
Muhammad, Khalil Gibran. *The Condemnation of Blackness: Race, Crime, and the Making of Modern Urban America* (Cambridge: Harvard University Press; 2010).
Murray, Charles. *Losing Ground: American Social Policy, 1950–1980* (New York: Basic Books, 1984).
Newton, Huey P. *To Die for the People: The Writings of Huey P. Newton* (New York: Vintage Books, 1972).
Newton, Huey P. *Revolutionary Suicide*, Ibooks Edition (New York: Penguin Books, 2009).
Spear, Allan. *Black Chicago: The Making of a Negro Ghetto* (Chicago: The University of Chicago Press, 1967).
Wacquant, Loic. *Urban Outcasts: A Comparative Sociology of Advanced Marginality* (Malden: Polity Press, 2008).
Warren, Calvin L. "Black Nihilism and the Politics of Hope," *The New Centennial Review* 15, no. 1 (2015): 215–248.
West, Cornel. *Race Matters* (Boston, Beacon Press: 2017).
West, Cornel. *Democracy Matters: Winning the Fight against Imperialism* (New York: Penguin, 2004).
West, Cornel. *Keeping Faith* (New York: Routledge, 1993).
Western, Bruce. *Punishment and Inequality in America* (New York: Russell Sage Foundation, 2006).
Wilson, James Q. *Thinking about Crime* (New York: Basic Books, 1975).

Chapter 13

Alternative Hip Hop Masculinity

On Hip Hop Hypermasculinity, Heteronormativity, and Radical Humanism

Reiland Rabaka

WE NEED A NEW "NIGGERATI" AND MORE ALTERNATIVES TO CONVENTIONALLY CONCEIVED BLACK MASCULINITY: THE HARLEM RENAISSANCE, THE HIP HOP MOVEMENT, MASCULINITY, AND SEXUALITY

As I observed in *Hip Hop's Amnesia*, black feminist and black queer radicals were at the heart of the revolt of the "Niggerati" of the Harlem Renaissance, just as many black feminist and black queer radicals have and continue to contribute to rap music and hip hop culture or, what Jeffrey Ogbar has termed, the "Hip Hop Revolution."[1] To put it plainly, if indeed hip hop constitutes a culture, instead of a group of "largely . . . male and heterosexist cultural icon[s]" or, rather, a sexist and heterosexist cult, then, progressive male and heterosexual hip hoppers must honestly open ourselves to the lives and struggles of female and queer hip hoppers.[2] Once we open ourselves, then it is important to solemnly open others, especially our friends and family members, to the lives and distinct struggles of the women and queer folk of the Hip Hop Movement. It is not, and never will be, enough for male and heterosexual hip hoppers to critique the myriad ways in which racism and capitalism are corroding American citizenship, democracy, and society. Similar to the radicals of the Harlem Renaissance, progressive hip hoppers must be willing to extend and expand what it means to be a hip hopper.

Men do not have a monopoly on what it means to be a hip hopper any more than heterosexuals have a monopoly on love, sex, marriage, or religion. Where the "Niggerati" of the Harlem Renaissance deconstructed and reconstructed the moniker "New Negro" to include women and queer folk, as well as "the low-down folks, the so-called common element," as Langston Hughes roared in his classic "The Negro Artist and the Racial Mountain," *it is time for hip hoppers to radically embrace humanism.*[3] Moreover, it is time for *hip hop radical humanists* to either deconstruct and reconstruct hip hop culture to make it inclusive of hip hop feminists and hip hop queer folk or, and I say this quite solemnly, leave the world of hip hop altogether and create a new, authentically humanist *post-hip hop culture.*[4]

There are many lessons that hip hop radical humanists can learn from the revolt of the "Niggerati" of the Harlem Renaissance, especially Langston Hughes's "The Negro Artist and the Racial Mountain," where he audaciously asserted:

> We younger Negro artists who create now intend to express our individual dark-skinned selves without fear or shame. If white people are pleased we are glad. If they are not, it doesn't matter. We know we are beautiful. And ugly too. The tom-tom cries and the tom-tom laughs. If colored people are pleased we are glad. If they are not, their displeasure doesn't matter either. We build our temples for tomorrow, strong as we know how, and we stand on top of the mountain, free within ourselves.[5]

Faithfully following, and to paraphrase, Hughes, hip hop radical humanists should say, in so many words:

> We [hip hop radical humanists] who create now intend to express our individual [black feminist, black queer, black trans, etc.] selves without fear or shame. If [male hip hoppers] are pleased we are glad. If they are not, it doesn't matter. We know we are beautiful. And ugly too. . . . If [heterosexual hip hoppers] are pleased we are glad. If they are not, their displeasure doesn't matter either. We build our temples for tomorrow, strong as we know how, and we stand on top of the mountain, free within ourselves.

The best of hip hop is about being "free within ourselves" and standing in solidarity with others, especially others whose lives and struggles might be or, in fact, are very different from our own. This is so because "real" hip hop has always been about daringly breaking down barriers and consciously crossing borders.

Radical humanist hip hoppers, both heterosexual and queer, must end hip hop's "don't ask, don't tell" policy. It is time to acknowledge our full *inheritance* from our cultural aesthetic ancestors, especially the radicals of the Harlem Renaissance.[6] How is it that the radicals of the Harlem Renaissance developed an antisexist and anti-heterosexist cultural aesthetic nearly six decades prior to the birth of hip hop, but yet postmillennial hip hop culture remains as misogynistic and queerphobic as the sky is blue and water is wet? This is a serious issue, one that demands that those of us who identify as both hip hoppers *and* radical humanists interrogate immediately. I write all of this consciously bearing in mind that I/we have been socialized in *sanitized or user-friendly sexist and heterosexist settings*: from the black church to black colleges and universities, from the expressions of black entertainers to the awe-inspiring acrobatics of black athletes. But, as I have illustrated in *Hip Hop's Inheritance* and *Hip Hop's Amnesia*, in the midst of every major modern black social and political movement there have been black women and black queer folk, as well as heterosexual radical humanists, who were willing to go against *the hegemony of heteronormativity* and consciously contribute to heterosexual and queer alliances.[7]

BLACKNESS, MALENESS, AND QUEERNESS: PATRIARCHAL QUEERNESS, INTERNALIZED (HETERO)SEXISM, AND THE QUEER HIP HOP MOVEMENT

As it was with the Harlem Renaissance, within the world of the Queer Hip Hop Movement, the artistry and activism of queer men have almost always eclipsed the artistry and activism of queer women.[8] The conception of hip hop radical humanism articulated here, then, does not give the *patriarchal queerness* and *internalized (hetero)sexism* promoted and practiced by many gay male rappers a pass.[9] As with white supremacy and anti-black racism, patriarchy and misogyny are utterly evil, no matter who the culprit is, whether black or white, male or female, heterosexual or queer.[10] In their groundbreaking article, "Sista Outsider: Queer Women of Color and Hip Hop," Eric Pritchard and Maria Bibbs interrogate the patriarchal queerness and internalized (hetero)sexism of many gay male rappers, writing:

> In the advent of the movement called "Homo-Hop," which serves to frame gay hip hop within a term acknowledging the larger LGBT community that is a part of the culture, males benefit from being the center of this "gay rapper" discourse while bisexual and lesbian women of color in the hip hop game remain maligned and subsequently ignored in media coverage and opportunities. In the popular news media, criticisms of homophobic rhetoric, the potential for "gay hip hop" to be a viable genre of hip hop culture, and even the homophobic rhetoric itself are all gendered male. We wish to stress here that this does not mean queer men are not marginalized in the hypermasculine, heteronormative and homophobic discourse of hip hop, however, in order to present the collective and diverse

voices of queer women of color in hip hop, it is necessary to critique the male privilege and sexism existing for queer men as well and how that affects women in the LGBT and hip hop communities.[11]

Bisexual and lesbian nonwhite women are faced with a set of serious problems within the world of hip hop. On the one hand, they must confront the sexism and heterosexism of mainstream hypermasculinist and heteronormative hip hop. On the other hand, they have to contest the patriarchal queerness of many gay male hip hoppers and critique the gender hierarchy within the Queer Hip Hop Movement. It is this double- (or triple-) bind that makes bisexual and lesbian women's relationship with rap music and hip hop culture qualitatively different than any of the other members of the hip hop community. Few dispute rap music's misogyny or hip hop's sexism in general. However, it is a rare (a very rare) Hip Hop studies scholar and/or activist who will break the long-standing silence surrounding hip hop's heterosexism and queerphobia. As a hip hop radical humanist who also happens to be a critical social theorist, I want to utilize my evolving interdisciplinary studies and ongoing emphasis on intersectionality to reach an audience who might not otherwise be aware of, or care for what has come to be called "critical queer theory."[12]

OFFERING AN ALTERNATIVE TO HIP HOP HYPERMASCULINITY AND HETERONORMATIVITY: AN AUTOBIOGRAPHICAL INTERLUDE

Truth be told, I have gone back and forth over whether I should raise the issue of the hegemony of heteronormativity in hip hop. I kept telling myself that there are so many other well-established Hip Hop studies scholars who are certainly much more qualified than I to speak on the hegemony of heteronormativity in hip hop. But, as I surveyed the postmillennial hip hop scene I became increasingly aware of the excruciating pain and suffering that many queer hip hoppers, many of whom are close colleagues and comrades of mine, have experienced during the more than four decades of the Hip Hop Movement's existence. It is not simply the silence surrounding queerness within the world of hip hop but, even more, the near erasure and/or invisibility of queer and trans folk as a result of the hegemony of heteronormativity within U.S. society as a whole.

Recently one of my queer colleagues told me that she could not wait for me to complete this chapter on blackness, maleness, queerness, and hip hop. I earnestly asked her why. Next she said something that has stuck with me since then. She patiently explained to me that I will be able to reach "straight folk" (i.e., heterosexuals) in ways that most queer and trans folk cannot. She, of course, was referring to me reaching black "straight folk" and the ways in which black queer and trans folk are silenced and, frequently, physically, psychologically, and verbally violated (e.g., Sakia Gunn, Rashawn Brazell, Duanna Johnson, Roger English, Roberto Duncanson, Queasha D. Hardy, Monika Diamond, Nina Pop, Helle Jae O'Regan, Dominique "Rem'mie" Fells, Riah Milton, Merci Mack, Shaki Peters, Bree Black, etc.) in the black community and wider world. Naïvely I responded by telling her that I know many black "straight folk" who love (or, at the least, greatly appreciate) Langston Hughes, Claude McKay, James Baldwin, Audre Lorde, Essex Hemphill, Barbara Smith, Tracy Chapman, Meshell Ndegeocello, Frank Ocean, and Big Freedia. Then, she solemnly checked me with impunity. She said:

> Listen, Rabaka, you ain't hearing me. I ain't never heard no straight black person talk about how Baldwin's gayness factored into his books and speeches, or how Audre Lorde's lesbianism is linked to her radical political activism. Most black people leave Langston Hughes's queerness "in the closet." They privilege black queer folk's blackness over their queerness.

I sat there silent for a moment, staring into the distance, thinking things over. She was on point. She was right and, not that she needed to hear it from me, I humbly told her so. Her weighted words helped me to think about how the various identities we either reject or embrace influence our ability to appreciate aspects of others' identities, and develop deep sensitivities to their distinct identity formation processes and ongoing identity politics.

Bisexual, lesbian, and otherwise queer nonwhite women in the world of hip hop are regularly asked to choose between being queer folk or hip hoppers, as well as being queer folk or members of their specific racial and cultural groups. The work of hip hop lesbian feminists has documented how gay men often play prominent roles in coercing bisexual, lesbian, and otherwise queer women to choose between their queer identities and their identities as hip hoppers. In other words, this is what has been termed "gay-on-gay violence" (also known as "queer-on-queer violence").[13] Clearly, then, a gay man's sexual orientation does not automatically preclude him from practicing patriarchy any more than a woman's gender somehow automatically precludes her from perpetuating patriarchy. For the record: Nonwhites can, and often do, internalize white supremacy and racism. Women can, and frequently have, internalized patriarchy and misogyny. And, queer folk can, and historically have, internalized heterosexism and homophobia. This is precisely why anti-racism, in and of itself, solves only part of the problem; feminism, in and of itself, solves only part of the problem; and, anti-heterosexism, in and of itself, solves only part of the problem. Without emphasizing that racism, classism, sexism, and heterosexism are all extremely important interlocking systems of exploitation, oppression, and violence that must be collectively combated, then all we are left with are drive-by, hit or miss movements meandering from one pressing issue to the next with no concrete or coherent radical humanist and authentically "universal" end-goal.[14]

THE HIP HOP MOVEMENT: MOVING AWAY FROM HIP HOP HYPERMASCULINITY AND HETERONORMATIVITY TOWARD HIP HOP RADICAL HUMANISM, ANTI-RACISM, ANTI-SEXISM, ANTI-HETEROSEXISM, AND ANTI-CAPITALISM

The Queer Hip Hop Movement gives us an almost ideal opportunity to explore the reasons why anti-racism, anti-classism, anti-sexism, and anti-heterosexism divorced from authentic radical humanism often yield little more than empty rhetoric and the continued social segregation of so-called progressive communities. How truly progressive are male antiracists if they, whether consciously or unconsciously, dehumanize women? How truly progressive are white feminists if they, whether consciously or unconsciously, dehumanize nonwhite people, especially nonwhite women? How truly progressive are anti-heterosexist gay male activists if they, whether consciously or unconsciously, dehumanize and marginalize bisexual and lesbian women? What about the ways in which white queer folk, whether consciously or unconsciously, dehumanize and marginalize nonwhite queer folks' lives and struggles?[15]

In her eye-opening essay, "'I Used to be Scared of the Dick': Queer Women of Color and Hip Hop Masculinity," Andreana Clay critically discusses white and male supremacy in the ways in which queerness is depicted in the United States and some of the reasons that nonwhite (especially black and brown) bisexual and lesbian women continue to identify with hip hop culture. She rhetorically and revealingly asks, "[s]o, who and why do queer women identify with this culture that is known for its homophobia and sexism? And, how do we continue to maintain queer feminist ideology and practice in this groove?"[16] First, she asserts that often when black queerness is discussed the conversation almost immediately turns to the "on the down low" phenomenon, which centers bisexual black men's closeted sex lives. Consequently, bisexual and gay black men's "promiscuity" and "unhealthy sexual practices" dominate the discourse on black queerness. Second, she writes, even though the larger gay community has pushed a national debate about same-sex marriage into the public eye . . . [m]ost of the poster children for the same-sex marriage debate are white: gay neighborhoods or scenes, like the Castro district in San Francisco, is predominantly white, male, and middle-class. In both of these contexts, queer black desire and identity has been erased, especially for women.[17]

Clay continues,

Because we are absent from a discussion of black same-sex sex on the one hand and one of gay and lesbian identity on the other, it's no surprise that young, queer women of color find reprieve anywhere we can—including the often sexist, homophobic, and hypermasculine genre of hip hop.[18]

Clay claims that "queer engagement with hip hop masculinity is mad full of complexity and contradiction."[19] This is so because, as Todd Boyd argued in *Am I Black Enough for You?: Popular Culture from the 'Hood and Beyond*, many black men have embraced the "nigga" identity, and "the nigga is not interested with anything that has to do with the mainstream, though his cultural products are clearly an integral part of mainstream popular culture."[20] In a sense, the "nigga" is mainstream America's unacknowledged alter ego, its "bastard" brother, sister, or—from mainstream America's paternalistic perspective—its "bastard" child. Therefore, ironically, "[t]he nigga rejects the mainstream even though he has already been absorbed by it."[21]

In U.S. culture and society, African American masculinity, as with African American sexuality, is situated in a sociocultural context that is simultaneously within and without, inside and outside of mainstream heteronormativity, because black men and their blackness is always being psychopathically and schizophrenically rejected *and* absorbed by mainstream American heteronormativity.[22] Hip hop masculinity has been expressed through the guises of the nigga, the playa, the hustla, the thug, the prisoner, and the ex-con, among others. Each of these expressions of hip hop masculinity has been much maligned by mainstream America. Therefore, one can comprehend why the bisexual and lesbian "sista outsiders" of the Hip Hop Movement could come to selectively embrace certain elements of rap music and hip hop culture—because rap music and hip hop culture, despite its mainstream absorption, continues to provide a, however "underground," polyvocal voice for the voiceless, a culture for the supposedly cultureless, and a sense of belonging for those who have been told in no uncertain terms that they do not belong, especially in mainstream America.[23]

Similar to many of the queer folk of the Harlem Renaissance, the queer folk of the Hip Hop Movement have long demonstrated their ability to appreciate and contribute to "mainstream" hip hop culture. However, similar to many of their heterosexist antecedents, very few of the heterosexuals of the Hip Hop Movement have challenged the hegemony of hip hop's heteronormativity. As with the New Negro Movement at the turn of the twentieth century, either hip hop culture will consciously extend and expand itself to include the lives and struggles of queer folk, completely freeing itself from heteronormativity, or else queer and radical humanist heterosexual hip hoppers are justified in leaving the world of hip hop and creating *a new, radically humanist post-hip hop culture that is decidedly antiracist, anti-sexist, anti-heterosexist, and anticapitalist.*

Neither queer folk nor heterosexual women should have to tolerate hip hop's sexism and heterosexism one minute longer. It is time for hip hop to clean its house. Since black men, straight and gay, are consistently at the center of hip hop discourse (including the Queer Hip Hop Movement), we have a special responsibility to combat hip hop hypermasculinity and heteronormativity. As many of the old church folk say, quoting Luke 12:48: "For unto whomsoever much is given, of him shall be much required: and to whom men have committed much, of him they will ask the more." Hip hop womenfolk and queer folk are justified in asking more of hip hop menfolk. I end here with the same words with which I began, by stating on behalf of the Hip Hop Movement, in the hallowed words of Langston Hughes: "We know we are beautiful. And ugly too."

NOTES

1. Reiland Rabaka, *Hip Hop's Amnesia: From Blues and the Black Women's Club Movement to Rap and the Hip Hop Movement* (Lanham: Rowman & Littlefield, 2012), 167–230; Jeffrey Ogbar, *The Hip Hop Revolution: The Culture and Politics of Rap* (Lawrence: University of Kansas Press, 2007). In *When Harlem Was in Vogue* (New York: Oxford University Press, 1989), David Levering Lewis discussed the growing disdain that younger New Negroes developed in relation to the older New Negro civil rights establishment:

> "Wallie" Thurman had become increasingly distressed by party-line art. Temporarily replacing [George] Schuyler in 1926 as editor of *The Messenger*, he lashed out repeatedly against the Victorian aesthetics of civil rights grandees—those whom he and novelist Zora Hurston later ridiculed as the "Niggerati." Before the end of the year, he decided to recruit younger artists and launch a magazine [i.e., *Fire!!!*] devoted to art for the artist's sake—and for the sake of the folk. His rent-free place on 136th Street—the infamous "267 House" . . . was the cradle of revolt against establishment arts. Thurman and Hurston also mocked themselves by calling 267 House "Niggerati Manor," and all the younger artists called Thurman their "leader"—the fullest embodiment of outrageous, amoral independence among them. Thurman never doubted that, freed from the prim guidance

of the leading civil rights organizations, the artists would recognize the need "for a truly Negroid note" and would go to the proletariat rather than to the bourgeoisie for characters and material (193).

As can be easily detected, the intentionally outrageous and ironic term "Niggerati" is a *portmanteau* of "nigger" and "literati" meant to mock the black bourgeois pretentions and "Victorian aesthetics of [New Negro] civil rights grandees" and their mealy mouthed minions. Although the "Niggerati" neologism took form as a rebuke of the Victorianism, conservatism, bourgeoisism, and unmitigated elitism of the New Negro civil rights establishment, observe how—similar to the artists and activists of both the Black Arts Movement and the Hip Hop Movement—a controversial new name and movement moniker was eventually embraced by the young radicals of the Harlem Renaissance. As the unrepentant "Niggerati" of the Harlem Renaissance, Hurston, Thurman, Langston Hughes, Helene Johnson, Richard Bruce Nugent, Gwendolyn Bennett, Jonathan Davis, and Aaron Douglass, among others, sought not only civil rights and social justice, but also democratic socialist and sexual revolution. For further discussion of the "Niggerati" of the Harlem Renaissance, and for the most noteworthy works that informed my analysis here, see Henry Louis Gates and Gene Andrew Jarrett (Eds.), *The New Negro: Readings in Race, Representation, and African American Culture, 1892–1938* (Princeton: Princeton University Press, 2007); Zora Neale Hurston, *Dust Tracks on a Road: An Autobiography* (Philadelphia: J.B. Lippincott, 1942); Zora Neale Hurston, *I Love Myself When I Am Laughing . . . And Then When I Am Looking Mean and Impressive: A Zora Neale Hurston Reader*, edited by Alice Walker (Old Westbury, NY: Feminist Press, 1979); Carole Marks and Diana Edkins (Eds.), *Power of Pride: The Style-Makers and Rule-Breakers of the Harlem Renaissance* (New York: Crown Publishers, 1999); and Wallace Thurman, *The Collected Writing of Wallace Thurman: A Harlem Renaissance Reader*, edited by Amritjit Singh and Daniel M. Scott III (New Brunswick: Rutgers University Press, 2003).

2. Jeffrey C. Stewart, "The New Negro as Citizen." In *The Cambridge Companion to the Harlem Renaissance*, edited by George Hutchinson (Cambridge: Cambridge University Press), 19.

3. Langston Hughes, "The Negro Artist and the Racial Mountain." In *Modern Black Nationalism: From Marcus Garvey to Louis Farrakhan*, edited by William L. Van Deburg (New York: New York University Press, 1997), 53.

4. For further discussion of my conception of "radical humanism" (as well as "revolutionary humanism"), which has been indelibly influenced by the insurgent intellectual and radical political legacies of W. E. B. Du Bois, Frantz Fanon, Amilcar Cabral, Langston Hughes, Audre Lorde, James Baldwin, Angela Davis, bell hooks, and Cornel West, among others, see Reiland Rabaka, *Du Bois's Dialectics: Black Radical Politics and the Reconstruction of Critical Social Theory* (Lanham: Rowman & Littlefield, 2008); Reiland Rabaka, *Africana Critical Theory: Reconstructing the Black Radical Tradition, from W.E.B. Du Bois and C.L.R. James to Frantz Fanon and Amilcar Cabral* (Lanham: Rowman & Littlefield, 2009); Reiland Rabaka, *Against Epistemic Apartheid: W.E.B. Du Bois and the Disciplinary Decadence of Sociology* (Lanham: Rowman & Littlefield, 2010); Reiland Rabaka, *Forms of Fanonism: Frantz*

Fanon's Critical Theory and the Dialectics of Decolonization (Lanham: Rowman & Littlefield, 2010); Reiland Rabaka, *Concepts of Cabralism: Amilcar Cabral and Africana Critical Theory* (Lanham: Rowman & Littlefield, 2014); Reiland Rabaka, *The Negritude Movement: W.E.B. Du Bois, Leon Damas, Aime Cesaire, Leopold Senghor, Frantz Fanon, and the Evolution of an Insurgent Idea* (Lanham: Rowman & Littlefield Publishers, 2015).

5. Hughes, "The Negro Artist and the Racial Mountain," 56. For more detailed discussion of Langston Hughes's life and legacy, see Arnold Rampersad, *The Life of Langston Hughes: I, Too, Sing America, 1902–1941, vol. 1* (2nd ed.) (New York: Oxford University Press, 2002); and Arnold Rampersad, *The Life of Langston Hughes: I Dream a World, 1941–1967, Vol. 2* (2nd ed) (New York: Oxford University Press, 2002).

6. For further discussion of "hip hop's inheritance" from previous social, political, cultural, and artistic movements, especially black popular movements and black popular musics, see Reiland Rabaka, *Hip Hop's Inheritance: From the Harlem Renaissance to the Hip Hop Feminist Movement* (Lanham: Rowman & Littlefield, 2011).

7. For further discussion of heterosexual and queer alliances in black America, see Eric Brandt (Ed.), *Dangerous Liaisons: Blacks & Gays and the Struggle for Equality* (New York: New Press, 1999); Charlene A. Carruthers, *Unapologetic: A Black, Queer, and Feminist Mandate for Radical Movements* (Boston: Beacon Press, 2018); E. Patrick Johnson and Mae G. Henderson, (Eds.), *Black Queer Studies: A Critical Anthology* (Durham: Duke University Press, 2005); Melanie Judge, *Blackwashing Homophobia: Violence and the Politics of Sexuality, Gender, and Race* (London: Routledge, 2017); James T. Sears and Walter L. Williams (Eds.), *Overcoming Heterosexism and Homophobia: Strategies That Work* (New York: Columbia University Press, 1997).

8. For further discussion of the Queer Hip Hop Movement, see Xin Ling Li, *Black Masculinity and Hip Hop Music: Black Gay Men Who Rap* (New York: Palgrave Macmillan, 2018); Shanté Smalls, "Queer Hip Hop: A Brief Historiography," in Fred Everett Maus and Sheila Whiteley (Eds.), *The Oxford Handbook of Music and Queerness* (New York: Oxford University Press, 2018) DOI: 10.1093/oxfordhb/9780199793525.013.103; D. Mark Wilson, "Post-Pomo Hip Hop Homos: Hip Hop Art, Gay Rappers, and Social Change" *Social Justice* 34, no. 1 (2007), 117–140.

9. For further discussion of *patriarchal homosexuality* and *internalized (hetero) sexism* among queer folk, and queer hip hoppers in specific, see Judith Halberstam, "Mack-Daddy, Superfly, Rapper: Gender, Race, and Masculinity in the Drag King Scene," *Social Text* 52/53 (1997), 104–131; Judith Halberstam, *Female Masculinity* (Durham: Duke University Press, 1998); Judith Halberstam, "Queer Voices and Musical Genders," In *Oh Boy!: Masculinities and Popular Music*, edited by Freya Jarman-Ivens (New York: Routledge, 2007), 183–196; Thomas Piontek, *Queering Gay and Lesbian Studies* (Urbana: University of Illinois Press, 2006); and Tamsin Wilton, *Lesbian Studies: Setting an Agenda* (New York: Routledge, 1995).

10. Roderick A. Ferguson, *Aberrations in Black: Toward a Queer of Color Critique* (Minneapolis: University of Minnesota, 2004); Kathryn B. Stockton, *Beautiful*

Bottom, Beautiful Shame: Where "Black" Meets "Queer" (Durham: Duke University Press, 2006); and Mason B. Stokes, *Color of Sex: Whiteness, Heterosexuality, and the Fictions of White Supremacy* (Durham: Duke University Press, 2001).

11. Eric Pritchard and Maria Bibbs, "Sista Outsider: Queer Women of Color and Hip Hop," In *Home Girls Make Some Noise!: The Hip Hop Feminism Anthology*, edited by Gwendolyn D. Pough, Elaine Richardson, Aisha Durham, and Rachel Raimist (Mira Loma, CA: Parker Publishing, 2007), 22. My analysis throughout this section has greatly benefitted from systemic readings of several noteworthy works in Lesbian, Gay, Bisexual, Transgender, and Queer Studies, for example: Diane Richardson and Steven Seidman (Eds.), *The Handbook of Lesbian and Gay Studies* (Thousand Oaks, CA: Sage, 2002); Donald E. Hall and Annamarie Jagose (Eds.), *The Routledge Queer Studies Reader* (New York: Routledge, 2013); Robert J. Corber and Stephen Valocchi (Eds.), *Queer Studies: An Interdisciplinary Reader* (Malden: Wiley-Blackwell, 2003); George E. Haggerty and Molly McGarry (Eds.), *A Companion to Lesbian, Gay, Bisexual, Transgender, and Queer Studies* (Malden: Blackwell, 2007); and Noreen Giffney and Michael O'Rourke (Eds.), *The Ashgate Research Companion to Queer Theory* (Farnham, Surrey, UK: Ashgate, 2009).

12. The discourse on "critical queer theory" or "queer critical theory" has been developing since the mid-1990s, and some of the earliest articulations can be found in Steven Seidman, "Deconstructing Queer Theory, or the Under-Theorization of the Social and the Ethical," in Linda J. Nicholson and Steven Seidman (Eds.), *Social Postmodernism: Beyond Identity Politics* (Cambridge: Cambridge University Press, 1995); Steven Seidman (Ed.), *Queer Theory/Sociology* (Cambridge: Blackwell, 1996); and Steven Seidman, *Difference Troubles: Queering Social Theory and Sexual Politics* (Cambridge: Cambridge University Press, 1997). Major postmillennial contributions to critical queer theory include: Kevin Floyd, *Reification of Desire: Toward a Queer Marxism* (Minneapolis: University of Minnesota Press, 2009); Michael Hames-Garcia, "Can Queer Theory Be Critical Theory?," in William S. Wilkerson and Jeffrey Paris (Eds.), *New Critical Theory: Essays on Liberation* (Lanham, MD: Rowman & Littlefield, 2001), 201–222; Ken Plummer, "Living with the Tensions: Critical Humanism and Queer Theory," in Norman K. Denzin and Yvonna S. Lincoln (Eds.), *The Sage Handbook of Qualitative Research* (Thousand Oaks, CA: Sage, 2005), 357–375; and Steven Seidman, Nancy Fischer and Chet Meeks (Eds.), *Handbook of New Sexuality Studies* (New York: Routledge, 2006). Critical queer theory constitutes theorizing about queerness in the interest of justice and fairness for queer and trans folk. It accents and criticizes queerphobia and heterosexism in social, political, and cultural thought, practices, and institutions.

13. For further discussion on "gay-on-gay violence" (also known as "queer-on-queer violence"), see John Dececco, Patrick Letellier, and David Island, *Men Who Beat the Men Who Love Them: Battered Gay Men and Domestic Violence* (New York: Haworth Press, 1991); Claire M. Renzetti, *Violent Betrayal: Partner Abuse in Lesbian Relationships* (Newbury Park, CA: Sage, 1992); Claire M. Renzetti and Charles H. Miley (Eds.), *Violence in Gay and Lesbian Domestic Partnerships* (New York: Harrington Park Press, 1996); and Sandra E. Lundy and Beth Leventhal, *Same-Sex Domestic Violence: Strategies for Change* (Thousand Oaks, CA: Sage, 1999).

14. Gregory M. Herek (Ed.), *Stigma and Sexual Orientation: Understanding Prejudice Against Lesbians, Gay Men, and Bisexuals* (Thousand Oaks: Sage, 1998); Patricia B. Jung and Ralph F. Smith, *Heterosexism: An Ethical Challenge* (Albany: State University of New York, 1993); James T. Sears and Walter L. Williams (Eds.), *Overcoming Heterosexism and Homophobia: Strategies That Work* (New York: Columbia University Press, 1997); and Samantha Wehbi (Ed.), *Community Organizing Against Homophobia and Heterosexism: The World Through Rainbow-Colored Glasses* (New York: Harrington Park Press, 2004).

15. Eric Brandt (Ed.), *Dangerous Liaisons: Blacks & Gays and the Struggle for Equality* (New York: New Press, 1999); E. Patrick Johnson and Mae G. Henderson, (Eds.), *Black Queer Studies: A Critical Anthology* (Durham: Duke University Press, 2005); Emmanuel S. Nelson (Ed.), *Critical Essays: Gay and Lesbian Writers of Color* (London: Haworth Press, 1993); Siobhan B. Somerville, *Queering the Color-Line: Race and the Invention of Homosexuality in American Culture* (Durham: Duke University Press, 2000); Kathryn B. Stockton, *Beautiful Bottom, Beautiful Shame: Where "Black" Meets "Queer"* (Durham: Duke University Press, 2006); and Mason B. Stokes, *Color of Sex: Whiteness, Heterosexuality, and the Fictions of White Supremacy* (Durham: Duke University Press, 2001).

16. Adreana Clay, "'I Used to be Scared of the Dick': Queer Women of Color and Hip Hop Masculinity," in *Home Girls Make Some Noise!: The Hip Hop Feminism Anthology*, eds. Gwendolyn D. Pough, Elaine Richardson, Aisha Durham, and Rachel Raimist (Mira Loma, CA: Parker Publishing, 2007), 151. See also Adreana Clay, "Like an Old Soul Record: Black Feminism, Queer Sexuality, and the Hip Hop Generation," *Meridians: Feminism, Face, Transnationalism* 8, no. 1 (2007), 53–73; Adreana Clay, *The Hip Hop Generation Fights Back!: Youth, Activism, and Post-Civil Rights Politics* (New York: New York University Press, 2012).

17. Adreana Clay, "'I Used to be Scared of the Dick'," 152–153.

18. Ibid., 153.

19. Ibid., 160.

20. Todd Boyd, *Am I Black Enough for You?: Popular Culture from the 'Hood and Beyond* (Indianapolis: Indiana University Press, 1997), 33.

21. Todd Boyd, *Am I Black Enough for You?*, 33. See also R. A. T. Judy, "On the Question of Nigga Authenticity," *boundary 2* 21 no. 3 (1994), 211–230; Robin D.G. Kelley, *Yo' Mama's Disfunktional!: Fighting the Culture Wars in Urban America* (Boston: Beacon, 1997); Eithne Quinn, *Nuthin' But A "G" Thang: The Culture and Commerce of Gangsta Rap* (New York: Columbia University Press, 2005); and Vershawn A. Young, *Your Average Nigga: Performing Race, Literacy, and Masculinity* (Detroit: Wayne State University Press, 2007).

22. Devon W. Carbado (Ed.), *Black Men on Race, Gender, and Sexuality: A Critical Reader* (New York: New York University Press, 1999); Darlene Clark Hine and Earnestine Jenkins (Eds.), *A Question of Manhood: A Reader in U.S. Black Men's History and Masculinity, Vol. 1* (Bloomington: Indiana University Press, 1999); Darlene Clark Hine and Earnestine Jenkins (Eds.), *A Question of Manhood: A Reader in U.S. Black Men's History and Masculinity, Vol. 2* (Bloomington: Indiana University Press, 2001); Rudolph P. Byrd and Beverly Guy-Sheftall (Eds.), *Traps:*

African American Men on Gender and Sexuality (Indianapolis: Indiana University Press, 2001); Patricia Hill Collins, *Black Sexual Politics: African Americans, Gender, and the New Racism* (New York: Routledge, 2005); Athena D. Mutua (Ed.), *Progressive Black Masculinities* (New York: Routledge, 2006); and Anthony J. Lemelle, *Black Masculinity and Sexual Politics* (New York: Routledge, 2010).

23. For further discussion of rap music and the Hip Hop Movement as a "polyvocal voice for the voiceless, a culture for the supposedly cultureless, and a sense of belonging for those who have been told in no uncertain terms that they do not belong, especially in mainstream America," see Reiland Rabaka, *The Hip Hop Movement: From R&B and the Civil Rights Movement to Rap and the Hip Hop Generation* (Lanham: Rowman & Littlefield, 2013).

BIBLIOGRAPHY

Boyd, Todd. *Am I Black Enough for You?: Popular Culture from the 'Hood and Beyond* (Indianapolis: Indiana University Press, 1997).

Brandt, Eric. (Ed.), *Dangerous Liaisons: Blacks & Gays and the Struggle for Equality* (New York: New Press, 1999).

Byrd, Rudolph P. and Beverly Guy-Sheftall (Eds.), *Traps: African American Men on Gender and Sexuality* (Indianapolis: Indiana University Press, 2001).

Carbado, Devon W. (Ed.), *Black Men on Race, Gender, and Sexuality: A Critical Reader* (New York: New York University Press, 1999).

Carruthers, Charlene A. *Unapologetic: A Black, Queer, and Feminist Mandate for Radical Movements* (Boston: Beacon Press, 2018).

Clay, Adreana. "'I Used to be Scared of the Dick': Queer Women of Color and Hip Hop Masculinity," in *Home Girls Make Some Noise!: The Hip Hop Feminism Anthology*, eds. Gwendolyn D. Pough, Elaine Richardson, Aisha Durham, and Rachel Raimist (Mira Loma, CA: Parker Publishing, 2007).

Clay, Adreana. "Like an Old Soul Record: Black Feminism, Queer Sexuality, and the Hip Hop Generation," *Meridians: Feminism, Face, Transnationalism*, 8(1), (2007): 53–73.

Clay, Adreana. *The Hip Hop Generation Fights Back!: Youth, Activism, and Post-Civil Rights Politics* (New York: New York University Press, 2012).

Collins, Patricia Hill. *Black Sexual Politics: African Americans, Gender, and the New Racism* (New York: Routledge, 2005).

Corber, Robert J. and Stephen Valocchi (Eds.), *Queer Studies: An Interdisciplinary Reader* (Malden: Wiley-Blackwell, 2003).

Dececco, John, Patrick Letellier, and David Island, *Men Who Beat the Men Who Love Them: Battered Gay Men and Domestic Violence* (New York: Haworth Press, 1991).

Ferguson, Roderick A. *Aberrations in Black: Toward a Queer of Color Critique* (Minneapolis: University of Minnesota, 2004).

Floyd, Kevin. *Reification of Desire: Toward a Queer Marxism* (Minneapolis: University of Minnesota Press, 2009).

Gates, Henry Louis and Gene Andrew Jarrett (Eds.), *The New Negro: Readings in Race, Representation, and African American Culture, 1892–1938* (Princeton: Princeton University Press, 2007).

Giffney, Noreen and Michael O'Rourke (Eds.), *The Ashgate Research Companion to Queer Theory* (Farnham, Surrey, UK: Ashgate, 2009).

Haggerty, George E. and Molly McGarry (Eds.), *A Companion to Lesbian, Gay, Bisexual, Transgender, and Queer Studies* (Malden: Blackwell, 2007).

Halberstam, Judith. "Mack-Daddy, Superfly, Rapper: Gender, Race, and Masculinity in the Drag King Scene." *Social Text* 52/53 (1997): 104–131.

Halberstam, Judith. *Female Masculinity* (Durham: Duke University Press, 1998).

Halberstam, Judith. "Queer Voices and Musical Genders," in *Oh Boy!: Masculinities and Popular Music*, ed. Freya Jarman-Ivens (New York: Routledge, 2007): 183–196.

Hall, Donald E. and Annamarie Jagose (Eds.), *The Routledge Queer Studies Reader* (New York: Routledge, 2013).

Hames-Garcia, Michael. "Can Queer Theory Be Critical Theory?," in *New Critical Theory: Essays on Liberation*, eds. William S. Wilkerson and Jeffrey Paris (Lanham, MD: Rowman & Littlefield, 2001): 201–222.

Herek, Gregory M. (Ed.), *Stigma and Sexual Orientation: Understanding Prejudice against Lesbians, Gay Men, and Bisexuals* (Thousand Oaks: Sage, 1998).

Hine, Darlene Clark and Earnestine Jenkins (Eds.), *A Question of Manhood: A Reader in U.S. Black Men's History and Masculinity, Vol. 1* (Bloomington: Indiana University Press, 1999).

Hine, Darlene Clark and Earnestine Jenkins (Eds.), *A Question of Manhood: A Reader in U.S. Black Men's History and Masculinity, Vol. 2* (Bloomington: Indiana University Press, 2001).

Hughes, Langston. "The Negro Artist and the Racial Mountain," in *Modern Black Nationalism: From Marcus Garvey to Louis Farrakhan*, ed. William L. Van Deburg (New York: New York University Press, 1997).

Hurston, Zora Neale. *Dust Tracks on a Road: An Autobiography* (Philadelphia: J.B. Lippincott, 1942).

Hurston, Zora Neale. *I Love Myself When I Am Laughing . . . And Then When I Am Looking Mean and Impressive: A Zora Neale Hurston Reader*, ed. Alice Walker (Old Westbury, NY: Feminist Press, 1979).

Johnson, E. Patrick and Mae G. Henderson, (Eds.), *Black Queer Studies: A Critical Anthology* (Durham: Duke University Press, 2005).

Judge, Melanie. *Blackwashing Homophobia: Violence and the Politics of Sexuality, Gender, and Race* (London: Routledge, 2017).

Judy, R. A. T. "On the Question of Nigga Authenticity," *boundary* 2, 21(3), (1994): 211–230.

Jung, Patricia B. and Ralph F. Smith, *Heterosexism: An Ethical Challenge* (Albany: State University of New York, 1993).

Kelley, Robin D. G. *Yo' Mama's Disfunktional!: Fighting the Culture Wars in Urban America* (Boston: Beacon, 1997).

Lemelle, Anthony J. *Black Masculinity and Sexual Politics* (New York: Routledge, 2010).

Lewis, David Levering. *When Harlem Was in Vogue* (New York: Oxford University Press, 1989).

Li, Xin Ling, *Black Masculinity and Hip Hop Music: Black Gay Men Who Rap* (New York: Palgrave Macmillan, 2018).

Lundy, Sandra E. and Beth Leventhal, *Same-Sex Domestic Violence: Strategies for Change* (Thousand Oaks, CA: Sage, 1999).

Marks, Carole and Diana Edkins (Eds.), *Power of Pride: The Style-Makers and Rule-Breakers of the Harlem Renaissance* (New York: Crown Publishers, 1999).

Mutua, Athena D. (Ed.), *Progressive Black Masculinities* (New York: Routledge, 2006).

Nelson, Emmanuel S. (Ed.), *Critical Essays: Gay and Lesbian Writers of Color* (London: Haworth Press, 1993).

Ogbar, Jeffrey. *The Hip Hop Revolution: The Culture and Politics of Rap* (Lawrence: University of Kansas Press, 2007).

Piontek, Thomas. *Queering Gay and Lesbian Studies* (Urbana: University of Illinois Press, 2006).

Pritchard, Eric and Maria Bibbs, "Sista Outsider: Queer Women of Color and Hip Hop," in *Home Girls Make Some Noise!: The Hip Hop Feminism Anthology*, eds. Gwendolyn D. Pough, Elaine Richardson, Aisha Durham, and Rachel Raimist (Mira Loma, CA: Parker Publishing, 2007).

Plummer, Ken. "Living with the Tensions: Critical Humanism and Queer Theory," in *The Sage Handbook of Qualitative Research*, eds. Norman K. Denzin and Yvonna S. Lincoln (Thousand Oaks, CA: Sage, 2005): 357–375.

Quinn, Eithne. *Nuthin' But A "G" Thang: The Culture and Commerce of Gangsta Rap* (New York: Columbia University Press, 2005).

Rabaka, Reiland. *Du Bois's Dialectics: Black Radical Politics and the Reconstruction of Critical Social Theory* (Lanham: Rowman & Littlefield, 2008).

Rabaka, Reiland. *Africana Critical Theory: Reconstructing the Black Radical Tradition, from W.E.B. Du Bois and C.L.R. James to Frantz Fanon and Amilcar Cabral* (Lanham: Rowman & Littlefield, 2009).

Rabaka, Reiland. *Against Epistemic Apartheid: W.E.B. Du Bois and the Disciplinary Decadence of Sociology* (Lanham: Rowman & Littlefield, 2010).

Rabaka, Reiland. *Forms of Fanonism: Frantz Fanon's Critical Theory and the Dialectics of Decolonization* (Lanham: Rowman & Littlefield, 2010).

Rabaka, Reiland. *Hip Hop's Inheritance: From the Harlem Renaissance to the Hip Hop Feminist Movement* (Lanham: Rowman & Littlefield, 2011).

Rabaka, Reiland. *Hip Hop's Amnesia: From Blues and the Black Women's Club Movement to Rap and the Hip Hop Movement* (Lanham: Rowman & Littlefield, 2012).

Rabaka, Reiland. *The Hip Hop Movement: From R&B and the Civil Rights Movement to Rap and the Hip Hop Generation* (Lanham: Rowman & Littlefield, 2013).

Rabaka, Reiland. *Concepts of Cabralism: Amilcar Cabral and Africana Critical Theory* (Lanham: Rowman & Littlefield, 2014).

Rabaka, Reiland. *The Negritude Movement: W.E.B. Du Bois, Leon Damas, Aime Cesaire, Leopold Senghor, Frantz Fanon, and the Evolution of an Insurgent Idea* (Lanham: Rowman & Littlefield Publishers, 2015).

Rampersad, Arnold. *The Life of Langston Hughes: I, Too, Sing America, 1902–1941, Vol. 1* (2nd ed.) (New York: Oxford University Press, 2002).

Rampersad, Arnold. *The Life of Langston Hughes: I Dream a World, 1941–1967, Vol. 2* (2nd ed.) (New York: Oxford University Press, 2002).

Renzetti, Claire M. *Violent Betrayal: Partner Abuse in Lesbian Relationships* (Newbury Park, CA: Sage, 1992).

Renzetti, Claire M. and Charles H. Miley (Eds.), *Violence in Gay and Lesbian Domestic Partnerships* (New York: Harrington Park Press, 1996).

Richardson, Diane and Steven Seidman (Eds.), *The Handbook of Lesbian and Gay Studies* (Thousand Oaks, CA: Sage, 2002).

Sears, James T. and Walter L. Williams (Eds.), *Overcoming Heterosexism and Homophobia: Strategies That Work* (New York: Columbia University Press, 1997).

Seidman, Steven. "Deconstructing Queer Theory, or the Under-Theorization of the Social and the Ethical," in *Social Postmodernism: Beyond Identity Politics*, eds. Linda J. Nicholson and Steven Seidman (Cambridge: Cambridge University Press, 1995).

Seidman, Steven. (Ed.), *Queer Theory/Sociology* (Cambridge: Blackwell, 1996).

Seidman, Steven. *Difference Troubles: Queering Social Theory and Sexual Politics* (Cambridge: Cambridge University Press, 1997).

Seidman, Steven. Nancy Fischer and Chet Meeks (Eds.), *Handbook of New Sexuality Studies* (New York: Routledge, 2006).

Smalls, Shanté. "Queer Hip Hop: A Brief Historiography," in *The Oxford Handbook of Music and Queerness*, eds. Fred Everett Maus and Sheila Whiteley (New York: Oxford University Press, 2018) DOI: 10.1093/oxfordhb/9780199793525.013.103.

Somerville, Siobhan B. *Queering the Color-Line: Race and the Invention of Homosexuality in American Culture* (Durham: Duke University Press, 2000).

Stewart, Jeffrey C. "The New Negro as Citizen," in *The Cambridge Companion to the Harlem Renaissance*, ed. George Hutchinson (Cambridge: Cambridge University Press).

Stockton, Kathryn B. *Beautiful Bottom, Beautiful Shame: Where "Black" Meets "Queer"* (Durham: Duke University Press, 2006).

Stokes, Mason B. *Color of Sex: Whiteness, Heterosexuality, and the Fictions of White Supremacy* (Durham: Duke University Press, 2001).

Thurman, Wallace. *The Collected Writing of Wallace Thurman: A Harlem Renaissance Reader*, eds. Amritjit Singh and Daniel M. Scott III (New Brunswick: Rutgers University Press, 2003).

Wehbi, Samantha. (Ed.), *Community Organizing Against Homophobia and Heterosexism: The World Through Rainbow-Colored Glasses* (New York: Harrington Park Press, 2004).

Wilson, D. Mark. "Post-Pomo Hip Hop Homos: Hip Hop Art, Gay Rappers, and Social Change." *Social Justice* 34, 1 (2007), 117–140.

Wilton, Tamsin. *Lesbian Studies: Setting an Agenda* (New York: Routledge, 1995).

Young, Vershawn A. *Your Average Nigga: Performing Race, Literacy, and Masculinity* (Detroit: Wayne State University Press, 2007).

Chapter 14

How Black Lives Matter and Why Revolutionary Philosophy Is Relevant

Philosophical Considerations on Ideological and Political Economic Contradictions

John H. McClendon III

When Dr. George Yancy extended the invitation about writing for his anthology, examining the dynamics of Black Lives Matter, and the killing of Black men by the State, he suggested approaching the topic from my personal viewpoint.[1] My first personal revelation is that I am presently experiencing immense joy due to my continuous political communications with my adult children as well as grandchildren, nieces, nephews, along with former and current students about multiple issues involving the Black Lives Matter movement (BLMM). The opportunity to pass the baton, in the relay race of protracted struggle, develops as no less than the summit for any elder scholar/activist. I have now reached the status, commonly termed Elder, Senior Person, or what my oldest grandson, Marquis, recently conveyed, in a text, with deep affection, "My Old Man." This clearly signals to me that by sharing past experiences, over the years, affirms that we are now forging ahead with new building blocks. This new energetic push embodies the spirit and fortitude of our younger generations.[2]

Indeed, Yancy's request instantaneously evoked ruminations on the formative stages of my very own activism. As a young Black activist, I often engaged in intense discussions—with various comrades—about the relationship holding between the personal and political dimensions of activism. At an early stage, I determined that political responsibilities quintessentially required an enduring personal commitment. Furthermore, it became graphically apparent to me how personal encounters repeatedly provide the primary catalyst for one's ensuing engagement in political activity for social change.[3] Likewise, personal experience can also provide both the motivation and subject matter for philosophical reflection. This chapter on "How Black Lives Matter" cannot be jettisoned from my deep sense of political engagement. Political experience explicitly frames my *method of presentation*, and correlatively all background assumptions coalesce with the *method of investigation*. Wherein, I unequivocally state, a great deal of my philosophical insights are considerably informed by experiences gained in the course of struggle.[4]

THE PLIGHT OF GEORGE FLOYD: PERSONAL REFLECTIONS ON PRESENT PROBLEMS AND FUTURE PROSPECTS

In the aftermath of the killing of George Floyd, I must acknowledge that the present problems surrounding the circumstances of his demise—the impending racist threat of State terrorism—are a very stark prospect with a deeply personal dimension for me. The aftermath of his brutal murder, with respect to the countrywide broadcasting of his funeral services, encapsulated a telling message that hit me at the very core of my being. In sum, Floyd was a cherished significant other and co-parent as well as son, grandson, father, brother, nephew, and cousin, not to mention a dear friend within the context of an extended Black family network and adjoining community life.

I share all of the above kinship networks and affiliated community relations, and additional common characteristics with George Floyd. The profound truth is that the same prospect lurks over the horizon for me and all the Black males in my extended (as well as fictive) kinship network. This transpires because Floyd was not murdered based on his unique persona. Consequently, the personal tragedy attendant with Floyd's death is intimately connected to the multifaceted veil of white supremacy—in the forms of institutionalized racism and national oppression—founded on capitalist class exploitation. This is why we observed on the very day that Floyd's murderer was declared guilty of his crime, other Black men were concurrently faced with violence and murder at the hands of the police. Such occurrences were not matters of irony or paradox, rather they were (and still remain) systematic functions of a violent and racist system where profit and property reign supreme over Black humanity. Therefore, the recent verdict in Floyd's case does not signal any kind of victory over the system of State terrorism. Instead, it is an important moment in our movement. Subsequently, the extent to which we can expect further changes concerning the lives of Black men—such as George Floyd and other victims of State terrorism—is ultimately linked to the crucial matter of traveling the road of mass resistance. The valuable lesson gained is that the struggle for Black lives remains an enduring one. The personal dimension is at root invariably tied to political action, that is, the politics of revolutionary struggle.

As an African American philosopher—inhabiting a vastly changing world—the BLMM reveals itself as supremely historic, and thus suitable for philosophical inquiry.[5] I contend that periods of rapid social change, resulting from the intensive acceleration of mass movements, provide an abundant reservoir, which contains the organic subject matter, readily available for philosophical consumption. Among African American philosophers, I do not singularly hold the belief about how mass movements are an invaluable subject matter for philosophical examination.[6] For example, in 1963, Black philosopher Dr. Carleton L. Lee published an influential article on "The Religious Roots of Negro Protest." Comparable social impulses—along the lines of BLMM—at that juncture actually swept throughout the country. Unmistakably, the 1960s Civil Rights movement evolved into a whirlwind of grassroot activity. Hence, this social upsurge sparked Dr. Lee's intellectual process, wherein creative thoughts were effectively adjoined with critical reflections about how religious motivations substantially influenced Black protest strategies.[7]

Assuredly, many among the ranks of professional philosophers would certainly disagree with my thesis. Some argue that the actual process of knowing reality must be relegated to the rigorous analysis of language. Leading analytic philosopher, Michael Dummett, ardently claims,

> What distinguishes analytic philosophy, in its diverse manifestations, from other schools is the belief, first, that a philosophical account of thought can be obtained through *a philosophical account of language*, and, secondly, that a comprehensive account can only be so obtained.[8] (*Emphasis Added*)

I fundamentally disagree with Dummett's metaphilosophical stance. This disagreement portends as not only theoretical and thus restricted within the confines of scholarly discourse, but, more relevantly, it is expressly practical, that is, inherently a political issue of immense measure. Indeed from my political encounters, I have learned that basic philosophical differences—respecting what are root theoretical alignments—ultimately reside at the level of ideological orientation.

In my personal sojourn as an activist/scholar, I have had the distinct opportunity to study with and learn from one of the few Marxist philosophers of African descent. The esteemed scholar, C. L. R. James, was not only a philosopher, but also made notable contributions as an historian, political economist, and literary theorist, among other intellectual pursuits.[9] James's work spotlighted how Black lives definitively matter to the future of humanity, specifically in the quest for revolutionary transformation.[10] In that context, James shined as both revolutionary theorist and Marxist activist. He did not abide by the assumption of removing philosophy from real-world issues and problems.[11] Thus, he was an archfoe of the analytic philosophical community. In his critique of analytic philosophy, James concluded that this particular school

> has various evil-smelling stagnant pools or little streams that babble as aimlessly and far less usefully than Alfred Lord Tennyson's "The Brook." One of the stagnant schools . . . begins from the premise that all previous philosophies misconceived language, and they have set out to make language more precise.[12]

According to James, what is at stake continues to be that analytic philosophy remains constrained by the linguistic turn. It stands to reason that Dummett would contest James's critique of analytic philosophy.[13] My viewpoint on analytic philosophy follows James's projection. In view of the multidimensional character of BLMM, the complexity of the intellectual challenge before us encompasses the problem of how philosophical investigation remains appreciably dialectical in character. By dialectical I mean that while philosophical investigation is saliently theoretical, it simultaneously continues in a tangible fashion, with concrete and indispensable implications and thus mediating as an invaluable guide for our practical undertakings. Dr. Kwame Nkrumah wisely proclaims, "Practice without thought is blind. Thought without practice is empty."[14] Long before BLMM, Black philosophers seriously addressed this matter pertaining to theoretical thought and practical action. In 1966, for example, African American philosopher Dr. Richard I. McKinney unambiguously stated:

> The question of the relationship of theory to practice has often been of concern to philosophers. Sometimes it is claimed that all action proceeds from some recognized philosophical presuppositions. On the other hand, there are those who maintain that we develop habits of action and then seek philosophical justification for them. In any case, we recognize that every philosophy represents some foundation for conduct, whether or not it is developed in advance of that conduct. It is probable that among the participants in the protest movement, examples of both claims may be discovered.[15]

Can we discern that BLMM—as protest movement—engenders or embodies any discernable philosophical currents? In other words, can we plausibly argue that BLMM actually extends itself beyond immediate practical concerns and consciously fosters what are distinctively innovative theories or philosophies of social transformation?[16] Have BLMM activists embarked on forming their own reflections on revolutionary theory? In summation, philosophy can offer—in a theoretical manner—indeed the conceptual instruments for navigating our collective actions. It is exactly revolutionary philosophy that functions as our intellectual compass and guide toward foundational social reconstruction via its theoretical apparatus, that is, its robust critical mode of inquiry.

In his penetrating essay, "Another World Is Possible: A Marxist Philosophy of Revolution," Black philosopher Dr. Stephen C. Ferguson judiciously declares, "A revolution is justified if the socio-political analysis demonstrates that the current mode of production cannot eliminate oppression and exploitation."[17] Ferguson offers keen insight for BLMM. He concretely explains what is to be done. Specifically, we must uncover the limitations adjoined to the bourgeois (capitalist) mode of production, as a rudimentary exercise for revolutionary struggle. This important procedure successively issues forth as our critical analysis of oppression and exploitation. Notably, bourgeois philosophy precisely has the same corresponding limitations, albeit in the form of idealizations.

BOURGEOIS PHILOSOPHY AND THE NEGATION OF BLACK LIFE

African American philosopher Broadus Butler is keenly aware that the dialectical relationship between critical theoretical comprehension and its application for social betterment continues as a marginal concern among professional philosophers. This is most apparent with respect to African American movements such as BLMM that focus on changing social conditions and relations that generate oppression and exploitation. Butler unmistakably stands in opposition to the philosophical establishment with its adjoining propensity toward marginalization of the African American struggle as worthy of philosophical examination.

He argues that the principal cause of this quagmire, among leading professional philosophers, is importantly rooted in a pronounced tendency concerning positivist metaphilosophy. Butler astutely states, "Almost all contemporary professional philosophers generally have abdicated their responsibility to profound moral and ethical issues in their theoretical pursuit of the image of the physical sciences and the image of the technological model of mathematics."[18]

At the heart of these contending notions about the content, tasks, and scope of philosophical inquiry emerges something that is greater than standard erudite issues regarding metaphilosophical deliberations. The question of what should be the subject matter of philosophical inquiry, and the ancillary presupposition that contrarily declares Black lives matter, is not appropriately suited here. The result that follows is an explicit affirmation of the viewpoint that Black lives *do not matter* as a serious concern for professional philosophers. This philosophical orientation comprises the intellectual congelation, the philosophical idealization, which signifies the explicit justification for legitimating the starkly material relationships and conditions surrounding Black existence. In contrast, there has been the fight to legitimate Black philosophy.[19]

Furthermore, this counter-position of legitimating Black philosophy not only offers its affirmation that philosophy must necessarily engage with the subject of Black lives, but also the point that such presumptions about philosophical inquiry explicitly affirm that, de facto, Black lives matter. The truth of this proposition holds even if the dominant philosophical schools of thought—what Professor Butler correctly identifies as the philosophical establishment—correspondingly abdicate such intellectual obligations and social responsibilities. There are determinate material circumstances that compel the philosophical establishment to consistently join on the side of reaction. Karl Marx's telling observations are most appropriately relevant:

> The ideas of the ruling class are in every epoch the ruling ideas, i.e. the class which is the ruling material force of society, is at the same time its ruling intellectual force.... The ruling ideas are nothing more than the ideal expression of the dominant material relationships, the dominant material relationships grasped as ideas; hence of the relationships which make the one class the ruling one, therefore, the ideas of its dominance.[20]

Sequentially, we can readily observe that there are two fundamentally different, indeed mutually exclusive, viewpoints about the significance of Black lives and how they matter. In a nutshell, the marginalization of Black lives, on the part of the philosophical establishment, is in fact the negation of the value afforded to Black humanity. We should not be dismayed, throw up our hands, and respond in horror. There is a concrete material basis that grounds the actions concerning the philosophical establishment. Born within an intellectual milieu, typically referred to as Anglo-American philosophy, the philosophical establishment absorbed the twin influences of the linguistic turn and neo-positivism resulting in a distinctive kind of formalism.[21] This philosophical formalism, in turn, eschewed addressing issues adjoined to social content, expressly the investigation of the systemic framing and institutionalization of class exploitation, national oppression, and racism. Given the philosophical establishment's attraction to empiricism—deemed as the apotheosis of scientific method—we observe that what transpired as hegemonic political/social philosophy simply followed suit. This meant that all manner of dialectical investigation respecting social relations were rejected. Bourgeois social and political philosophers refused to dig beneath the formal declarations about democratic principles, which are said to be based on justice before the law, along with equality of economic opportunity.

For this establishment, the triad of class, nationality, and race exists as benign factors in a vibrant meritocracy founded on individual freedom. It assumes that the present state of affairs is rendered as a neutral haven, dedicated to the cause of prosperity and justice for all. If this is true, we must ask, Why has BLMM emerged as an oppositional force to the status quo? What are the immediate dangers affixed to white supremacy that persistently looms over the daily lives of the Black working class?

PHILOSOPHICAL CONSIDERATIONS ON POLITICAL ECONOMIC CONTRADICTIONS

An effectively suited critique of white supremacy obviously involves identifying and critically examining its ideological expressions via its manifest forms as racism and nationalism. Additionally, there is the need for demonstrating how capitalist political economic interests address the question of the value of Black lives.[22] During and after slavery, African Americans were systematically hindered in acquiring *access* to meaningful occupational opportunity, along with any measurable quality of education, health care, housing, recreational activity for youth, and the like. Ideological rationalization found racism and national oppression as its most useful tools. The prevailing value matrix essentially involves dehumanization by degree, with enslavement fostering the notion of subhuman status as justification for the legal proclamation of chattel. From an historical standpoint, how Black lives come to matter, in terms of the ruling class, emerges as an accounting on capitalist commodity exchange. Initially as slaves, Black people were accorded status entirely presumed as commodities. The political economic contradiction issuing between Black slave labor and industrial wage labor directly resulted in how slaveholders and industrial capitalists persistently sought political measures leading to reactionary compromises, always at the expense of Black lives. Black lives within the realm of exchange values pertaining to the status afforded to sharecroppers and tenant farmers, principally remained outside the capacity of selling labor power as a commodity. Hence, this grouping was essentially relegated to neo-slavery. With the next stage of industrial capitalist relations, we uncover that the majority of African Americans finally reached the status of wage workers. Although the affixed location presumes the capacity to sell one's labor power, nevertheless, this progression corresponds with entering the lowest rungs of the proletariat. Lastly, we observe the current stage, which is marked by structural erosion of the industrial sector. The existing state of the Black working class, where the majority are forcefully pushed into the low paying service sector wherein the median wage, indeed, falls miserably short of providing a meaningful living.[23]

The presently declining material conditions suffocating Black people have accelerated the contradictions surrounding class exploitation, as well as national and racial oppression. In addition to the immediate catalyst of police terror, the combined intensity of such material forces aptly illuminates the dynamics for understanding the escalation of BLMM. In sequence, the ruling class's compelling need to co-opt BLMM—by an assortment of ideological props that appear as progressive alternative solutions—prevails as an impending danger. Therefore, the current disposition toward emphasizing identity politics—while concurrently embracing some type of residual common U.S. national identity—should not obscure what are fundamental contradictions: ones that are rooted in African American national oppression and class exploitation.

White nationalism has never been a fringe phenomenon in this country. Contrastingly, to the objectives of BLMM, the pinnacles of "American" patriotism such as George Washington and Thomas Jefferson, not to mention (early on in his life) Benjamin Franklin, were slaveholders.[24] The contradiction between their political declarations about democracy and economic interests in slavery requires our considerable modification or caveat, one that I term bourgeois democracy. Successively, when BLMM activists (such as Colin Kaepernick, LeBron James, and Bubba Watson) face-threatening retaliatory calls about their lack of patriotism, one cannot overlook what are antagonistic contradictions. In the United States, the symbolic expression of nationalism via patriotism has always been supported by its substantive content adjoined to white supremacy. Whether it is the Confederate flag or the tradition of standing for the national anthem ("The Star-Spangled Banner"), we unearth that what is lurking in the background stands white supremacy.[25]

Of course, the Confederate flag needs no explanation. It is immediately and symbolically bound to the institution of slavery.[26] Less known is the fact that Francis Scott Key—the author of what is known as the "National Anthem"—was a slaveholder and lawyer. In the latter capacity, he prosecuted Abolitionists, and also held the racist idea that free Black people should be sent back to Africa. As with his best friend and brother-in-law, Roger Taney, Key was a staunch defender of slavery in all of its legality. The inspiration for the song results from the U.S. defeat in the War of 1812. At the Battle of Bladensburg, Black soldiers (Colonial Marines) fighting on behalf of Great Britain defeated U.S. troops. Key was a lieutenant among the defeated. He later witnessed another military defeat at Fort McHenry. Key reported that the troops were gallant in defeat and this inspired him to write the song. What should not be neglected is that Key viewed patriotism as integral to the defense of slavery.[27] Both Key and Taney were fervent white supremacists. In the Dred Scott decision, Chief Justice Roger Taney made it abundantly clear that a Black man has no rights that a white man is bound to respect. The Constitutional Convention not only legally sanctioned the institution of slavery, but also made any attempt to run away from it or destroy "the peculiar institution" as the commission of a federal crime. "Criminal while Black" has a rather prolonged history.[28] Nonetheless, white supremacy is not solitarily racism. With the formation of the U.S. empire, Indigenous Nations faced genocide and African Americans endured the burden of enslavement. Hence, when patriotism is evoked as the measure for the legitimacy of BLMM, it should be viewed as an ideological attack.

PHILOSOPHICAL CONSIDERATIONS ON PRACTICAL CONCERNS

Practically, we cannot overlook that BLMM is constantly under ideological attack. Philosophy can assist in this ideological battle. Foremost, there is the constant reframe, "All lives matter," which issues as a counterstatement to Black lives matter. This counterstatement openly intends to subvert not only the conceptualization of Black lives matter, but more significantly the BLMM itself. The following exercise effectively demonstrates why "All lives matter" is not a valid counter-position regarding the notion, Black lives matter. First, the statement, "All lives matter," when rationally stated, converts to "All human life matters." Now we have derived the first premise, "All human life matters." The second premise accordingly converts to, "Black people are human beings." Here the conclusion is most evident, namely, given that all human life matters and Black people are human beings, therefore, Black lives matter. Only with the assertion of the negative proposition—Black people are not human—is it possible that "All lives matter," would reasonably stand in contradiction to the proposition, Black lives matter.

Another practical subject concerns the fight for police reform. Undoubtedly, police reform is an immediate necessity. However, it is only the first step in a protracted struggle. It is not coincidental that the attorney general of Kentucky, despite Breonna Taylor dying at the hands of police, rejected bringing murder charges respecting the cops. Crucially, he misinformed the Grand Jury. The members of the jury, post facto, determined that the public should know why and how they reached their decision. The attorney general, a Black man, blocked their efforts for transparency. From this case are many lessons: (1) the few "bad" cops versus the "fine majority" claim fails to account for systemic violence; (2) the attorney general's actions reveal that increased Black participation in law enforcement does not guarantee a real solution to police abuse and legal injustice; (3) police power is State sanctioned and its exercise crucially engages the violent termination of Black lives; (4) State terrorism best defines #3, wherein State terrorism includes such laws as "No Knock," "Stop and Frisk," and "The Police Exercise of Self-Defense." The last legal doctrine directly applies to Taylor's murder. This doctrine also parallels "Stand Your Ground." In Trayvon Martin's murder, Stand Your Ground legally sanctioned armed self-defense by civilians. These instruments of systemic violence are accumulatively designated "Law and Order."[29] The demand for police reform must shift toward demolishing State power. Thus, the need for a political philosophy that relentlessly critiques the bourgeois State apparatus. *Sans* critique, then the mass struggle eventually falls into the trap of *reformism*. Reformism is the political doctrine which upholds that reforms are the *only viable* means for social change.

In conclusion, the task for BLMM rests on securing its continued progressive development. This process entails transitioning from an amorphous movement—largely based on spontaneity—to building concrete organizational forms. What is necessary are the type of organizations which consciously prepares for and carries out the compulsory mission of the protracted and revolutionary struggle for socialism.

NOTES

1. For a comprehensive collection of this view on the personalized methodological approach to philosophy, consult George Yancy, ed., *The Philosophical I: Personal Reflections on Life in Philosophy* (Lanham: Rowman & Littlefield, 2002).

2. Although my statement covers my personal family experience, family connections by actively relating to BLMM are now expanding into a common practice of widespread proportion. On how BLMM presently influences the nature of family conversations, see Patti Neighmond, "'Change Can Happen': Black Families on Racism, Hope and Parenting" *NPR.org* (July 19, 2020). Also read, Emily Bloch, "'Our Voice Is Crucial': How Jacksonville's Young People Are Fighting for Black Lives" *Florida Times-Union* (September 4, 2020). Also read, Camille Furst, "In the Effort to Change the Nation Teens and young adults are on the Front Lines" Newton NorthJersey.com (June 30, 2020). For an account of BLM political education efforts with youth in public schools, consult Peter Myers, "Black Lives Matter Comes to the Classroom" *City-Journals.org* (Summer 2019).

3. There is some documentation relating to my student activism as a member of the Student Organization for Black Unity. Consult, A Guide to the Microfilm Addition of Black Studies Research Sources, Microfilm from Major Archival and Manuscript Collections. The Black Power Movement, Part 1: *Amiri Baraka from Black Arts to Black Radicalism*, Komozi Woodard, Editorial Adviser, Randolph H. Boehm, Project Coordinator, Daniel Lewis, guide compiled by, a microfilm project

of University Publications of America (2001) observed the Table of Contents, Reel 4 Series 8: Student Organization for Black Unity.

4. The most detailed account pertaining to the evolution of my political orientation, which successively influences my philosophical method of analysis, that is, expressly along the definitive lines of dialectical materialism, which is Marxist-Leninist philosophy, read Azuka Nzegwu, "Interview with Professor John H. McClendon III" *Journal on African Philosophy* Issue 16 (2017).

5. The reader should note that my use of the acronym BLMM also includes the definite article "the." Hence, BLMM reads as "the Black lives matter movement."

6. Two African American philosophers of particular interests are Everett F.S. Davies, "Negro Protest Movement: The Religious Way." *The Journal of Religious Thought* 24(2) (1967): 13–25. Richard I. McKinney, "Ethics of Dissent." *The Journal of Religious Thought* 29(2) (1972): 68–79.

7. Carleton L. Lee, "The Religious Roots of Negro Protest" in Arnold M. Rose, ed., *Assuring Freedom to the Free* (Detroit: Wayne State University Press, 1963). For a philosophical treatment of black liberation theology, consult John H. McClendon III, *Black Christology and the Quest for Authenticity: A Philosophical Appraisal* (Lanham: Lexington Books, 2019).

8. Michael Dummett, *Origins of Analytic Philosophy* (London: Duckworth, 1994): 4. Michael Dummett, *Truth and Other Enigmas* (London: Duckworth, 1978):441.

9. I address my relationship with Professor James in John H. McClendon III, *C. L. R. James's Notes on Dialectics: Left Hegelianism or Marxism-Leninism?* (Lanham: Lexington Books, 2005). Specifically review, Chapter 1 "Reminiscences of the James Legacy." Also read, C. L. R. James *Notes on Dialectics: Hegel-Marx-Lenin* (Westport: Lawrence Hill, 1980).

10. C. L. R. James, "Revolution and the Negro" in *C. L. R. James and Revolutionary Marxism: Selected Writings of C. L. R. James 1939–1949*, S. McLemee and P. LeBlanc, editors, (Atlantic Highlands: Humanities Press, 1994). "Dialectical Materialism and the Fate of Humanity" in *Spheres of Existence: C. L. R. James Selected Writings* (Westport: Lawrence Hill, 1980). C. L. R. James, *The Black Jacobins* (New York: Vintage Books//Random House, 1963). C. L. R. James, *A History of Pan-African Revolt* (Washington, DC: Drum and Spear Press, 1969).

11. Stephen C. Ferguson, "C. L. R. James, Marxism and Political Freedom" *APA Newsletter on Philosophy and the Black Experience* 2(2) (Spring 2003): 72–82.

12. C. L. R. James, *Facing Reality* (Highland Park: Friends of Facing Reality, 1958):6.

13. A considerable number of philosophers, from divergent camps, generally agree that analytic philosophy principally develops from specifically focusing on the linguistic turn toward, with an eye in molding philosophy. Henry B. Veatch and M. S. Gram, who are not in the analytic school, nonetheless, collectively assert, "the peculiar features of our human language and logic that are responsible for our coming to see and understand things only as patterned and structured by such logico-linguistic features." H. B. Veatch and M. S. Gram, "Philosophy and Ethics" in *The Great Ideas Today 1970* (Chicago: Encyclopedia Britannica, 1970): 230. Respecting ideological

critique, read John H. McClendon III, "Black and White contra Left and Right? The Dialectics of Ideological Critique in African American Studies" *APA Newsletter on Philosophy and the Black Experience* 2(1) (Fall 2002): 47–56.

14. Kwame Nkrumah, *Consciencism: Philosophy and Ideology for Decolonization and Development with Particular Reference to the African Revolution* (New York: Monthly Review Press, 1970), 78.

15. Richard I. McKinney, "Existentialist Ethics and Protest Movement" *Journal of Religious Thought* 22(2) (1965–1966): 108–109. Additional information on Professor McKinney can be found in John H. McClendon III, "Dr. Richard Ishmael McKinney: Historical Summation on the Life of a Pioneering African Americans Philosopher" *APA Newsletter on Philosophy and the Black Experience* 5(2) (Spring 2006): 1–4.

16. While not entirely philosophical in substance, there is a fine article that clearly advocates for moving beyond immediate issues such as the BLM concerns about police reform, please read, Antonio Darder and Bill Fletcher Jr., "Black Lives Matter is Part of a Global Struggle against Oppression" *Jacobin Magazine* (August 2020) https://jacobmag,com/2020/black-oppression-racism-dr-king. Darder and Fletcher keenly observed, "It is easy for us to forget, in the aftermath of George Floyd's murder by the Minneapolis police, that this fatal atrocity is not just a matter of brutality against black communities. Instead, what the world witness was the barbarous enactment of racism, as part of a wider system of exploitation." p. 1.

17. Stephen C. Ferguson, "Another World is Possible: A Marxist Philosophy of Revolution" *APA Newsletter on Philosophy and the Black Experience* 18(2) (Spring 2019): 13.

18. Broadus Butler, "In Defense of Negro Intellectuals" *Negro Digest* 11(10) (August 1962): 43.

19. William R. Jones, "The Legitimacy and Necessity of Black Philosophy: Some Preliminary Considerations" *The Philosophical Forum* 9(2–3) (Winter–Spring 1977–1978): 149–160. See also John H. McClendon III and Stephen C. Ferguson II, *African American Philosophers and Philosophy: An Introduction to the History, Concepts and Contemporary Issues* (New York: Bloomsbury, 2019).

20. Karl Marx and Frederick Engels, *The German Ideology* in *Marx/Engels Collected Works*, V. 5 (New York: International Publishers, 1976): 59.

21. On the influence of neo-positivism and its intimate connection to the linguistic turn, Robert Klee states, "The positivist held that a scientific theory is a linguistic representation, not of external reality (which they were not sure was a notion that even make sense), but of actual and possible human experiences." Robert Klee, *Introduction to the Philosophy of Science: Cutting Nature at Its Seams* (New York: Oxford University Press, 1997): 28.

22. For a treatment on the contemporary conditions that point to the national oppression of African Americans, consult Sergio Pecanha, "These Numbers show that Black and White People Live in Two Different Americas" Washington Post.com (June 23, 2020). Pecanha reports, "Blacks live in a country where the economy is always in recovery. Even though white Americans haven't seen an unemployment rate near 15 percent in decades, African Americans have seen it many times-about

once a decade over the past 50 years. . . . The bottom line is clear. Here's how the numbers add up: Whites live in one America and Blacks live in another."

23. Anthony Carnevale et al., *The Unequal Race for Good Jobs: How Whites Made Outsized Gains in Education and Good Jobs Compared to Blacks and Latinos* (Center on Education and the Workforce, Georgetown University, 2019).

24. Of the sixteen presidents of the United States elected between 1788 and 1848, half were Southern slaveholders. In fact, a total of twelve U.S. presidents owned slaves and eight of them owned slaves while serving as president. The following U.S. presidents owned slaves: George Washington, Thomas Jefferson, James Madison, James Monroe, Andrew Jackson, Martin Van Buren, William Henry Harrison, John Tyler, James K. Polk, Zachery Taylor, and Andrew Jackson. The following presidents owned slaves while serving as president: George Washington, Thomas Jefferson, James Madison, James Monroe, Andrew Jackson, John Tyler, James Polk, and Zachary Taylor. See Rob Lopresti, "Which U.S. Presidents Owned Slaves?" https://pres-slaves.zohosites.com/ (accessed July 13, 2021).

25. Jamie Stiehm accurately states, "Francis Scott Key and Colin Kaepernick are perfect opposites in the drama of privilege versus protest in America." See Jamie Stiehm, "'The Star-Spangled Banner's' Racist Lyrics Reflect its Slave Owner Author, Francis Scott Key" *theundefeated.com* (September 6, 2018).

26. My comments about the Confederate flag as obviously racist, of course is not to overlook the intense debates and conflicts over the legitimacy of the Confederate flag and monuments. When I began drafting this chapter, here in Michigan there was a controversy over a Michigan legislator who wore a Confederate flag mask as protection during the present COVID-19 crisis. Read, Meryl Kornfield and Hannah Knowles, "Michigan Lawmaker denies Wearing Confederate Flag Mask, Calls it History, then Apologizes" *The Washington Post* (April 25, 2020).

27. Jason Johnson, "Star-Spangled Bigotry: The Hidden Racist History of the National Anthem" *The Root* (July 14, 2016). The legacy of white supremacy in association with patriotism today find full measure with how police enforcement is intimately linked with far right-wing elements. Read the following report, Michael German, *White Supremacy, and Far-Right Militancy in Law Enforcement*, Brennan Center for Justice (August 27, 2020).

28. For an excellent Marxist examination and the most contemporary legal treatment, from a historical standpoint, concerning Africa Americans and law, consult Malik Simba, *Black Marxism and American Constitutionalism* (Dubuque: Kendall Hunt, 2016). Especially read chapter 13, "The Hegemonic Racial American Culture, Criminal Justice, and Black Lives Matter."

29. After the mass rebellion in Ferguson, Missouri, in response to the police killing of Michael Brown, an unarmed eighteen-year-old Black man, the progressive think tank, the Sentencing Project issued a report on racism and legal punitive action. The report documented that a great number of white people consistently associate crime with African Americans. Consult Nazgol Ghandnoosh, *Race and Punishment: Racial Perceptions of Crime and Support for Punitive Policies* The Sentencing Project (September 3, 2014).

BIBLIOGRAPHY

Bloch, Emily. "'Our Voice Is Crucial': How Jacksonville's Young People Are Fighting for Black Lives" *Florida Times-Union* (September 4, 2020).

Butler, Broadus. "In Defense of Negro Intellectuals" *Negro Digest* 11(10) (August 1962): 43.

Carnevale, Anthony et al., *The Unequal Race for Good Jobs: How Whites Made Outsized Gains in Education and Good Jobs Compared to Blacks and Latinos* Center on Education and the Workforce, Georgetown University (2019).

Darder, Antonio and Bill Fletcher Jr., "Black Lives Matter is Part of a Global Struggle against Oppression" *Jacobin Magazine* (August 2020) https:// jacobmag,com/20 20/black-oppression-racism-dr-king.

Davies, Everett F. S. "Negro Protest Movement: The Religious Way." *The Journal of Religious Thought* 24(2) (1967): 13–25.

Dummett, Michael. *Origins of Analytic Philosophy* (London: Duckworth, 1994).

Dummett, Michael. *Truth and Other Enigmas* (London: Duckworth, 1978).

Ferguson, Stephen C. "C. L. R. James, Marxism and Political Freedom." *APA Newsletter on Philosophy and the Black Experience* 2(2) (Spring 2003): 72–82.

Ferguson, Stephen C. "Another World is Possible: A Marxist Philosophy of Revolution" *APA Newsletter on Philosophy and the Black Experience* 18(2) (Spring 2019): 13.

Furst, Camille. "In the Effort to Change the Nation Teens and Young Adults are on the Front Lines" Newton NorthJersey.com (June 30, 2020).

German, Michael. *White Supremacy, and Far-Right Militancy in Law Enforcement*, Brennan Center for Justice (August 27, 2020).

Ghandnoosh, Nazgol. *Race and Punishment: Racial Perceptions of Crime and Support for Punitive Policies* The Sentencing Project (September 3, 2014).

James, C. L. R. "Revolution and the Negro" in *C. L. R. James and Revolutionary Marxism: Selected Writings of C. L. R. James 1939–1949*, S. McLemee and P. LeBlanc, editors, (Atlantic Highlands: Humanities Press, 1994).

James, C. L. R. "Dialectical Materialism and the Fate of Humanity" in *Spheres of Existence: C. L. R. James Selected Writings* (Westport: Lawrence Hill, 1980).

James, C. L. R. *The Black Jacobins* (New York: Vintage Books//Random House, 1963).

James, C. L. R. *A History of Pan-African Revolt* (Washington, DC: Drum and Spear Press, 1969).

James, C. L. R. *Facing Reality* (Highland Park: Friends of Facing Reality, 1958).

Johnson, Jason. "Star-Spangled Bigotry: The Hidden Racist History of the National Anthem" *The Root* (July 14, 2016).

Jones, William R. "The Legitimacy and Necessity of Black Philosophy: Some Preliminary Considerations" *The Philosophical Forum* 9 (2–3) (Winter-Spring 1977–1978): 149–160.

Klee, Robert. *Introduction to the Philosophy of Science: Cutting Nature at Its Seams* (New York: Oxford University Press, 1997).

Kornfield, Meryl and Hannah Knowles. "Michigan Lawmaker denies Wearing Confederate Flag Mask, Calls it History, then Apologizes" *The Washington Post* (April 25, 2020).

Lee, Carleton L. "The Religious Roots of Negro Protest," in Arnold M. Rose, ed., *Assuring Freedom to the Free* (Detroit: Wayne State University Press, 1963).

Lopresti, Rob. "Which U. S. Presidents Owned Slaves?" https://pres-slaves.zohosites.com/ (accessed July 13, 2021).

Marx, Karl and Frederick Engels, *The German Ideology* in *Marx/Engels Collected Works*, V. 5 (New York: International Publishers, 1976): 59.

McClendon, John H., III. *Black Christology and the Quest for Authenticity: A Philosophical Appraisal* (Lanham: Lexington Books, 2019).

McClendon, John H., III. *C. L. R. James's Notes on Dialectics: Left Hegelianism or Marxism-Leninism?* (Lanham: Lexington Books, 2005).

McClendon, John H., III. "Black and White contra Left and Right? The Dialectics of Ideological Critique in African American Studies" *APA Newsletter on Philosophy and the Black Experience* 2(1) (Fall 2002): 47–56.

McClendon, John H., III. "Dr. Richard Ishmael McKinney: Historical Summation on the Life of a Pioneering African Americans Philosopher" *APA Newsletter on Philosophy and the Black Experience* 5(2) (Spring 2006): 1–4.

McClendon, John H., III and Stephen C. Ferguson II, *African American Philosophers and Philosophy: An Introduction to the History, Concepts and Contemporary Issues*. New York: Bloomsbury, 2019.

McKinney, Richard I. "Ethics of Dissent." *The Journal of Religious Thought* 29(2) (1972): 68–79.

McKinney, Richard I. "Existentialist Ethics and Protest Movement" *Journal of Religious Thought* 22(2) (1965–1966): 108–09.

Myers, Peter. "Black Lives Matter Comes to the Classroom" *City-Journals.org* (Summer 2019).

Neighmond, Patti. "Change Can Happen': Black Families on Racism, Hope and Parenting" *NPR.org* (July 19, 2020).

Nkrumah, Kwame. *Consciencism: Philosophy and Ideology for Decolonization and Development with Particular Reference to the African Revolution* (New York: Monthly Review Press, 1970), 78.

Nzegwu, Azuka. "Interview with Professor John H. McClendon III" *Journal on African Philosophy* Issue 16 (2017).

Pecanha, Sergio. "These Numbers show that Black and White People Live in Two Different Americas" Washington Post.com (June 23, 2020).

Simba, Malik. *Black Marxism and American Constitutionalism* (Dubuque: Kendall Hunt, 2016).

Stiehm, Jamie. "'The Star-Spangled Banner's' Racist Lyrics Reflect Its Slave Owner Author, Francis Scott Key" *theundefeated.com* (September 6, 2018).

Veatch, H. B. and M. S. Gram, "Philosophy and Ethics" in *The Great Ideas Today 1970* (Chicago: Encyclopedia Britannica, 1970).

Yancy, George (Ed). *The Philosophical I: Personal Reflections on Life in Philosophy* (Lanham: Rowman & Littlefield, 2002).

Chapter 15

The Spectacle Lynching and Modern-Day Crucifixion of George Floyd

When the World Is a Witness to Murder

Aaron X. Smith

As George Floyd screamed his soul from his body under the perverse pressure of callous, racist police murder, I viewed the contemporary manifestation of the age-old struggle between White power and Black existence. I watched a man suffocated by the full weight of Manifest Destiny, Plymouth Rock, Mount Rushmore, and the demonic disregard for Black life which is White supremacy. I witnessed the spirits of Emmett Till, Eric Gardner, Breonna Taylor, and so many others intermingle with the cries of a man who sensed the very real possibility of his imminent death. I felt the ancestors looking on and weeping as the pounding of the warrior's drum grew faint. I watched every Black man and woman who has ever had a tense encounter with police murdered as if in effigy. I felt tragically compelled to behold the modern-day crucifixion of George Floyd[1]—another Black man murdered by the power of the state.

We witnessed once again the social contract of America being torn asunder—a thinly stitched, tattered veil of equal protection splitting repeatedly along the racial periphery of the bruised banner. The blood of George Floyd has been spangled across the starry-eyed hopes of a post-Obama generation, left with the daunting task of making America great for Black people for the first time in history.

There is a long-sorted history of murder, marginalization, and emasculation of Black men in American society. Writer and abolitionist, David Walker, describes the powerlessness of too many Black men in a pre-emancipated America. The problematics of power denied continue to resonate today in a world where slave masters and slave patrollers have evolved in slavish police forces. "They can neither protect their wives and children, nor can they themselves escape the all-encompassing power of Whites whose malicious hunger, Walker says gnaws into our very vitals."[2]

This *gnawing*, described Walker, reached beyond the veins and into the deepest recesses of George Floyd's spirit. He cried out to/for his mother!![3] His mother, a woman who is no longer among the living! I was forced to wonder whether he was seeking ancestral assistance, or simply announcing his expected reuniting with the one who gave him life at the same time another was actively taking it away. His body lay prostrate, a painfully symbolic timeline of Black bondage, repression, and death. Upon this emblematic continuum of racist terror, the weight of three men rested, each representing a different period of Black oppression in America. Slavery/Convict Leasing, Jim Crow/Segregation, and Police Brutality/Mass Incarceration were all reflected in the sick symbolism of this callous rampant abuse of authority.[4] This overreaching of power on the part of numerous representatives of police departments in America represents a small portion of a global system of racial oppression. Frances Welsing, in her article "The Cress Theory of Color Confrontation and Racism,"[5] states:

> Racism is viewed as a global behavior power system with a constant and specific set of power relationships. Racism evolved with a singular goal of White supremacy or White power domination by the global White minority over the vast non-White global majority. This "colored global collective" has been forced into the position of relative powerlessness compared to the global White collective.[6]

Slave patrols came out of the tradition of slave hunters who were originally privately contracted by slave masters and later organized officially under State control and funding.[7] Remnants of various expressions of oppression coupled with flashes of the slave patrol and the buck breaking process encircled my psyche. I watched a Black body bound and struggling until it went limp and lifeless. I watched George Floyd murdered. He was murdered by a peace officer. This contradictory paradox reflects the entirety of the toxic cultural cocktail, that is, American history for African Americans encapsulated within 9 minutes and 29 seconds. "There have been new lows in American law enforcement's tenuous relationship with its Black citizens and, unfortunately, no shortage of fatal incidents involving police officers and Black People."[8]

Men deputized to clean up the streets, instead littered the thoroughfare with George Floyd's unfulfilled plans, broken dreams, and a lifetime of memories. They murdered him with the callousness of a slave owner's wife, protected by the accidental killing act of 1669.[9] They murdered him with the demonic arrogance of George Zimmerman posting pictures of Trayvon Martin's lifeless corpse on social media, before signing a skittles wrapper for a racist who fetishizes the murder of Black children. They murdered George Floyd in the twisted tradition of fatal spectacle, like the lynching of Mary Turner, the lynching of Claude Neal, and countless others who dared to exercise their full humanity and communicate their own divinity. They, murdered, him.

> Let us understand that death is only part of the fact that African American (Black) males have the least life expectancy of any group in the country; that we are more likely to die before the age of twenty and least likely to reach sixty than anybody else in this country; that we are most likely to be killed before we reach the age of thirty.[10]

The individual acts of violence are a natural outgrowth from a system rooted in the destruction of Black life systemically and the structural negation of African humanity. A deeper statistical analysis of the system appears to be very effective. "The life expectancy of African-American men is 65.5, European men, 69.9, African American women, 74.5, and European women, 77.8. These figures have much significance. African American men die before anybody else."[11]

The very institutions contribute to such glaring racial disparities that the conditions are culturally corrosive.

> Societal inequity is killing people. The act of moving about and navigating spaces with those whom society has trained us to believe are inherently different from us is killing people, and not just the targets. Studies are showing that prejudice itself can be deadly.[12]

The initial abuse, torture, and murder, followed by the ensuing fear, blame, exploitation, and rationalization which surrounds the murder of George Floyd, was nothing new. "I think the best word to accurately describe the impact that the White nation is having upon Black people is terror. The Black community is being terrorized by Whites at all levels of human involvement."[13] Insecurity, fear, brutality, and pure evil are often on full display in an age where the hoods of police cars and store fronts have replaced the stocks and the whipping posts of the antebellum period as primary locations of Black degradation.

There was something expressly troubling about the lack of violent resistance in the video. Assassination despite cooperation is a difficult psychological reality to digest. Watching a Black man murdered through public, extrajudicial means, presents a tragic retrospective representation of some of the country's most abhorrent racial realities. Beyond the public nature of this form of persecution existed institutional expressions of historical degradation by police, which harken back to the earlier legal apparatuses labeled slave patrols.

The prideful connection with death that appeared to emanate from the officer's frame at the time of the murder was reminiscent of the fulfillment manifested in photos of successful big game hunters posing over their recently killed prey. In the same manner White men and women have taken photographs with lions and rhinos, we find an urban hunter positioned comfortably over a corpse which still has warm blood coursing through its veins. This sadistic modern-day urban game hunting has resulted in an epidemic of police brutality and Black Death at the hands of State funded, hunters of men who kill both mind and spirit with impunity.

There are also invisible binds and ties which White America tags on Black men before birth that grow with us, designed to constrict us through adolescence, with intentions to restrict our potential and sometimes lifespan. These societal shackles however silent ring consistently in our conscious/subconscious, creating a sick symphony of self-doubt, self-hatred, racial profiling, and racist abuse for the world to hear and dance to our destruction accordingly. The question remains, how does Black America (emblematized in the death of George Floyd) escape the deadly dangers of racial pathologies and implicit biases which plague so many White minds in positions of power? Where the Black man is concerned, the restrictive road to full humanity has been marked with numerous legal and societal setbacks. From the three-fifths compromise,[14] to signs that read "I AM A MAN" during the infamous sanitation worker demonstrations in Memphis and other places to follow, the seemingly never-ending quest for racial reciprocity looms large.[15]

In order to better understand the personal paradox which is the prison of existence within a world predicated upon the denial of Black liberty, I submit a description of the struggle articulated by author Tommy J. Curry in his work, *The Man-Not: Race, Class, Genre, and the Dilemmas of Black Manhood*. Curry inquires about the Black Man's ability to transcend xenophobic racial pathologies throughout history, asking:

> How possible is it for him to be thought of, studied, or engaged beyond the historical characterization(s) that relegate him to the Macho, the criminal, the liar, the rapist, the murderer, the thug, the deadbeat father, the abuser, the misogynist, the beast, the beast cub, the super-predator, or the devil. Is he nothing more than an unactualized (hu)man, a fatally flawed thing, struggling not against the

murderous logics that rationalize his death but against the savageness assigned to him that continues to justify treating him as a non-human entity.[16]

Despite the commonplace of lethal acts of police brutality, it would be difficult to say that the response to this instance of violence met with an expected response. The killing of George Floyd marked the beginning of the largest social justice movement in the history of the world.

> Four recent polls—including one released this week by Civis Analytics, a data science firm that works with businesses and Democratic campaigns—suggest that about 15 million to 26 million people in the United States have participated in demonstrations over the death of George Floyd and others in recent weeks. These figures would make the recent protests the largest movement in the country's history.[17]

The movement for drastic police reform and greater accountability spread quickly, shortly after the protests in the United States began.

> As the protests continued in the United States for a second week in response to the killing of George Floyd, people around the world began to stand with them. From London to Pretoria to Sydney, people took to the streets to express the need for police reform and racial equality.[18]

The undeniable popularity of the moment turned movement caused many to wonder why this time was so different. One of the differences appeared to be a tipping point being met in the hearts and minds of marginalized and oppressed people while social media technological capabilities began to be maximized for the sake of social justice.

While many were encouraged by the apparent exponential increase in progressive allies who have been screaming Black Lives Matter while organizing, protesting, and waving signs, I have concerns and reservations as a historian regarding the timing and intention of certain efforts. This strategic protest as a possible means of avoiding otherwise inevitable consequences left me wondering if whether some of these signs were more political than personal.

People from various walks of life have been engaged in similar progressive work long before the tragic killing of George Floyd, others were faced with a racial reckoning inspired by the tragic events which have spurred them into action. Notwithstanding, there have also been displays of opportunistic engagement and the potential exploitation of the moment which I argue contain unfortunate biblical parallels. There is an old church saying, inspired by biblical teachings, that discusses what it means to be absent from the body but spiritually secure with the creator of all. Yet, we watched the soul of George Floyd leave his body because justice is absent in the streets. What we are bearing witness to is the confluence of numerous perversions. At times I have witnessed signs which read "Black Lives Matter" plastered in the windows and on the lawns of houses in recently gentrified neighborhoods which conjures connections to Exodus 12:13. The scripture reads:

> And the blood shall be to you for a token upon the houses where ye are: and when I see the blood, I will pass over you, and the plague shall not be upon you to destroy you, when I smite the land of Egypt.[19]

Here we find exoneration from condemnation through a vehicle which is predicated upon the death of the innocent (lamb). I question if the legacy of George Floyd is being utilized as a proverbial sacrificial lamb upon the triangular alter of White guilt, mainstream media manipulation, and the racially polarized American history of property protection. Could the promotion of the cause, *Black Lives Matter*, be manipulated to protect the subtext of White Property Matters?

At times being a Black Man in America feels like you are constantly being discounted even among the larger disregarded segments of society. How do you explain the tragedy of being viewed and treated as a minor minority? The confusion, anxiety, misplaced anger, repression, overcompensation, and resistance to emasculation which many Black Men struggle with are all compounded by White insecurity, ignorance, and police brutality.

In some regards, the term witness does a disservice to the intimate connection often experienced by Black people, who by extension are virtually assaulted by the triggering historical and contemporary realities of State-sanctioned violence. As we say his name, recognizing that we are George Floyd, beyond this connective transcendental identification exists the tragic recognition of the uncertainty of our own national safety. Unprotected, not fully free, still fighting desperately for the recognition of our own citizenship, equal protection under the law, and full humanity.

In the same way that I wanted to have the power to remove George Floyd from the wicked weight of his mortal enemy, I am eternally motivated to prevent the same racist restrictions to life from impacting my fellow citizens of the world and the generations to come. The world we exist in currently must not be the world we pass on to our future. We must lift this 400 plus year weight of oppression off of our collective backs. We must resist the arresting temptation to give up and give in to complacency, pessimism, and defeatist mentality. This is an age of courageous transformation, where protests of many types are being used to evoke sustained, transformative, intergenerational change. We must rise up together for the ancestors, for George Floyd, and for the future of America.

NOTES

1. Crucifixion: extreme and painful punishment, affliction, or suffering. *The Merriam-Webster Dictionary*. https://www.merriam-webster.com/dictionary/crucifixion.
Mathew 27:50. *King James Bible*. https://www.kingjamesbibleonline.org/Matthew-27-50/.
2. Vincent Woodard, *The Delectable Negro: Human Consumption and Homoeroticism within U.S. Slave Culture* (New York University Press, 2014): 13.
3. John 19:26. *King James Bible*. https://www.kingjamesbibleonline.org/John-19-26/.
4. Molefi Kete Asante and Maulana Karenga. *The Handbook of Black Studies* (Sage Publications, 2006).
5. Francis Cress Welsing, The Cress Theory of Color-Confrontation. In Ellis Cashmore & James Jennings (Eds.), *Racism: Essential Readings* (SAGE, 2001): 181–187.
6. Jawanza Kunjufu, *Countering the Conspiracy to Destroy Black Boys* (African American Images, 1985): 1.
7. Damian A. Pargas, *Fugitive Slaves and Spaces of Freedom in North America* (University Press of Florida, 2018).
8. Joy DeGruy, *Post Traumatic Slave Syndrome: America's Legacy of Enduring Injury and Healing* (Rev. ed.). (Joy DeGruy Publications Inc., 2017): 90.
9. Don Fehrenbacher, *The Dred Scott Case* (Oxford University Press, 1978): 34.
10. Na'im Akbar, *Visions for Black Men* (Mind Productions & Associates, Inc., 1991): 22.
11. Jawanza Kunjufu, *Countering the Conspiracy to Destroy Black Boys*, 24.
12. Isabel Wilkerson, *Caste: The Origins of Our Discontents* (Random House, 2020): 304.
13. Haki Madhubuti, *Black Men Obsolete, Single, Dangerous? The Afrikan American Family in Transition* (Third World Press, 1991): vi.
14. Mamie Locke, "From Three-Fifths to Zero: Implications of the Constitution for African-American Women, 1787–1870." *Women & Politics*, *10*(2), (1990): 33–46. DOI: 10.1300/J014v10n02_04.
15. Howard Ohline, "Republicanism and Slavery: Origins of the Three-Fifths Clause in the United States Constitution." *The William and Mary Quarterly*, 28(4), (1971): 563–584. DOI: 10.2307/1922187.
16. Tommy Curry, *The Man-Not: Race Class Genre, and the Dilemmas of Black Manhood* (Temple University Press, 2017): 197.
17. Larry Buchanan, Quoctrung Bui, & Jugal K. Patel. *Black Lives Matter May Be the Largest Movement in U.S. History. The New York Times* (July 3, 2020): para. 2–3. https://www.nytimes.com/interactive/2020/07/03/us/george-floyd-protests-crowd-size.html.

18. Anne-Christine Poujoulat, *Protests across the Globe after George Floyd's Death*. CNN. para. 1 https://www.cnn.com/2020/06/06/world/gallery/intl-george-floyd-protests/index.html.

19. Exodus 12:13. *King James Bible*. https://www.kingjamesbibleonline.org/Exodus-12-13/.

BIBLIOGRAPHY

Akbar, Na'im. *Visions for Black Men* (Mind Productions & Associates, Inc., 1991).

Asante, Molefi Kete, & Maulana Karenga. *The Handbook of Black Studies* (Sage Publications, 2006).

Buchanan, Larry, Quoctrung Bui, & Jugal K. Patel. *Black Lives Matter May Be the Largest Movement in U.S. History*. The New York Times (July 3, 2020). https://www.nytimes.com/interactive/2020/07/03/us/george-floyd-protests-crowd-size.html.

Curry, Tommy J. *The Man-Not: Race Class Genre, and the Dilemmas of Black Manhood* (Temple University Press, 2017).

DeGruy, Joy. *Post Traumatic Slave Syndrome: America's Legacy of Enduring Injury and Healing* (Rev. ed.). (Joy DeGruy Publications Inc., 2017).

Fehrenbacher, Don E. *The Dred Scott Case* (Oxford University Press, 1978).

Kunjufu, Jawanza. *Countering the Conspiracy to Destroy Black Boys* (African American Images, 1985).

Locke, Mamie E. "From Three-Fifths to Zero: Implications of the Constitution for African-American Women, 1787–1870." *Women & Politics, 10*(2), (1990): 33–46. DOI: 10.1300/J014v10n02_04.

Madhubuti, Haki R. *Black Men Obsolete, Single, Dangerous? The Afrikan American Family in Transition* (Third World Press, 1991).

Ohline, Howard A. "Republicanism and Slavery: Origins of the Three-Fifths Clause in the United States Constitution." *The William and Mary Quarterly, 28*(4), (1971): 563–584. DOI: 10.2307/1922187.

Pargas, Damian A *Fugitive Slaves and Spaces of Freedom in North America* (University Press of Florida, 2018).

Poujoulat, Anne-Christine. *Protests Across the Globe After George Floyd's Death*. (CNN, June 6, 2020). https://www.cnn.com/2020/06/06/world/gallery/intl-george-floyd-protests/index.html.

Welsing, Francis Cress. (2001). The Cress Theory of Color-Confrontation. In Ellis Cashmore & James Jennings (Eds.), *Racism: Essential Readings* (SAGE, 2001): 181–187.

Wilkerson, Isabel. *Caste: The Origins of Our Discontents* (Random House, 2020).

Woodard, Vincent. *The Delectable Negro: Human Consumption and Homoeroticism within U.S. Slave Culture* (New York University Press, 2014).

Chapter 16

Blood on the Check

Semassa Boko

I remember the last time I watched police lynch someone. Or rather, I remember the last time I went online and pressed play on a video because, in my dreams, I have unwillingly been subject to scenes of black death at the hands of the State. I have had many chances to press play on such videos since and will have many chances again as long as antiblackness continues its surreal ruptures of space and time, making narrative a tenuous form for me to communicate these remarks. It was the summer of 2016 and I was participating in a research program at the University of Colorado Boulder. Every morning I would head to the cafeteria to fix a breakfast consisting of an omelet with a side of fruit and perhaps some hash browns if I was feeling hungry. As I ate and scrolled through twitter, I saw a number of distressed posts. Something about police, a shooting, a black man in a car with his daughter and girlfriend, a video. It was a few minutes before I actually saw the footage. The scene was hypnotic, grabbing hold of me and freezing the movement of time around me. After several watches, I was still numb, frozen in the spot. But then I looked up, and I looked around: Hundreds of people for whom this was just another weekday of work or otherwise attending to their lives. Smiles, laughter, coffee sips, and the buzz of casual conversation filled my ears at a frequency that I felt barred from. "I must be dreaming." I remember myself thinking, less an observation than me trying to talk myself out of accepting the reality of the color line separating me from so many people around me.

My sense of the world had just been upended. Philando Castile's life had ended. The reality I was experiencing was entirely incommensurate with whatever reality the other folks in the room were. The feelings that I experienced that day remain the most visceral perception of social death I have ever experienced. A profound sense of estrangement between the (almost entirely nonblack) people I encountered while moving through campus and the town prevented me from feeling as if I was part of the same community as them. In his groundbreaking work *Slavery and Social Death*, Orlando Patterson defines social death by three elements: generalized dishonor, natal alienation, and gratuitous violence. Each element gripped me in a barrage of simultaneity and quick succession. The video was proof of gratuitous violence—a warning to all black people that no violation of conduct is necessary to become a victim of State-sanctioned violence. The nonblack people watching the video—whether their emotions were akin to pity, rage, or *pleasure*—felt a sense of relief knowing that this sort of brutality would never happen to them, at least not without a transgression on their part. It is only black people who wear dishonor on their skin, in spite of whatever other borrowed identities they have managed to accumulate. But it is only now after years of reflection that I am able to understand how natal alienation fit into that day.

I called my mom later on that day. We packed a lot of gravitas into what I remember to have been a fairly brief conversation. Sometimes when I talk to people I play a soundtrack in my head that tacitly helps me remember the content of those conversations. ScHoolboy Q's raspy and wearily animated voice chanting "We might die for this shit nigga,"[1] played in a loop in my head. "It's a war outside, mom, and I don't know what I gotta do but the stakes are too high for me to sit here and do nothing." I knew what I wanted to communicate, but the thoughts seemed unspeakable. How could I tell my mom that I was ready to relinquish the life that she had birthed and worked so hard to cultivate and nourish? And yet, with her characteristic calming grace, she reassured me that God had a plan for me, and that she trusted in that plan AND in me. What did/do I owe my mother? Grappling with that question led to the phone call in the first place. But was the call more for me, or for her? I still do not have definitive answers. What I know is that her faith continues to carry me as I move through a world spirited by black death. I think that such profound faith exhibited by her and many other black mothers comes from the condition—consciously acknowledged or not—of not being able to protect one's offspring. Black people are denied that capacity in the face of an antiblack world. Natal alienation names that condition that prevents black people from having legitimately recognized claims of ownership over each other. But in that space of alienation my mother was able to bestow upon me a gift that keeps me going in the midst of gratuitous violence, generalized dishonor, and natal alienation.

A couple of years ago, I received a phone call from one of my closest friends. "Are you ready to be a godfather?" I nearly dropped the phone. This was his way of killing two birds with one stone: letting me know he was getting ready to have a baby, and bestowing upon me the honor inherent in the question itself. On my father's side, many West African cultures treat the "godparent" as a legitimate entry into kinship relations. Blood could, quite literally, not add to the depth of that relationship. That is the attitude I take with my godchild and his parents who are so dear to me. In the Western world, so much emphasis is placed upon genetics and blood relations that notions like godparenthood seem anachronistic, or at the very least subordinate to "real" (which is to say legally recognized) ties of kinship. What will my relationship to this child be outside of ownership, and outside of the capacity to shield them from the worst that this world has to give? What inheritance can I provide them in a world that allows black people to lay claim to nothing? I could tell them lies about how there are certain actions they can take to reduce their risk of encountering violence in the world, or how they can be anything they want to be if they just work hard enough (actions I would never judge black people for choosing to do—if "choice" is even an appropriate word here). I cannot give them safety, and I cannot promise them futurity. As two abject beings in an antiblack world, I can only give my godchild "nothing." But I cannot forget that nothingness produced everything in the universe.

There is an anime show on Netflix called *Violet Evergarden*. The protagonist of the show is a former child soldier who has been severely traumatized by war and a military that used her as a tool, preventing her from developing authentic emotional connections with most people. After the war and her injuries, she is forced to find new work and finds a job where she writes letters for customers who have ideas but do not have the ability to put those ideas onto a page. In one episode, a sickly mother hires the protagonist to write a series of letters. The big reveal comes at the end of the episode when the mother dies and viewers are greeted to a montage of the daughter opening up a letter dictated by her mother for every year of her life. My godchild was born just before the chaos of pandemic lockdowns and street rebellions. While the fires raging in the streets affected me in different ways, I turned toward fictionalized worlds for ideas. Between *Violet Evergarden* and James Baldwin's letter to his nephew in *Notes of a Native Son*, I started writing a series of letters for my godchild to read as they grow older, whether I am around or not. Embracing the reality of a world saturated with black death, and accepting my own vulnerability to that, actually frees me to engage in this morbid yet grounding project. I cannot give my godchild safety, but I can give something like the gift my mother carved out for me. Whereas the mother in *Violet Evergarden* was assured of her imminent demise, I am constantly reminded of my living death, the decrepit sociality that has no identifiable beginning even if its end is repeated on endless video loops. Whether I am physically around or not as my godchild reads those letters makes no difference. I inherited a profound sense of faith from my mother. In this space of natal alienation I wish to leave my godchild something that is profoundly unidentifiable in advance. The letters will be one exercise for them to eventually hold and wrestle with, building their own inheritance from the substance I leave behind.

Most famously embodied in the infamous Moynihan Report entitled *The Negro Family: A Case for National Action*—which was a 1963 United States federally sponsored document that argued that black families in the United States were pathological due to their matriarchal structures that went against the hegemonic heteropatriarchal nuclear family structure—is the idea that the black family is always already rendered as deviant. In order to resist this narrative, many black men lean more deeply into a black patriarchal narrative that ultimately reifies white hegemony. But there is a way in which we can affirm the black family as pathological inasmuch as its interdiction from hegemonic norms creates the potential for new forms of familial relations. This would be an affirmation "of pathology sans pathos,"[2] that is, an invitation to study the relationship between the figure of blackness and the concept of pathology sans pathos. The black family is pathological inasmuch as the sorts of hierarchical relations of domination present in "normative" family structures fail to cohere in the black intramural. This is not to deny the often violent damage caused by those who attempt to sediment such normative familial relations—relations that Frantz Fanon pointed out are always already cutouts of the State.[3] It is through reflecting on where my private relations with my mother, godchild, and others meet with the unrelenting and totalizing force of antiblackness in the world that I am able to imagine familial relations beyond those of negative debt and hierarchical domination.

Almost four full years passed between that conversation with my mother and George Floyd's murder. In those years I had come of age, so to speak, along many registers—politically, intellectually, emotionally. I went from being midway through my undergraduate degree to being a couple of years into a PhD program. What became most salient during those sweltering days and weeks immediately following Floyd's execution, however, was not my own continuing development, but the counsel I was fortunate enough to have in my ear. Internally, I was gripped by the same fervor as four years prior. But this time, there was an outlet. People were in the streets nationwide and I wanted to be right there with them, fanning the flames to the end of this antiblack world. The old heads put me in my place.

> Who are you in community with that you won't be out there on your own? Are you willing to potentially derail your academic trajectory in a moment of fervor? You think this will be the last time people are in the streets?

All these questions and more were posed to me to de-romanticize my desire to cosplay a street warrior. I had skills and access to resources that could be utilized in other ways. I had faith in my ability to prepare for the aftermath and support people in the streets in other ways.

Sometimes, though, that fervor possesses you beyond the point of self-discipline. I can only point to one truly out-of-body experience in my life (as opposed to the day I watched Philando Castile's murder, which was more so an out-of-this-world experience). It was the type of night I have been out in a thousand times, hanging out drinking with friends and heading out to a party. My younger brother was the designated driver and unfortunately got caught speeding on a stretch of highway where the speed limit changed but the sign was difficult to see. The police pulled us over and made him get out the car. At first, I was alert but relatively calm, assured in the fact that my brother was completely sober. But for some reason, when I looked back and saw that cop interrogating my brother at the back of the car, outside of my line of sight, my body erupted. I forced the door open and yelled "What are you doing with him?!" I myself was taken aback. The weight of over a thousand years of antiblack violence and their attendant scenes of subjection welled up inside me. I was simply a receptacle for the mangled chaos of feelings accumulated by black ancestors. There was no way I could shield my brother, but I did not have time to work through that shame and was instead taken over. Sometimes I wonder if this is the emotion felt by the person who burned down the Third Police Precinct in Minneapolis on May 28, 2020. Or perhaps it's the feeling that motivates the countless actors engaging in spontaneous acts of rebellion against a force attempting to dominate them. I will not rehearse the rest of the scene, but I am only able to refer to that moment today because the incoherence of antiblackness means that sometimes you survive for no reason, in the same way your earthly life ends for no reason.

In the wake of George Floyd's assassination, I am committed to studying the black radical tradition in order to strengthen my criticism of the ways his death, and police violence in general, is often used to reify heteropatriarchal visions of black male leadership and entitlement. In such a world, the image of the mangled black male body overdetermines spectacularized scenes of police violence. What does a black man do with that? One way is to buy into the false belief that black men somehow have it worse off than black women, willfully obfuscating the "deformed equality of equal oppression"[4] that underwrites intramural relations between black people of all genders. Every black person dies by antiblackness, according to the black intellectual Fred Moten. Visibility is a trap when the spotlight burns like sulfuric acid.

Within such a context, I wonder if perhaps instead of trying to shine the same brutal spotlight on black women, other sorts of work can be done to address the deformed equality of violence all black people are subject to in the world. It is glaringly apparent that screaming "Protect black women" has not changed the fundamental contradictions between black men who wish to claim community with black women while also striving for patriarchal domination. Or maybe it is that "protection," under these conditions, should not be understood as a shield from violence, but rather as a process of giving over to each other that refuses the myth of individualism that names black sociality as always-already pathological. Still, I want to shield my own godchild from the pain of this antiblack world, the same way I wanted to shield my little brother.

Let me be clear: lynchings are ritualized community events. As a social phenomenon, they demand an audience—a participatory one at that. The desire to participate cuts through all categories of difference for nonblack people. I would argue that when societies are built on structures of violence, they have a need to perpetuate those rituals, albeit in new forms. Lynchings of black people were picnics, family affairs for the white community to come and enjoy. And for those who were not able to be physically present, photos of mangled bodies formed the backdrop for postcards and memorabilia. It takes a certain astuteness to recognize the ritualistic participation today. For example, during the rebellions following George Floyd's murder, many nonblacks took the liberty of reenacting Floyd's scene of death by kneeling for the amount of time he was tortured. This symbolic act was meant to pay tribute. However, in all actuality it provided an outlet for nonblack peoples to obliterate the black body again, again, again, and again. Watching the video allows one to participate in the scene on an ocular level. The symbolic gesture allows for a fleshly participation that reached its apex when Pelosi and the Democrats kneeled in front of Congress with Kente cloth.[5]

The neoliberal university is also a site for this ritualistic community grounded in the consumption of black death. Antiblackness becomes the raw material for voyeuristic discourses that cause funds to be redistributed under the rubrics of "diversity and inclusion" without affecting the structural conditions that create and perpetuate black death in the streets. For black people toiling on the academic plantation, anything that you receive—fellowships, accolades, time off from work—comes with a debt attached. Now, this is no different than black people's relationship to any institution. We are always supposed to be grateful that we are being given anything at all, no matter how hard we worked for it. But the neoliberal university is quite cognizant of the disruptions that black-led movements can cause, and does its damnedest to neutralize one's potential commitment to radical politics. As a black male academic, who is attempting to nurture the black radical tradition, I have to watch out for the traps of contemporary academia and black neoliberal culture. How do I work to resist the seduction of borrowed institutionality that manifests transparently as black capitalism or renewed black patriarchy, but manifests more obliquely as emotional expression without an interrogation of desire and affect? When black people bleed, somebody gets cut a check. And more and more often that check is cashed by other black individuals in service of their career aspirations under the guise of black liberation or community uplift. I retch at some of the ways black men take up the space cleared by spectacular antiblack violence in order to minimize the violence black non-men experience. Some of those same aspiring black patriarchs opportunistically ignore the fact that black women, queer, and trans folk have been at the forefront of the organizing and intellectual work necessary to resist the particularities of black male subjection in an antiblack world. And seeing as antiblackness makes it impossible for any black person to perform gender in a manner recognizable as normative, I don't believe that black women have the structural capacity to exclude or erase black men. Therefore, the phobic danger is nothing but misplaced projection. I work to stay attuned to the always-already failed nature of black masculinity while also accounting for the wicked identifications between black people and a certain fixed figure of black male-hood.

I also have to grapple more seriously with the fact that so much of my growth across registers was perversely gained at the expense of black women around me. I won't rehearse those harms here—that is internal work for myself and those I am in close community with to work through. The question I am left with is how to grapple with those personal histories in relation to the larger wake of violence wrought by black people who thought they could be men. It seems to me that in order to struggle against violence perpetrated by black men upon black women, and those otherwise marginalized along the lines of gender and sexuality, it is important to recognize vulnerability as both a condition that variously structures the gratuitous violence that all black people have to contend with, and also the building blocks for new and dynamic forms of community. Black people are always vulnerable to gratuitous violence, but those same mechanisms of domination mean that we exist in the space of opening. Wounds are a sort of opening. There was a time when I based my self-worth on my ability to protect the people closest to me. I wanted to accumulate power because I identified with the figure of the benevolent black male patriarch who could earn the privileges of masculine entitlement via an intricate dance of force, respect, fear, strength, and wisdom. But no one is strong enough to protect themselves, let alone the ones they love, from a world where antiblackness constitutes the weather.[6]

In the wake of Black Lives Matter I have seen more and more advertisements and workshops geared toward black men that essentially say "Black men just need to talk to each other" or "Black men need to go to therapy." I am not sure about much in this surreal, antiblack world. But I do know that therapy will not free us, though I do not wish to discount the important work of black psychologists and the reprieve that the therapeutic process can bring to individual black men. Increased emotional expression without a concomitant commitment to divesting from antiblack figures of what it means to be a cisheteropatriarchal black man will only obscure ongoing black intramural violence. Psychoanalysis—particularly as it has been rendered through black thinkers—has given me the tools to not only see but take for granted my brokenness. No matter how much I try to convince myself, getting free is not the only thing that I want. It is through meditating upon and working through that ambivalence alone and in community with others that I am able to bulwark my faith in black folk. Let me be a little clearer about what I mean by faith. I have replaced hope with faith, a move that does not necessarily "get" us anywhere. Even if parts of myself desire guarantees, or a vision of success, I am able to check myself. I know better. Joy James said "I don't believe in dreams that don't include the possibility of nightmares,"[7] and I take that assertion quite seriously.

I feel that there is much to be gained for black men to embrace the death-saturated condition of our existence without fetishizing the violence that can easily be warped and turned inward against other black people. Dealing with questions of death and violence will be paramount for a capacious vision of black male transformation. Perhaps there is a way to paradoxically claim nothingness as an inheritance. And perhaps what black men have to offer to other black people we are in community with—dancing together in that space of nothingness where the horizon of death may even conjure forth the end of the world. Even though I refer to myself as a black man, over the years my ability to identify with the category has become less and less assured. I know that I am not invested in recuperating black masculinity—I remain ambivalent even as I recognize that there are legitimate arguments for maintaining black masculinity as an open signifier that is not tethered to the brutality of hegemonic masculinity. Black people of all genders have engaged and refashioned black masculinity to advance a powerful ethics of care, community, and creative destruction. "Black man" functions for me as a temporary heuristic rather than an aspiration or a statement on my essence.

There is no post-George Floyd world inasmuch as that scene of spectacular violence continues to repeat and, more insidiously, continues to evolve in terms of sophistication and incoherence. However, the time of that video is the time of now, the time of the past, and will be the time of the future until a temporal rupture yanks us from the timeline of antiblackness and into an entirely new set of relations between the sentient beings we provisionally call humans. As a black male academic, critic, and cultural worker, I do not believe that my job is to provide some sort of blueprint for how to move forward. And it damn sure is not to ask nonblack people for anything either. I take comfort in these words from the Haitian historian Michel-Rolph Trouillot's seminal text *Silencing the Past: Power and the Production of History*: "The demands of the revolution were too radical to be formulated in advance of their deeds."[8] If the demand I heed comes from anyone/where, it comes from black people of all genders who have suffered under the perverse collusion between antiblackness and patriarchy. That demand might read something like: Let us move toward a new world that can cultivate fresh modes of sociality that allow for black self-determination along all registers of identity and being.

NOTES

1. ScHoolboy Q, "Tookie Knows II," Blank Face LP, 2016.
2. This phrase comes from a lecture by Jared Sexton called "People of Color Blindness." See UCBerkeleyEvents. "People-of-Color-Blindness: A Lecture by Jared Sexton." YouTube, October 27, 2011. https://www.youtube.com/watch?v=qNVMI-3oiDaI. Last accessed July 26, 2021.
3. Frantz Fanon, *Black Skins, White Masks* (New York: Grove Press, 1967).
4. Angela Davis, "Reflections on the Black Woman's Role in the Community of Slaves." *The Massachusetts Review* 13 (1972): 81–100.
5. https://www.bbc.com/news/world-africa-52978780.
6. I am referring to Christina Sharpe's formulation advanced in her 2016 book *In the Wake: On Blackness and Being* (Duke University Press).
7. Joy James, "The Plurality of Abolitionism BY GROUNDINGS." Interviewed by Devon Springer and Felicia Denaud on Podchaser. Accessed July 27, 2021. https://www.podchaser.com/podcasts/groundings-621369/episodes/the-plurality-of-abolitionism-81944385.
8. Michel-Rolph Trouillot, *Silencing the Past: Power and the Production of History* (Beacon Press, 2015): 88.

BIBLIOGRAPHY

Davis, Angela. "Reflections on the Black Woman's Role in the Community of Slaves." *The Massachusetts Review* 13 (1972): 81–100.
Fanon, Frantz. *Black Skins, White Masks* (New York: Grove Press, 1967).
James, Joy. "The Plurality of Abolitionism BY GROUNDINGS." Interviewed by Devon Springer and Felicia Denaud on Podchaser. Accessed July 27, 2021. https://www.podchaser.com/podcasts/groundings-621369/episodes/the-plurality-of-abolitionism-81944385.
Rovner, Josh, et al. "Racial Justice." *The Sentencing Project*, July 15, 2021, www.sentencingproject.org/issues/racial-disparity/.
ScHoolboy Q, "Tookie Knows II," Blank Face LP, 2016.
Sharpe, Christina. *In the Wake: On Blackness and Being* (Duke University Press, 2016).
Trouillot, Michel-Rolph. *Silencing the Past: Power and the Production of History* (Beacon Press, 2015).
UCBerkeleyEvents. "People-of-Color-Blindness: A Lecture by Jared Sexton." YouTube, October 27, 2011. https://www.youtube.com/watch?v=qNVMI3oiDaI.

Index

ableism, 121
Abreit mach frei, 123, 129n4
absolute idealism, 82
abstract individual, 29
academic policing, 30–33
activism, 119–20
African Americans, 12, 15–16, 19–21, 116, 131–32, 154, 185; masculinity, 169; sexuality, 169
African Caribbean, 116–17
Afro-nihilism, 150
Afro-pessimism, 73
Akan people, 13
Alexander, Michelle, 12, 21
Alford, C. Fred, 136–37
Alger, Horatio, 20
Ali, Muhammad, 40
All Lives Matter movement, 54–56, 187
American (in)justice system, 131–42
American war on blackness, 49–56
Am I Black Enough for You?: Popular Culture from the 'Hood and Beyond (Boyd), 169
Anglo-Saxon community, 42
"Another World Is Possible: A Marxist Philosophy of Revolution" (Ferguson), 183
antiblack juridical system, 133

antiblackness, 3, 7–8, 11, 21–23, 208–11; within contemporary theory, 72–73; criminogenic gaze of, 11
antiblack oppressive forces, 149
Anzaldúa, Gloria, 126–27, 129
Arbery, Ahmaud, 2, 11
arbitrary-set discrimination, 67–68
Aristotle, 122
Atlantic Slave Trade, 131

Baldwin, James, 4–6, 29–30, 59, 141, 205
Bell, Derrick, 140
Beloved (Morrison), 156
Bernstein, Nell, 19
Bibbs, Maria, 165
Bible, 87–89
bigotry, 121
Black Arts Movement, 170n1
black bodies, 16–17, 30, 52, 127
Black Bodies, White Gazes: The Continuing Significance of Race (Yancy), 30
Black Boy (Wright), 19
black critical consciousness, 156
black family, 206
black female incarceration, 20
black feminist/women, 7, 68–71
black firsts, 21

black freedom struggle, 151–57
black ghettos, 21, 149–50, 153–54, 157n1, 158n7
Black Lives Matter movement (BLMM), 5, 105, 109, 117, 179–88, 199–200, 209; activists, 186; bourgeois philosophy, 183–85; Floyd, plight of, 180–83; negation of black life, 183–85; political economic contradictions, philosophical considerations on, 185–87; practical concerns, philosophical considerations on, 187–88
black male/people, 1–8, 11–23, 203–11; academic policing and, 30–33; and American (in)justice system, 131–42; beliefs about, 67; breath, 84–85; breathing/breathlessness, phenomenology of, 85–87; credibility deficit of, 33–36; criminals, viewed as, 12, 17, 112–15; Du Bois, W. E. B. on, 1–3, 111, 116; elimination from society, 69; employment discrimination, 12; as exceptional, 28–29; existence, 27–30, 33–36; as freak of nature, 28–29; gender-based theorizations of, 81–93; with hypersexuality, 35; identity, 7, 27–30, 33–36; as inhabitants of philosophical problem of truth, 81–84; injustice to, 12–23; as Man-Not, 31–32; mortality in police encounters, significance of, 65–74; portrayal of, 2–3; rapacious, 3; recognition, 115; skin, 90–91; slavery, 49–50, 116–17, 124, 132–33; in social space, 16–17; and state of union, 49–56; surveillance of, 16–18; vulnerability, 32–33; whiteness and, 4
blackness, 5, 119–29, 165–66; incarceration, 11–23; policing, 11–23; recognition, 115; war on, 49–56
black nihilism, 7, 139–40, 150–57

Black Panther Party, 103, 149
black philosophy, 183–88
Black Power: The Politics of Liberation (Ture and Hamilton), 98
black queer, 7, 119–20, 127, 163–70
"black stuff," 120
black trans modes, 7
black underclass, 153–54
BLMM. *See* Black Lives Matter movement
body, 129n5
Boyd, Todd, 169
breathing, 85–87
breathlessness, 85–87
Brooks, Gwendolyn, 62
Brown, Claude, 19–20
Brown, Michael, 66
brown youth, 19
Bryant, Roy, 42
Burning Down the House: The End of Juvenile Prison (Bernstein), 19
Bushwick, 98–105
Butler, Broadus, 183–84
Butler, Paul, 97

Campbell, Joseph, 126
capitalism, 109–10
carceral society, 12–23
Carel, Havi, 85–87
Castile, Philando, 2, 207
Castoriadis, Cornelius, 110
chattel enslavement, 131–32, 135, 143n12
Chauvin, Derek, 6, 11, 27, 65, 131
Christianity, 82–83
Civil Rights movement (1960), 181
Clarke, John Henrik, 111
class exploitation, 184
Clay, Andreana, 168–69
Coates, Ta-Nehisi, 118
colonialism, 98
colonialization of identity, 121–24
The Communist Manifesto (Marx and Engels), 123
Compounded Other, 127, 129n8

conversion, politics of, 150–57
"Copernican Revolution" (Kant), 81
corporate market forces, 152
Corredor, Mercy, 44
Cose, Ellis, 20
COVID-19 pandemic, 85, 90, 105, 119
credibility, black male, 33–36
Crenshaw, Kimberlé, 89–90, 110
criminality, 112–15
crisis, nature of, 90–91
Critique of Judgment (Kant), 82
Critique of Pure Reason (Kant), 82, 89
Crow, Jim, 12, 17; convict lease system, 19; economy, 19, 21; justice system, 19; laws, 19
crucifixion, 195–201
culture of poverty, 154
Curry, Tommy J., 30–33, 198–99

Darwin, Charles, 123
Davis, Jordan, 42–43
Dawson, William, 62
De Genova, Nick, 150, 154
dehumanization of black people, 50–52, 65–66, 85–93, 109, 131–32, 135, 185
Del Zotto, Augusta, 68–69
Derrida, Jacques, 83–84
Descartes, René, 81–82
Diallo, Amadou, 2
disillusionment, 141–42
divorce, 134–35
documentary (Till, Emmett), 41–45
Dorrien, Gary, 150
Douglas, Frederick, 55
drag queen, 128
Du Bois, W. E. B., 1–3, 111, 116
Dummett, Michael, 181–82

Edwards, Frank, 69–70
Eibach, Richard, 68
emotions, 1
Engels, Friedrich, 123
enslavement, 98
The Envy of the World: On Being a Black Man in America (Cose), 20

epistemic failure, 87–90
Esposito, Michael, 69–70
exceptionalism, 109
experiences, 81–84

Fagan, Robbie, 44–46
Fanon, Frantz, 111, 132, 206
Federal Housing Administration (FHA), 99
feminism, 88–90, 119–20
Ferguson, Stephen C., 183
FHA. *See* Federal Housing Administration
Floyd, George Perry, Jr., 1–2, 6–8, 11, 33–36, 59–60, 65–74, 85–86, 90–91, 97–98, 109, 117, 131; lynching of, 195–201; modern-day crucifixion of, 195–201; murder, 2, 6, 11, 27–28, 50, 55–56, 65–74, 97, 131, 206–7; plight of, 180–83; and significance of black male mortality in police encounters, 65–74; and war on black men, 55–56
formalism, 184
Foucault, Michel, 12
founding murder, 53–55
Fowler, Gary, 90–91
"free" black labor, 19
Fricker, Miranda, 33–35

Garner, Davell, Jr., 105
Garner, Eric, 2, 85–86, 195
Garvey, Marcus, 117
Gaye, Marvin, 62
gay-on-gay violence, 167, 173n13
gender, 120
gender non-conforming, 120
generalized dishonor, 204
The German Ideology (Marx), 49–50
Girard, Rene, 53–54
Glissant, Edouard, 125
God, 87
good black *versus* bad nigger, 13
Goplen, Joanna, 70
Gordon, Lewis, 150

gratuitous violence, 204
growth, 125–26

Hamilton, Charles, 98
Hampton, Fred, 101
Harlem Renaissance, 163–65, 170n1
Hart, William, 1
Hayes, Chris, 98
Hayes III, Floyd W., 150
Headley, Clevis, 150
heroin, 99
heteronormativity, 7
heterosexism, 166
hip hop culture, 7
hip hop masculinity, 169–70
Hip Hop Movement, 163–70, 170n1
Hip Hop's Amnesia (Rabaka), 163, 165
Hip Hop's Inheritance (Rabaka), 165
Hobbes, Thomas, 51
Hobbesian theory, 51–52
homicide, 69
homonegativity, 121
homophobia, 168
"(Hue)Man" suffering, 81–93
Hughes, Langston, 164
human being, 119
humanity, 88–89
Hume, David, 81–82
Hunter, Corey D., 13–16, 21
Hurston, Zora Neale, 60
Husserl, Edmund, 89
hypermasculinity, 7, 21, 163–70
hypervisibility, 30

identity, 119–20; colonization of, 121–24; social power, 33–34
(il)legal decadence, awakening to, 137, 141–42
(il)legal humiliation, dialectics of, 135–37
incarceration: blackness, 11–23; mass, 16, 21
Incarnation of Christ, 82
injustice: racial, 12–23; testimonial, 34–35. *See also* black male/people

interhuman order, 92–93
internalized (hetero)sexism, 165–66
"'I Used to be Scared of the Dick': Queer Women of Color and Hip Hop Masculinity," (Clay), 168–69

James, C. L. R., 181–82
James, Joy, 210
Jones, Claudia, 117
Joseph, Peniel E., 150

Kaepernick, Colin, 54
Kant, Immanuel, 81–84, 89
Key, Francis Scott, 186–87
Kierkegaard, Søren, 82–84
King, Martin Luther, Jr., 99–100
kinship, 12–13, 180, 204–5
knowledge, 81–82
Kunstman, Jonathan, 70

The Last Year of Malcolm X (Breitman), 103
lawlessness, 137–38
law of inequality, 97
Lee, Carleton L., 181
Lee, Hedwig, 69–70
Leibniz, Gottfried, 88–89
Levinas, Emmanuel, 85, 88, 92
Lindsay, John, 100
loss, 137–38
lynchings, 195–201, 208

Macpherson, C. B., 51
magic, 121–24
Mahler, Jonathan, 101
Makes Me Wanna Holler: A Young Black Man in America (McCall), 19–20
Malanga, Steve, 104
maleness, 31–32, 165–66
Manchild in the Promised Land (Brown), 19
The Man-Not: Race, Class, Genre, and the Dilemmas of Black Manhood (Curry), 30, 198–99

Man-Not(ness), 31–32
Mapping Prejudice project, 157n5
Markman, Morgan, 43–44
Marriott, David, 30–31
Martin, Trayvon, 2, 42–43, 52–53, 188, 197
Marx, Karl, 49–50, 123, 184
masculinity, 163–65
Maslow, Abraham, 121
mass incarceration, 16, 21
Mbembe, Achille, 97–98
McCall, Nathan, 19–20
McKinney, Richard I., 182
McPherson, James Alan, 60
Milam, J. W., 42
Miles, Branden, 42–43
Mills, Charles, 92, 150
misogyny, 165
Moore, Wes, 20
Morrison, Toni, 4, 156
mortality in police encounters, black male, 65–74
Moten, Fred, 207
Moynihan, Daniel P., 100–101
Muhammad, Khalil, 20
Murray, Albert, 60

naguala, 121, 126, 129n1
natal alienation, 204–5
national oppression, 184
Neal, Claude, 2, 197
necropolitics, 97–98
"The Negro Artist and the Racial Mountain" (Hughes), 164
The Negro Family: A Case for National Action (Moynihan), 206
negrophobogenesis, 111
Nelson, Stanley, 41
nepantla, 126–29, 129n7
New Negroes, 170n1
Newton, Huey P., 149–50
Nietzsche, Friedrich, 139
"Niggerati" of Harlem Renaissance, 163–65, 170n1

nihilism in black America, 139–40, 150–57
Nkrumah, Kwame, 182

Ogbar, Jeffrey, 163
On Black Men (Marriott), 30–31
oppression, 27, 65, 67–68, 90, 112, 134, 141, 149–51, 154, 180, 183–86
The Origins of Species (Darwin), 123
Other, 122, 129n3
The Other Wes Moore: One Name, Two Fates (Moore), 20

Parallel Time: Growing Up in Black and White (Staples), 19
patriarchal queerness, 165–66
Patterson, Orlando, 204
phenomenological intervention, 90–91
philosophy, 27–36
A Plague on Your Houses (Wallace and Wallace), 99
planned shrinkage, 100–101
Plant, Ashby, 70
pleasure, 152, 154
Poetics of Relation (Glissant), 125
police, 11–23
The Political Theory of Possessive Individualism: Hobbes to Locke (Macpherson), 51
politics of conversion, 150, 155–57
poverty, 5, 110–11, 158n7; culture of, 150, 154; Rodney's observation, 110–11; skin color and, 111
Pritchard, Eric, 165
proliferation of theory, 87–90
pro-slavery democracies, 97–98
public health crisis, 109
Purdie-Vaughns, Valerie, 68

queer, 119–20, 127, 163–70
queer critical theory, 166, 173n12
queer folks, 163–65, 167–70
Queer Hip Hop Movement, 165–70
queerness, 165–70

Race Matters, Democracy Matters, and *Keeping Faith* (West), 150, 153–54
racial dyslexia, 22
racial injustice, 12–23
racial misandry, 3, 7–8
racial profiling, 113–14
racism in America, 21–23, 39–47, 49–56, 98, 101, 109–10, 116–17, 120–24, 131–32, 180, 184, 195–201; antiblack, 8, 69–70; slavery and, 49–50; violence and, 8, 52–55, 65–74. *See also* black male/people
radical humanism, 7, 165, 168–70, 171n4
reactionary suicide, 149–50, 157n4, 158n7
recognition, 115
revolutionary suicide, 149–50, 157n4
Revolutionary Suicide (Newton), 149
Rice, Tamir, 2
Rios, Victor, 19
rituals, 54
Rodney, Walter, 110–11
Roof, Dylan, 17–18
rules of law, 139–40
RuPaul, 128–29

#SayHerName initiative, 110
scientism, 121
self-censorship, 112
self-deprecation, 112
self transformation, 138–39
senses, 129n5
sexism, 121, 168
sexuality, 121, 163–65
Sidanius, Jim, 68
"Sista Outsider: Queer Women of Color and Hip Hop" (Pritchard and Bibbs), 165
skin, black male body, 90–91
slavery, 49–50, 116–17, 124, 132–33
Slavery and Social Death (Patterson), 204
social death, 204–5
social inequity, 109, 197

social justice movement. *See* Black Lives Matter movement (BLMM)
social opprobrium, 115
social policies, 21
social power, 33–34
Solo Song for Doc (McPherson), 60
Staples, Brent, 19–20
State terrorism, 180, 188
stereotypes, 34
Stinney, George, Jr., 2
structure/agent relationship, 12–13
subordinate male target hypothesis, 67–68
subversive memory, 151–53, 156–57

Taney, Roger, 186–87
Taylor, Breonna, 11, 97–98, 187–88, 195
testimonial injustice, 34–35
theory, 87–90
Thurmond, Strom, 23
Till, Emmett, 2, 7, 39–47, 59–60, 195
Touré, Kwame, 116
trans, 120
transformative communities, 155–56
Trauma and Forgiveness: Consequences and Communities (Alford), 136–37
trauma of black people, 131–42; decadence, 141–42; degradation, 138–41; disillusionment, 141–42; divorce, 134–35; (il)legal decadence, awakening to, 137; (il)legal humiliation, dialectics of, 135–37; lawlessness and loss, 137–38; memory, 138–41
Trouillot, Michel-Rolph, 210–11
truths, 81–84, 122
Ture, Kwame, 98
Turner, Mary, 197

Universal Negro Improvement Association, 117
"Useless Suffering," (Levinas), 92

Veniegas, Rosemary, 68

violence, 8, 52–55, 65–74, 101, 132, 180–81. *See also* lynchings
Violet Evergarden, 205

Walker, David, 195–96
war on blackness, 49–56; Floyd, George and, 55–56; founding murder and, 53–55; overview, 49–50; state of, 51–53
Welsing, Frances, 195–96
West, Cornel, 150–57
western hegemony, 121–24
whiteness, 4–6, 18

white people, 4, 18
white supremacy, 21–23, 50, 97, 109–18, 180, 195
white *versus* black boys, 18
Wilderson, Frank, 73
Wilderson, Frank B., 4, 73
Wright, Richard, 19, 131–32

Yancy, George, 30–31, 114, 133, 179
Yoakam, Dwight, 61

Zimmerman, George, 55, 197
zone of nonbeing, 132

About the Contributors

Houston A. Baker Jr. is distinguished university professor of English and African American and Diaspora Studies at Vanderbilt University. He has published a number of critical books, essays, and reviews devoted to African American art, music, and life worlds.

Semassa Boko is a cultural worker, freelance writer, and current PhD student in sociology and critical theory at the University of California, Irvine. He is driven by the need to pose rigorous and generative questions regarding social change, violence, war, black music, and aesthetics, grounded in the insights of Cameroonian and Francophone revolutionaries. In addition to his academic research, he uses various forms of scholarly engagement beyond the academy including music reviews, poetry, speeches, and creative writing. Black study is his way of life and black liberation defines his dreams.

Tommy J. Curry is a professor of Philosophy and holds a personal chair in Africana Philosophy and Black Male Studies at the University of Edinburgh. His research interests are nineteenth-century ethnology, Critical Race Theory, and Black Male Studies. He is the author of *The Man-Not: Race, Class, Genre, and the Dilemmas of Black Manhood* (Temple University Press, 2017), which won the 2018 American Book Award, and *Another white Man's Burden: Josiah Royce's Quest for a Philosophy of white Racial Empire* (SUNY, 2018), which won the Josiah Royce Prize for American Idealist Thought. He is the editor of Black Male Studies: A Series Exploring the Paradoxes of Racially Subjugated Males at Temple University Press.

Arnold L. Farr is professor of Philosophy at University of Kentucky. He specializes in German idealism, Marxism, critical theory, and philosophy of race. He is coeditor and coauthor of *Marginal Groups and Mainstream American Culture* (2000) and author of *Critical Theory and Democratic Vision: Herbert Marcuse and Recent Liberation Philosophies* (2009). He is author of dozens of articles and book chapters on German Idealism, critical theory (mainly Marcuse and Honneth), and philosophy of race. He is the founder and president of the International Herbert Marcuse Society.

A. Todd Franklin is professor of Philosophy and Africana Studies at Hamilton College. Franklin's research focuses on the existential, social, and political implications of various critical and transformative discourses aimed at cultivating individual and collective self-realization. He teaches courses on existentialism and critical race theory and is the recipient of numerous teaching awards. The author of several scholarly works on the existential, social, and political significance of various dimensions of race, Franklin's writings focus on forms of praxis that take up matters of race in ways that frame and foster empowerment.

Timothy J. Golden is professor of Philosophy at Walla Walla University in College Place, Washington. He is the editor of *Racism and Resistance: Essays on Derrick Bell's Racial Realism* (forthcoming, SUNY Press), and author of *Frederick Douglass and the Philosophy of Religion: An Interpretation of Narrative, Art, and the Political* (forthcoming, Lexington Books), and *Reason's Dilemma: Subjectivity, Transcendence, and the Problem of Ontotheology* (forthcoming, Palgrave Macmillan).

William David Hart (PhD, Princeton, 1994) is the Margaret W. Harmon Professor of Religious Studies at Macalester College. He is the author of *The Blackness of Black: Key Concepts in Critical Discourse* (Lexington 2020); *Afro-Eccentricity: Beyond the Standard Narrative of Black Religion* (Palgrave (2011); *Black Religion: Malcolm X, Julius Lester, and Jan Willis* (Palgrave 2008); and *Edward Said and the Religious Effects of Culture* (Cambridge 2000). His research interests include black studies, social theory, philosophy of race, American philosophy, and the intersections of religion, ethics, and politics.

Floyd W. Hayes III is retired senior lecturer and coordinator of Programs and Undergraduate Studies in the Center for Africana Studies at Johns Hopkins University. He is the editor of *A Turbulent Voyage: Readings in African American Studies* and the author of numerous scholarly articles and book chapters. His research and writing focus on Africana political philosophy and politics, public policy, urban politics, and jazz and politics.

About the Contributors

Clevis Headley is currently associate professor of Philosophy at Florida Atlantic University. He has served in various positions during his tenure at Florida Atlantic University: chair of the Department of Philosophy, director of the Ethnic Studies Certificate Program, director of the Master's in Liberal Studies, and special assistant to the dean for Diversity. Professionally, he was a founding member and served as the first vice-president and treasurer of the Caribbean Philosophical Association. Professor Headley has published in the areas of Critical Philosophy of Race, Africana/Afro-Caribbean philosophy, Pragmatism, Philosophy of language, and Analytic philosophy.

Linden F. Lewis is a presidential professor of Sociology at Bucknell University. He is the editor of *The Culture of Gender and Sexuality in the Caribbean*, the coeditor of *Color, Hair and Bone: Race in the Twenty-first Century*, and editor of *Caribbean Sovereignty, Development and Democracy in an Age of Globalization*. He has published widely in areas such as gender, race, labor, globalization, and culture. Professor Lewis has also lectured throughout the Caribbean, Europe, and Africa.

John H. McClendon III is a professor in the Department of Philosophy at Michigan State University. McClendon is the author of the following books, *African American Philosophers and Philosophy: An Introduction to the History, Concepts, and Contemporary Issues*, coauthored with Dr. Stephen C. Ferguson II (Bloomsbury Publishers (2019); *Black Christology and the Quest for Authenticity: A Philosophical Appraisal* (Lexington Books, 2019); *Philosophy of Religion and the African American Experience: Conversations with My Christian Friends* (Brill/Rodopi, 2017), *Beyond the White Shadow: Philosophy, Sports, and the African-American Experience*, coauthored with Dr. Stephen C. Ferguson II (Kendall Hunt, 2012); *C. L. R. James's Notes on Dialectics: Left-Hegelianism or Marxism-Leninism?* (Lexington Books, 2005).

Sterlin Mosley is an assistant professor in the Department of Human Relations at the University of Oklahoma. Dr. Mosley earned his bachelor's degree in English Composition and his master's degree in Human Relations before finishing a PhD in Communication, all from the University of Oklahoma in 2015. Dr. Mosley's master's research focused on personality theories and human relations counseling. His doctoral and ongoing research focuses on theorizing alternative, culturally inclusive and holistic models and pedagogies of human communication from the perspective of marginalized identities.

Reiland Rabaka is the inaugural director of the Center for African and African American Studies at the University of Colorado Boulder, where he is also professor of African, African American, and Caribbean Studies in the Department of Ethnic Studies. Rabaka has published fifteen books and more than seventy-five scholarly articles, book chapters, and essays. He has been the recipient of numerous awards and honors, including funding from the National Endowment for the Humanities, the National Endowment for the Arts, and the National Council for Black Studies' Distinguished Career Award.

Aaron X. Smith currently serves as an assistant professor in the Department of Africology and African American Studies at Temple University. He is the author of "The Murder of Octavius Catto" featured in the Encyclopedia of Greater Philadelphia (2015), and a chapter on James Baldwin titled "Boundless Baldwin" published in *Contemporary Critical Thought in Africology and Africana Studies* (2015). He has also published multiple entries in *The SAGE Encyclopedia of African Cultural Heritage in North America* (2015).

Joseph L. Smith received his PhD in Philosophy from Southern Illinois University Carbondale in 2020. He is presently working on *The Niggarization of Black Male Bodies*, a book under contract with SUNY Press. In 2021, Smith graduated from the International Economic Law LL.M. program at Xiamen University in Xiamen, China. Smith has recently accepted an assistant professor position with a joint appointment in Africana Studies and Philosophy departments at Southern Illinois University Carbondale.

George Yancy is the Samuel Candler Dobbs Professor of Philosophy at Emory University, a Montgomery Fellow at Dartmouth College, and the University of Pennsylvania's inaugural fellow in the Provost's Distinguished Faculty Fellowship Program (2019–2020). Yancy is cited as one of the top ten influential philosophers in the last ten years, 2010–2020, based upon the number of citations and web presence. He is the author, editor, and coeditor of over twenty books. He has published over 190 combined scholarly articles, chapters, and interviews that have appeared in professional journals, books, and at various news sites such as at the *New York Times* philosophy column "The Stone," and at the prominent political website, *Truthout*.

Josiah Ulysses Young III is professor of Systematic Theology at Wesley Theological Seminary. He has authored several books and numerous articles. His forthcoming book, *Black Lives Matter: A Study in Theological Anthropology*, is to be published by Lexington Books.

www.ingramcontent.com/pod-product-compliance
Lightning Source LLC
Chambersburg PA
CBHW061712300426
44115CB00014B/2654